SCII TEACHERS' LEARNING

Enhancing Opportunities, Creating Supportive Contexts

Committee on Strengthening Science Education
through a Teacher Learning Continuum

Suzanne Wilson, Heidi Schweingruber, and Natalie Nielsen, *Editors*

Board on Science Education
Teacher Advisory Council
Division of Behavioral and Social Sciences and Education

The National Academies of
SCIENCES · ENGINEERING · MEDICINE

THE NATIONAL ACADEMIES PRESS
Washington, DC
www.nap.edu

THE NATIONAL ACADEMIES PRESS   500 Fifth Street, NW   Washington, DC 20001

This activity was supported by a contract between the National Academy of Sciences and the Merck Company Foundation. Any opinions, findings, conclusions, or recommendations expressed in this publication do not necessarily reflect the view of the organization or agency that provided support for the project.

International Standard Book Number-13:   978-0-309-38018-8
International Standard Book Number-10:   0-309-38018-9
Library of Congress Control Number: 2015957314

Additional copies of this report are available for sale from the National Academies Press, 500 Fifth Street, NW, Keck 360, Washington, DC 20001; (800) 624-6242 or (202) 334-3313; http://www.nap.edu.

Copyright 2015 by the National Academy of Sciences. All rights reserved.

Printed in the United States of America

Cover credits: (left to right) iStock image #4700119, ©Chris Schmidt; iStock image #34730760, ©Susan Chiang; iStock image #14532979, ©Steve Debenport.

Suggested citation: National Academies of Sciences, Engineering, and Medicine. (2015). *Science Teachers Learning: Enhancing Opportunities, Creating Supportive Contexts.* Committee on Strengthening Science Education through a Teacher Learning Continuum. Board on Science Education and Teacher Advisory Council, Division of Behavioral and Social Science and Education. Washington, DC: The National Academies Press.

The National Academies of
SCIENCES · ENGINEERING · MEDICINE

The **National Academy of Sciences** was established in 1863 by an Act of Congress, signed by President Lincoln, as a private, nongovernmental institution to advise the nation on issues related to science and technology. Members are elected by their peers for outstanding contributions to research. Dr. Ralph J. Cicerone is president.

The **National Academy of Engineering** was established in 1964 under the charter of the National Academy of Sciences to bring the practices of engineering to advising the nation. Members are elected by their peers for extraordinary contributions to engineering. Dr. C. D. Mote, Jr., is president.

The **National Academy of Medicine** (formerly the Institute of Medicine) was established in 1970 under the charter of the National Academy of Sciences to advise the nation on medical and health issues. Members are elected by their peers for distinguished contributions to medicine and health. Dr. Victor J. Dzau is president.

The three Academies work together as the **National Academies of Sciences, Engineering, and Medicine** to provide independent, objective analysis and advice to the nation and conduct other activities to solve complex problems and inform public policy decisions. The Academies also encourage education and research, recognize outstanding contributions to knowledge, and increase public understanding in matters of science, engineering, and medicine.

Learn more about the **National Academies of Sciences, Engineering, and Medicine** at **www.national-academies.org**.

COMMITTEE ON STRENGTHENING SCIENCE EDUCATION THROUGH A TEACHER LEARNING CONTINUUM

Suzanne Wilson (*Chair*), University of Connecticut, Storrs, CT
Betsy Davis, University of Michigan, Ann Arbor
Zoe Evans, Central Middle School, Carrollton, GA
Adam Gamoran, William T. Grant Foundation, New York, NY
Kris Gutiérrez, University of Colorado, Boulder
Paula Hooper, Institute for Inquiry at the Exploratorium,
    San Francisco, CA
Judith Warren Little, University of California, Berkeley
Julie Luft, University of Georgia, Athens
Barbara Miller, Education Development Center, Waltham, MA
Kathleen Roth, Biological Sciences Curriculum Study,
    Colorado Springs, CO
Irwin Shapiro, Harvard-Smithsonian Center for Astrophysics,
    Cambridge, MA
Patrick Shields, SRI International, Menlo Park, CA
Warren Simmons, Brown University, Providence, RI
Mark Windschitl, University of Washington, Seattle
James Wyckoff, University of Virginia, Charlottesville
Carla Zembal-Saul, Pennsylvania State University, University Park

Natalie Nielsen, *Study Director* (until January 2014)
Anthony Brown, *Program Assistant* (until June 2013)
Joanna Roberts, *Program Assistant* (from May 2014 to April 2015)
Miriam Scheiber, *Program Assistant* (from April 2015)
Rebecca Krone, *Program Associate* (until March 2014)
Ryan Stowe, *Christine Mirzayan Science and Technology Fellow*
Jay Labov, *Director*, Teacher Advisory Council
Heidi Schweingruber, *Study Director* and *Director,* Board on Science
    Education
Martin Storksdieck, *Director*, Board on Science Education (until June
    2014)

BOARD ON SCIENCE EDUCATION

Adam Gamoran (*Chair*), William T. Grant Foundation, New York, NY
George Boggs, Palomar College, San Marcos, California (emeritus)
Melanie Cooper, Department of Chemistry, Michigan State University
Rodolfo Dirzo, Department of Biology, Stanford University
Jacquelynne Eccles, Department of Psychology, University of Michigan,
    Ann Arbor
Joseph Francisco, Department of Chemistry, University of Nebraska,
    Lincoln
Margaret A. Honey, New York Hall of Science, New York City
Matthew Krehbiel, Kansas State Department of Education, Topeka
Michael Lach, Urban Education Institute, University of Chicago
Lynn S. Liben, Department of Psychology, Pennsylvania State
    University
Cathy Manduca, Science Education Resource Center, Carleton College
John Mather, NASA Goddard Space Flight Center
Brian Reiser, School of Education and Social Policy, Northwestern
    University
Marshall "Mike" Smith, Carnegie Foundation for the Advancement of
    Teaching, Stanford, CA
Roberta Tanner, Retired Physics Teacher, Thompson School District,
    Loveland, Colorado
Suzanne Wilson, Neag School of Education, University of Connecticut
Yu Xie, Department of Sociology, University of Michigan, Ann Arbor

Heidi Schweingruber, *Director*
Margaret Hilton, *Senior Program Officer*
Kery Brenner, *Program Officer* (from December 2014)
Kenne Dibner, *Program Officer* (from October 2015)
Matthew Lammers, *Program Coordinator*
Miriam Scheiber, *Program Assistant*

TEACHER ADVISORY COUNCIL

Mary Marguerite Murphy (*Chair*), Camden Hills Regional High School, Rockport, ME
Kenneth Huff (*Cochair*), Mill Middle School, Williamsville, NY
Sarah Bax, Hardy Middle School, Washington, DC
Winnie Gilbert, Los Altos High School, Covina, CA
K. Renae Pullen, Caddo Parish School Board, Shreveport, LA
Steve Robinson, Democracy Prep Charter High School, New York, NY
Sheikisha Thomas, Jordan High School, Durham, NC
Mike Town, Tesla STEM High School, Redmond, WA
Claudia Walker, Murphey Traditional Academy, Greensboro, NC
Bruce Alberts [Ex Officio], Department of Biochemistry and Biophysics, University of California, San Francisco

Jay Labov, Staff Director
Betty Carvellas, Teacher Leader
Matthew Lammers, Program Coordinator

Acknowledgments

This report is made possible by the important contributions of the National Academies of Sciences, Engineering, and Medicine staff, the study committee, and many other experts. First, we acknowledge the sponsorship of the Merck Company Foundation. We particularly thank Carlo Parravano and Margo Bartiromo for their guidance in conceptualizing the study, their support throughout the process, and their long-term commitment to the ongoing support of science educators.

Over the course of the study, committee members benefited from discussion and presentations by the many individuals who participated in our three fact-finding meetings. At the second committee meeting, Joseph Krajcik (Michigan State University) provided an overview of *A Framework for K-12 Science Education: Practices, Crosscutting Concepts, and Core Ideas* (National Research Council, 2012, Washington, DC: The National Academies Press and shared examples of instruction based on the Framework. Margo Murphy (Camden Hills Regional High School, Maine; Teacher Advisory Council member) shared reflections on the current state of curriculum and instruction. Margo Bartiromo (Merck Institute for Science Education) provided background on the goals of the study's sponsor.

At the third meeting, the committee heard reports on the data available on the science teaching workforce. Three experts presented results of commissioned analyses: Kelli Bird (University of Virginia) presented national data; Luke Miller (University of Virginia) presented data from New York; and Tim Sass (Georgia State University) presented data from

Florida. The committee also heard about international examples of systems for supporting science teachers' learning. John Loughran (Monash University, Australia) described an example from Australia; Catherine Lewis (Mills College) described an example from Japan; and John Holman (York University) described an example from England. Gerald Le Tendre (Pennsylvania State University) then discussed cross-national trends. Given the challenges of locating centralized and comprehensive data on science teacher learning opportunities in the United States, all of these presentations and the ensuing discussions helped the committee broaden and deepen its expertise. The committee also had the opportunity to discuss science teachers' professional development with science teachers, administrators, and science specialists. Participants in the discussion included Ford Morishita, science specialist, Science & Math Education Resource Center ESD 112, Vancouver, Washington; Mary Lynn Riggs, director of curriculum and instruction, Franklin West Supervisory Union, Fairfax, Vermont; Katherine Ward, biology teacher, Aragon High School, San Mateo, California; Carol Williamson, UKanTeach master teacher, University of Kansas. The perspectives of these teachers and leaders who work directly in and with schools was especially important to the committee, as practitioners are crucial to any attempts to improve U.S. science education.

At the fourth meeting, a panel discussed state-level decision making around deploying resources for science teachers' professional development. Panel participants included Ellen Ebert, State of Washington Office of Superintendent of Public Instruction; John Olson, Minnesota Department of Education; and Sam Shaw, South Dakota Department of Education. A second panel discussed district-level decision making around deploying resources for science teachers' professional Learning. Panelists included Xavier Botana, Michigan City Area Schools; Pauline Dow, Austin Independent School District, Texas; David Evans, National Science Teachers Association; Melanie Hobbs, American Federation of Teachers; and Mike Kaspar, National Education Association. All provided responses to the panel discussions. Again, insights from practice helped the committee understand the complexities associated with the ongoing support of a high-quality science teacher workforce.

This report has been reviewed in draft form by individuals chosen for their diverse perspectives and technical expertise, in accordance with procedures approved by the Report Review Committee of the National Academies of Sciences, Engineering, and Medicine. The purpose of this independent review is to provide candid and critical comments that will assist the institution in making its published report as sound as possible and to ensure that the report meets institutional standards for objectivity, evidence, and responsiveness to the charge. The review comments and draft manuscript remain confidential to protect the integrity of the process.

I thank the following individuals for their review of this report: Angela Calabrese Barton, Department of Teacher Education, Michigan State University; Laura M. Desimone, Graduate School of Education, University of Pennsylvania; Brenda J. Dietrich, Data Science, IBM Watson Group; Michael Lach, STEM Policy and Strategic Initiatives, University of Chicago; Marcia C. Linn, Graduate School of Education, University of California, Berkeley; Margo M. Murphy, science teacher, Camden Hills Regional High, Rockport, Maine; Cynthia Passmore, Graduate Group in Education, School of Education, University of California, Davis; William Penuel, School of Education, University of Colorado Boulder; Peter J. Polverini, University of Michigan School of Dentistry, University of Michigan Medical School; James Short, Gottesman Center for Science Teaching and Learning, Education Department, American Museum of Natural History, New York, New York; Norman H. Sleep, Department of Geophysics, Stanford University; Mark Smylie, The Center for Urban Education Leadership, University of Illinois at Chicago.

Although the reviewers listed above provided many constructive comments and suggestions, they were not asked to endorse the content of the report nor did they see the final draft of the report before its release. The review of this report was overseen by, Robert Floden, Institute for Research on Technology and Learning, Michigan State University and Caswell A. Evans, College of Dentistry, University of Illinois at Chicago. Appointed by the Academies, they were responsible for making certain that an independent examination of this report was carried out in accordance with institutional procedures and that all review comments were carefully considered. Responsibility for the final content of this report rests entirely with the committee and the institution.

Thanks are also due to the project staff and staff of the Division of Behavioral and Social Sciences and Education (DBASSE). Anthony Brown, Rebecca Krone, and Joanna Roberts managed the study's logistical and administrative needs, making sure meetings and workshops ran efficiently and smoothly. We are also grateful to Jay Labov and Ryan Stowe (Christine Mirzayan Science and Technology Fellow) for their contributions and to Margaret Hilton for her invaluable writing and editorial help. Kirsten Sampson Snyder of the DBASSE staff expertly guided us through the review process, and Yvonne Wise of the DBASSE staff oversaw the production of the report. Most importantly, Natalie Nielsen and Heidi

Schweingruber, of the Board on Science Education, directed the study and played a key role in the report drafting and review process with intelligence and grace. Their stewardship of the process and willingness to help in all matter of ways were essential to the completion of this project.

Suzanne Wilson, *Chair*
Committee on Strengthening Science Education
through a Teacher Learning Continuum

Contents

Summary

The United States today has an extraordinary opportunity to re-establish its preeminence in science and scientific discovery. More than thirty years ago the National Commission on Excellence in Education issued *A Nation at Risk*, which warned of the risks to education in general and science education in particular if the nation neglected to improve the quality of teaching in its public schools (National Commission on Excellence in Education, 1983). A series of reports published since then suggests that little has changed and that as a result the nation has paid a price in its standing internationally, in its economic well-being, and in the quality of its everyday interactions (see National Academy of Sciences, 2007). *The Next Generation Science Standards: For States, By States* (hereafter referred to as the NGSS), which call for *all* students to have opportunities to be actively engaged in investigating scientific phenomena and designing solutions to compelling problems offer an opportunity to respond to this challenge (Next Generation Science Standards Lead States, 2013). Indeed, the NGSS represent just the type of response called for in *A Nation at Risk* for the teaching of science (p. 25). The NGSS represent a fundamental change in the way science is taught and, if implemented well, will ensure that all students gain mastery over core concepts of science that are foundational to improving their scientific capacity.

Ultimately, the task of realizing this vision rests with teachers. To provide students these opportunities, teachers will need new knowledge of the ideas and practices in the disciplines of science, an understanding of instructional strategies that are consistent with the NGSS vision, and the skill to implement those strategies in their classrooms. To enable teachers to acquire this kind of learning will in turn require profound changes to current systems for supporting teachers' learning across their careers, including induction and professional development. Recognizing the challenges entailed in making these changes and the need for guidance on how to address them, the Board on Science Education within the Division of Behavioral and Social Sciences and Education of the National Academies of Sciences, Engineering, and Medicine, with support from the Merck Company Foundation, convened a 14-member expert committee to undertake a comprehensive study of how to provide coherent support for elementary, middle, and high school science teachers' learning across their careers.

The committee considered science teachers' learning from a perspective that acknowledges the rich and complex contexts of their work—the diversity of students and communities, the pressures of resource limitations, and the array of salient district and state policies. Further, the committee considered a variety of learning experiences: formal and informal, structured and unstructured, individual and collective, planned and serendipitous, mandated and sought out. The committee explored the evidence related to all of these mechanisms for supporting science teachers' learning.

One main message of this report is the need to adopt a broad view of where and what teachers learn to teach over the course of their careers. Teachers participate in occasions specifically designed to educate them, such as induction programs and professional development workshops, but they also learn a great deal in their own classes on a daily basis while interacting with their students (Ball and Cohen, 1999; Ball and Forzani, 2011; Luft et al., 2015). In many schools and districts, however, science teachers' work is not organized to provide the time and the opportunities for collaboration with other teachers needed to best support their learning. The committee also found that the evidence base related to science teachers' learning has focused mainly on programs, with many fewer studies examining learning opportunities embedded in the school day.

CONCLUSIONS

In reviewing the evidence, the committee drew the following conclusions about the gap between what science teaching and learning could be and the reality of current practices.

Conclusion 1: An evolving understanding of how best to teach science, including the NGSS, represents a significant transition in the way science is currently taught in most classrooms and will require most science teachers to alter the way they teach.

Conclusion 2: *The available evidence suggests that many science teachers have not had sufficiently rich experiences with the content relevant to the science courses they currently teach, let alone a substantially redesigned science curriculum. Very few teachers have experience with the science and engineering practices described in the NGSS. This situation is especially pronounced both for elementary school teachers and in schools that serve high percentages of low-income students, where teachers are often newer and less qualified.*

Conclusion 3: *Typically, the selection of and participation in professional learning opportunities is up to individual teachers. There is often little attention to developing collective capacity for science teaching at the building and district levels or to offering teachers learning opportunities tailored to their specific needs and offered in ways that support cumulative learning over time.*

Conclusion 4: *Science teachers' learning needs are shaped by their preparation, the grades and content areas they teach, and the contexts in which they work. Three important areas in which science teachers need to develop expertise are*

- *the knowledge, capacity, and skill required to support a diverse range of students;*
- *content knowledge, including understanding of disciplinary core ideas, crosscutting concepts, and scientific and engineering practices; and*
- *pedagogical content knowledge for teaching science, including a repertoire of teaching practices that support students in rigorous and consequential science learning.*

Conclusion 5: *The best available evidence based on science professional development programs suggests that the following features of such programs are most effective:*

- *active participation of teachers who engage in the analysis of examples of effective instruction and the analysis of student work,*
- *a content focus,*
- *alignment with district policies and practices, and*
- *sufficient duration to allow repeated practice and/or reflection on classroom experiences.*

Conclusion 6: Professional learning in online environments and through social networking holds promise, although evidence on these modes from both research and practice is limited.

Conclusion 7: Science teachers' professional learning occurs in a range of settings both within and outside of schools through a variety of structures (professional development programs, professional learning communities, coaching, and the like). There is limited evidence about the relative effectiveness of this broad array of learning opportunities and how they are best designed to support teacher learning.

Conclusion 8: Schools need to be structured to encourage and support ongoing learning for science teachers, especially given the number of new teachers entering the profession.

Conclusion 9: Science teachers' development is best understood as long term and contextualized. The schools and classrooms in which teachers work shape what and how they learn. These contexts include, but are not limited to school, district, and state policies and practices concerning professional capacity (e.g., professional networks, coaching, partnerships), coherent instructional guidance (e.g., state and district curriculum and assessment/accountability policies), and leadership (e.g., principals and teacher leaders).

Conclusion 10: School and district administrators are central to building the capacity of the science teacher workforce.

Conclusion 11: Teacher leaders may be an important resource for building a system that can support ambitious science instruction. There is increasing attention to creating opportunities for teachers to take on leadership roles to both improve science instruction and strengthen the science teacher workforce. These include roles as instructional coaches, mentors, and teacher leaders.

Conclusion 12: Closing the gap between the new way of teaching science and current instruction in many schools will require attending to individual teachers' learning needs, as well as to the larger system of practices and policies (such as allocation of resources, use of time, and provision of opportunities for collaboration) that shape how science is taught.

Conclusion 13: The U.S. educational system lacks a coherent and well-articulated system of learning opportunities for teachers to continue developing expertise while in the classroom. Opportunities are unevenly distributed across schools, districts, and regions, with little attention to sequencing or *how to support science teachers' learning systematically. Moreover, schools and districts often lack systems that can provide a comprehensive view of teacher learning; identify specific teacher needs; or track investments—in time, money, and resources—in science teachers' professional learning.*

RECOMMENDATIONS FOR PRACTICE AND POLICY

These conclusions are broad, with implications for programs, policy and practice. The committee chose to focus its recommendations at the district and school level, since those are crucial locations for investments in the science teacher workforce. The seven recommendations that follow, based on the above conclusions, highlight how districts and schools can improve the learning opportunities available to science teachers. These recommendations are intended to help both in determining science teachers' learning needs and in developing a comprehensive approach to meeting those needs, with particular attention to the ways that the current education system needs to be changed in order to support teachers' ongoing learning as they respond to the demands placed by current reforms in science education.

Recommendation 1:

Take stock of the current status of learning opportunities for science teachers: School and district administrators should identify current offerings and opportunities for teacher learning in science using a broad conceptualization of teacher learning opportunities, and including how much money and time are spent (as well as other associated costs). Throughout this process, attention should be paid to the opportunities available for teachers to learn about

- approaches for teaching all students,
- science content and scientific practices, and
- science pedagogical knowledge and science teaching practices.

When identifying costs, administrators should consider both traditional professional development time and other supports for learning, such as curriculum, teacher evaluation, and student assessment/accountability. Given differences in the learning needs of elementary, middle, and high school teachers, expenditures and time allocations should be broken down by grade level and by school and district level. Plans to address any inequities across classrooms or schools should be developed with an eye toward policies and practices that will equitably distribute teacher expertise and teacher learning opportunities across the system.

Recommendation 2:

Design a portfolio of coherent learning experiences for science teachers that attend to teachers' individual and context-specific needs in partnership with professional networks, institutions of higher education, cultural institutions, and the broader scientific community as appropriate: Teachers and school and district administrators should articulate, implement and support teacher learning opportunities in science as coherent, graduated sequences of experiences toward larger goals for improving science teaching and learning. Here, too, attention should be paid to building teachers' knowledge and skill in the sciences and scientific practices, in science pedagogical content knowledge, and in science teaching practices. It is critical to support teachers' opportunities to learn how to connect with students of diverse backgrounds and experiences and how to tap into relevant funds of knowledge of students and communities.

District personnel and school principals, in collaboration with teachers and parents, should identify the specific learning needs of science teachers in their schools and develop a multiyear growth plan for their science teachers' learning that is linked to their growth plan for students' science learning. Central to this work are four questions:

- In light of our school's/district's science goals for our students, what learning opportunities will teachers need?
- What kinds of expertise are needed to support these learning opportunities?
- Where is that expertise located (inside and outside of schools)?
- What social arrangements and resources will enable this work?

Using a variety of assessments/measures designed to provide the kind of concrete feedback necessary to support teacher and program improvement, the school principals, in collaboration with teachers and school partners, should regularly consult data from such sources as teacher observations, student work, and student surveys or interviews to assess progress on the growth plan. It will also be important to consider the larger contexts in which the plan will unfold and how existing policies and practices regarding personnel (hiring, retention, placement) and instructional guidance (curriculum and assessment) can enable or limit the plan.

Recommendation 3:

Consider both specialized professional learning programs outside of school and opportunities for science teachers' learning embedded in the work day: A coherent, standards and evidence-based portfolio of professional learning opportunities for science teachers should include both specialized programs that occur outside of the school day and ongoing learning opportunities that are built into the work day and enhance capacity in schools and districts. Development of this portfolio will require some restructuring of teachers' work in schools to support new learning opportunities. School and district leaders will need to develop policies and practices that provide the necessary resources (fiscal, time, facilities, tools, incentives).

As school and district leaders identify professional learning opportunities for science teachers, they should work to develop a portfolio of opportunities that address teachers' varied needs in ways that are sensitive to the school or district context. School and district leaders should not only make this portfolio of opportunities available to teachers but also actively encourage, through their leadership and provision of resources, teachers' engagement in these opportunities, and provide time during the school day for teachers to engage meaningfully in them. Furthermore, school and district leaders should work with teams of teachers to build coherent programs of science teaching learning opportunities, tailored to individual teachers and the school as a whole. The portfolio of teacher learning opportunities should include structured, traditional professional development; cross-school teacher professional communities; and collaborations with local partners.

Recommendation 4:

Design and select learning opportunities for science teachers that are informed by the best available research: Teachers' learning opportunities should be aligned with a school system's science standards, and should be grounded in an underlying theory of teacher learning and in research on the improvement of professional practice and on how to meet the needs of the range of adult and student learners in a school or district. Learning opportunities for science teachers should have the following characteristics:

- Designed to achieve specific learning goals for teachers.
- Be content specific, that is, focused on particular scientific concepts and practices.
- Be student specific, that is, focused on the specific students served by the school district.
- Linked to teachers' classroom instruction and include analysis of instruction.
- Include opportunities for teachers to practice teaching science in new ways and to interact with peers in improving the implementation of new teaching strategies.

- Include opportunities for teachers to collect and analyze data on their students' learning.
- Offer opportunities for collaboration.

Designers of learning opportunities for teachers, including commercial providers, community organizations, institutions of higher education and districts and states, should develop learning opportunities for teachers that reflect the above criteria.

When selecting learning opportunities for teachers, district and school leaders and teachers themselves should use the above criteria as a guide for identifying the most promising programs and learning experiences. District and state administrators should use these criteria to provide guidance for teachers on how to identify high-quality learning experiences.

District administrators and state agencies should use (and make public) quality indicators to identify, endorse, and fund a portfolio of teacher learning opportunities, and should provide guidance for school leaders and teachers on how to select high-quality learning experiences in science appropriate to specific contexts.

Recommendation 5:

Develop internal capacity in science while seeking external partners with science expertise: School and district leaders should work to build school- and district-level capacity around science teaching. These efforts include creating learning opportunities for teachers but might also include exploring different models for incorporating science expertise, such as employing science specialists at the elementary level or providing high school science department heads with time to observe and collaborate with their colleagues. When developing a strategy for building capacity, school and district leaders should consider the tradeoffs inherent in such choices.

School and district leaders should also explore developing partnerships with individuals and organizations—such as local businesses, institutions of higher education, or science-rich institutions—that can bring science expertise.

Crucial to developing relevant expertise is developing the capacity of professional development leaders. Investing in the development of professional developers who are knowledgeable about teaching all students the vision of science education represented in the *Next Generation Science Standards* and *A Framework for K-12 Science Education* (National Research Council, 2012) is critical. It is not sufficient for these leaders to be good teachers themselves; they must also be prepared and supported to work with adult learners and to coordinate professional development with other policies and programs (including staffing, teacher evaluation, curriculum development, and student assessment).

Recommendation 6:

Create, evaluate, and revise policies and practices that encourage teachers to engage in professional learning related to science: District and school administrators and relevant leaders should work to establish dedicated professional development time during the salaried work week and work year for science teachers. They should encourage teachers to participate in science learning opportunities and structure time to allow for collaboration around science. Resources for professional learning should include time to meet with other teachers, to observe other classrooms, and to attend discrete events; space to meet with other teachers; requested materials; and incentives to participate. These policies and practices should take advantage of linkages with other policies. For example, natural connections can be made between policies concerning professional development and teacher evaluation. Similarly, administrators could develop policies that more equitably distribute qualified and experienced science teachers across all students, schools, districts, and school networks.

At the elementary level, district and school leaders should work to establish parity for science professional development in relationship to other subjects, especially mathematics and English language arts.

Recommendation 7:

The potential of new formats and media should be explored to support science teachers' learning when appropriate: Districts should consider the use of technology and online spaces/resources to support teacher learning in science. These tools may be particularly useful for supporting cross-school collaboration, providing teachers with flexible schedules for accessing resources, and enabling access to professional learning opportunities in rural areas where teachers may be isolated and it is difficult to convene in a central location.

Finally, the committee also identified gaps in the existing research base on science teachers' learning. Accordingly, the committee offers in the full report recommendations for research in several areas that would inform the work of education leaders interested in supporting ongoing learning for science teachers.

REFERENCES

Ball, D.L., and Cohen, D.K. (1999). Developing practice, developing practitioners: Toward a practice-based theory of professional education. In L. Darling-Hammond and G. Sykes (Eds.), *Teaching as the Learning Profession: Handbook of Policy and Practice* (pp. 3-32). San Francisco, CA: Jossey-Bass.

Ball, D.L., and Forzani, F.M. (2011). Building a common core for learning to teach, and connecting professional learning to practice. *American Educator, 35*(2), 17-21, 38-39.

Luft, J.A., Dubois, S., Nixon, R., and Campbell, B. (2015). Supporting newly hired teachers of science: Attaining professional teaching standards. *Studies in Science Education, 51*(1), 1-48. Available: http://dx.doi.org/10.1080/03057267.2014.980559 [November 2015].

National Academy of Sciences. (2007). *Rising Above the Gathering Storm: Energizing and Employing America for a Brighter Economic Future.* Committee on Prospering in the Global Economy of the 21st Century: An Agenda for American Science and Technology. Committee on Science, Engineering, and Public Policy, and Policy and Global Affairs. Washington, DC: The National Academies Press.

National Commission on Excellence in Education. (1983). *A Nation at Risk: The Imperative for Educational Reform.* A report to the Nation and the Secretary of Education, U.S. Department of Education. Washington, DC: U.S. Government Printing Office.

National Research Council. (2012). *A Framework for K-12 Science Education: Practices, Crosscutting Concepts, and Core Ideas.* Committee on a Conceptual Framework for New K-12 Science Education Standards, Board on Science Education. Division of Behavioral and Social Sciences and Education. Washington, DC: The National Academies Press.

Next Generation Science Standards Lead States. (2013). *Next Generation Science Standards: For States, By States.* Washington, DC: The National Academies Press.

1

Introduction

Individuals increasingly must understand science and technology to thrive in today's society, and schools accordingly are challenged to provide high-quality science learning experiences to all students. Teachers are at the forefront of meeting this challenge, and the quality of their instruction therefore acts as a major fulcrum for improving science education.

Efforts to improve the quality of science teaching and learning have been under way for decades. Yet results of international comparisons (Martin et al., 2012; OECD, 2014) and indicators of general science literacy (Miller, 2010) reveal that many American students and adults still fail to grasp fundamental scientific concepts and to understand the process of scientific discovery.

To address these challenges, the most recent improvement efforts draw heavily on the past 30 years of research and development in cognitive science, education in general, and science education in particular. This research elucidates what is important for students to know and be able to do in science, how they learn, and how to help teachers support that learning.

At the K-12 level, the *Next Generation Science Standards* (hereafter referred to as the NGSS) (Next Generation Science Standards Lead States, 2013) represent the most recent effort to focus the reform of science education. The NGSS, developed by a consortium of educators and scientists from 26 states, specify what students should know and be able to do in science at the end of particular grades or grade bands. These standards are based on *A Framework for K-12 Science Education* (hereafter referred to as the Framework) (National Research Council, 2012), which was informed by research on science learning and on the science standards of the 1990s—the *National Science Education Standards* (National Research Council, 1996) and the *Benchmarks for Science Literacy* (American Association for the Advancement of Science, 1993). The vision of science education set forth in the Framework and the NGSS calls for classrooms that bring science and engineering alive for students,[1] emphasizing the satisfaction of pursuing compelling questions and the joy of discovery and invention.

Realizing this vision will be a challenge for teachers, administrators, and students. Many teachers are unlikely to have experienced this kind of science instruction themselves and may not be prepared to teach in the ways envisioned by the Framework and the NGSS. In many schools and districts, moreover, science is considered a lower priority than mathematics and English language arts—particularly in the elementary grades, where less time is allocated for science instruction than for instruction in these latter two disciplines (Center on Education Policy, 2007; Dorph et al., 2011). Achieving the vision will require more than increased time for science in the curriculum; it will require a pedagogical shift away from memorization of facts and presentation of information by teachers to student-led investigations and in-depth examination of core ideas. New curricula will need to be created, new assessments devised, and new instructional approaches employed.

Teachers embracing this vision will themselves need new kinds of learning opportunities and considerable support. This is true for experienced educators encountering new conceptions of science teaching as well as for novice teachers being apprenticed into the profession. It is as true of schools and districts that have long taken pride in their science programs as it is for those where science has been neglected. But this is not a challenge of simply preparing individual teachers. Rather, it is a challenge of preparing a teacher workforce, and creating a system of policies, programs, and practices at the federal, state, district, and school levels that support teachers as they progressively deepen their own expertise and challenge their students to learn, enjoy, and appreciate science.

---

[1]Current education reforms focus on the broad set of disciplines under the umbrella of science, technology, engineering, and mathematics (STEM). Especially important is a commitment to capitalize on the interdisciplinary nature of these fields. Thus while this report focuses on science teachers, the committee acknowledges the importance of considering how science teachers learn to integrate technology, engineering, and mathematics, into their instruction. The NGSS focus particular attention on how to integrate engineering practices into science instruction.

STUDY BACKGROUND AND COMMITTEE CHARGE

Currently, many states are adopting the NGSS or are revising their own state standards in ways that reflect them. Ultimately, the task of implementing science standards rests with teachers. To implement the NGSS, or similar standards based on them, teachers will need learning opportunities that reinforce and expand their knowledge of the major ideas and concepts in science and of science and engineering practices, facility with a range of instructional strategies in science, and the skill to implement those strategies in their classrooms. Supporting this kind of learning for teachers will likely require changes in current approaches to supporting teachers' learning across their careers, including induction and professional development. Despite decades of efforts to improve science education, most districts and schools lack a coherent approach to supporting science teachers' learning. Recognizing these challenges and the need for guidance in how to address them, the Board on Science Education, within the Division of Behavioral and Social Sciences and Education in collaboration with the Teacher Advisory Council of the Academies, with support from the Merck Company Foundation, convened a 14-member expert committee to undertake a comprehensive study of how to provide coherent support for elementary, middle, and high school science teachers' learning across their careers. (The full charge to the committee is presented in Box 1-1.) This report synthesizes the committee's findings.

BOX 1-1
Charge to the Committee

The committee will identify the learning needs for teachers throughout their careers. The committee will identify how these needs might differ depending on school level (elementary, middle, and high school), and across the span of one's career. To the extent possible the committee will characterize the current state of the learning opportunities and support for learning that exist for teachers and identify the characteristics of effective learning opportunities. The committee will also consider how school and district contexts shape teachers' learning opportunities and limit or promote teachers' efforts to implement new classroom practices. They will consider the roles of school and district administrators and the professional development opportunities they may need in order to provide effective support for teachers. If possible, the committee will develop guidance for schools and districts for how best to support teachers' learning and how to implement successful programs for professional development. This will include considerations of the trade-offs and benefits of different approaches to professional development (e.g., costs, time, staffing needs, etc.).

continued

BOX 1-1 Continued

With regard to the evidence base, the committee will assess and describe the strengths and weaknesses of the available research evidence related to each component of a teacher learning continuum. It will identify major gaps and develop a research agenda for future work on professional development continuums in science. The committee will review and analyze research challenges, such as appropriate measures of student outcomes and teacher learning and the difficulty of establishing causal links between professional development, teachers' instructional practices, and students' outcomes. The committee will outline the research needed to more clearly define learning continuums for science teachers at each stage of their careers.

Specific questions the committee may consider include

- How do teachers' learning and professional needs differ by the stage of their careers and school level (elementary, middle, or high school)?
- What is known about the characteristics of effective approaches to supporting science teachers' learning? What are the implications for schools and districts?
- What is known about the kind of training teacher educators and providers of professional development need in order to support teachers' learning?
- What is known about how local, district, and state contexts shape the learning opportunities available for teachers and influence the outcomes of teachers' learning activities? What are the implications for schools, districts, and states?
- What is known about how to design and implement professional development and what guidance can be given to states, districts, and schools about implementation of effective professional development? What are the tradeoffs, limitations, and benefits of different approaches to induction and professional development?
- What are the major gaps and weaknesses in the currently available research on teacher development?
- What measures are used to evaluate the outcomes of teacher development activities, and what are the strengths and weaknesses of these measures? How are assessments used to diagnose teachers' learning needs and assess their progress?

SCOPE AND FOCUS OF THE STUDY

Understanding how best to support practicing science teachers at all grade levels throughout their careers is an ambitious undertaking. Although this committee acknowledges the central importance of teacher preparation to how science teachers are launched in the profession, this subject has been the focus of other National Academies of Sciences, Engineering, and Medicine reports (National Research Council, 2000, 2010).

Therefore, the committee used those previous reports as foundational for the present study and focused primarily on understanding the literature on professional support for practicing science teachers.

Key Concepts and Assumptions

The committee began by considering several framing assumptions in its charge (see Box 1-1). First, we defined a "teacher of science" to include elementary school teachers, who are likely to teach science as one of several subjects in the elementary curriculum, as well as those at the middle and high school levels where science teaching is the province of specialists. Second, we considered common assumptions about the teaching profession. For many, "career-long" evokes images of teachers who teach for a lifetime, sometimes even in the same school. However, the median length of a teacher's career has been declining steadily for almost a decade (Carroll and Foster, 2010). While nearly half of all science teachers at the high school level and 42 percent of those at the middle school level have more than 10 years of science teaching experience (Banilower et al., 2013), up to 50 percent of entering science teachers at those levels leave teaching within the first 5 years of their career (Miller, 2013; Sass, 2013). While many of those teachers may reenter the workforce in the future, the current workforce includes a substantial number of early-career teachers. This observation has direct implications for strategies for supporting the improvement of classroom instruction, as well as personnel policies concerning staffing arrangements, mentoring policies, professional development, and leadership training.

Another common assumption is that a teacher learning continuum is best conceptualized in stages (preservice, early career [sometimes referred to as induction], and experienced). In reality, those distinctions can be blurry: as initial preparation programs continue to experiment with new arrangements for launching teachers, it becomes increasingly difficult to have a common definition of a first-year teacher (Britton et al., 2003; Feuer et al., 2013; Wilson et al., 2011). Other dimensions of context matter as well; for example, if an experienced elementary teacher is assigned to a middle school or if a teacher moves from a highly resourced to an underresourced school, he or she may feel like a novice all over again. If a school district radically changes its assessments, curricula, or instructional approaches, experienced teachers can feel as unprepared as they did in their first years of teaching. These challenges call for teachers' continual learning. Further, attempts to standardize that learning or develop "one-size-fits-all" models rarely work.

The committee also challenged the assumption that the best frame for understanding teachers and teaching is one that treats the teacher as the unit of analysis. Teachers work in schools, and their identities, instruction, and growth are shaped by the school community, including both the school's leadership and culture. The learning opportunities available to a teacher are shaped profoundly by the local context in which he or she works—a teacher may be challenged or isolated, supported or frustrated, made to feel that the advancement of instruction is a professional obligation or that it is low on the list of priorities. Thus, promoting and supporting teacher quality needs to be understood from a collective standpoint, whether that collective be a professional learning community in a school, a diffuse set of teachers linked in an online learning network (e.g., as discussed in National Research Council, 2007), or a professional association of teachers. Whatever form it takes, mounting evidence suggests that a learning culture is essential to sustaining both teacher and school improvement, and that teachers are best able to develop in professional cultures characterized by a consistent focus on student learning (Bryk et al., 2010; Gamoran et al., 2003; Johnson et al., 2012; Kraft and Papay, 2014; McLaughlin and Talbert, 2001; Vescio et al., 2008).

Finally, the committee considered a broad range of learning opportunities for science teachers: formal and informal, structured and unstructured, individual and collective, planned and serendipitous, mandated and sought out. Teachers participate in organized, formal events designed specifically to educate them, such as induction programs and professional development workshops. Yet while it is important to understand the content and character of such discrete professional development events, the shifting landscape of education has created a much broader array of teacher learning opportunities. Teachers learn a great deal in their own classrooms on a daily basis while interacting with their students (Ball and Cohen, 1999; Ball and Forzani, 2011). They access ideas online, through networks of likeminded colleagues, or by individual experimentation with new instructional strategies. They belong to learning communities in their schools or through their professional associations. Experienced teachers work with prospective teachers. Schools increasingly hire coaches and mentors to support teachers who are charged with adopting and implementing new curricula. Moreover, many teachers assume formal or informal leadership roles that offer opportunities for professional learning, such as participation in curriculum review committees and the collective scoring of student work.

This is not to deny the important role played by the organized, formal events that commonly come to mind when one mentions "professional development." A main message of this report, however, is the need for a broad, expansive view of where and how teachers learn to teach over the course of their careers. Programs can offer powerful learning opportunities for teachers, but so can the schools and classrooms in which they work. In summary, "professional learning" is a much broader phenomenon than the conventional view of "professional development."

The Importance of the Educational Context

As noted above, the committee recognized that understanding and improving teachers' learning requires considering policies, practices, and norms that transcend the individual teacher and classroom. Teachers work within a larger, ever-expanding and shifting education system, characterized by ongoing state and federal reform efforts and a changing student and teacher population (Cuban, 2010; Cusick, 2014). Within that ecology, new learning needs and opportunities arise, where novices can be experts and experts can be novices.

The Current Policy Context

Issues of accountability are especially important in the current policy context, which shapes standards, curriculum frameworks, and requirements (including testing requirements) for science and other subjects alike. Since 2002, the No Child Left Behind Act has mandated that students in grades 3-8 be tested annually and that states demonstrate adequate yearly progress in raising test scores. The law gives priority to mathematics and English language arts, and these subjects accordingly account for the bulk of states' accountability formulas. As a result, pressures related to testing in mathematics and English language arts have largely squeezed science out of the elementary curriculum (Blank, 2013; Dorph et al., 2011). Nationally, elementary students have had fewer opportunities to experience sound science instruction relative to students at other levels, and their teachers report feeling inadequately prepared for and supported in teaching science (Banilower et al., 2013; Dorph et al., 2007, 2011; Hartry et al., 2012; Smith et al., 2002; see the further discussion in Chapter 2). Even at the high school level, where science enjoys a relatively secure position, federal and state accountability metrics generally weigh performance in mathematics and English language arts more heavily than performance in science. In California, for example, mathematics and English language arts account for nearly 86 percent of the weight of the state's Academic Performance Index, and science for only about 7 percent (Hartry et al., 2012).

Accountability policies do not focus on students alone. Increasingly, the performance of teachers, administrators, and schools is being measured. Notably, the U.S. Department of Education's Race to the Top initiative provided incentives for states to seek ways to tie teacher evaluations more closely to student learning (Institute for Education Sciences, 2014).

The initiative promoted educator evaluation policies using multiple measures and multiple rating categories, which could help provide more valid and reliable measures of teacher quality. Many states have responded to the Race to the Top initiative, instituting new educator evaluation systems that include teachers and school leaders making plans for teacher learning over the course of the year, repeated observations of teachers' practice, and the use of standardized tests to gather evidence of student learning. Prominent in this work have been efforts to model the contribution or "value added" of teachers' instruction to their students' learning. These policies can have a positive or negative influence on teachers' taking the risks necessary to implement the vision of science instruction embodied in the Framework and NGSS, a point to which we return in Chapter 8.

Regardless of a state's or district's policies and priorities, successful implementation depends on the availability of resources—human (e.g., knowledgeable personnel), social (e.g., teacher networks), and physical (e.g., time, money, materials) (Cohen et al., 2003). In recent years, state departments of education, district or county offices of education, and intermediary units have been decimated, significantly reducing the curricular and instructional expertise available to teachers in all subjects. As one example, funding for the statewide California Science Project declined from more than $9 million in 2002 to $1.2 million in 2011 (Hartry et al., 2012). The lack of funding and other resources limits effective science teaching (or any science teaching at all) and confounds attempts to improve practice over time in myriad ways.

The New Educational Marketplace

Recent years have seen a proliferation of publicly funded charter schools and networks, as well as other providers of education-related services outside of public school systems. Especially in larger urban settings, these providers are changing the landscape of education for students and of professional learning for teachers. The traditional school district is not the only unit managing schools, and traditional public schools are partnering in new ways with outside actors as well. The implications for this report are twofold. First, any report on science teachers' learning ought to speak to educators across the contexts in which they work. Second, a growing literature documents how these new actors approach organizing schools for student—and, at times, teacher—learning, and the committee sought out relevant information to inform our perspective on these developments. In particular, many of these organizations operate with clearly articulated theories of human capital development and the ways in which resources might best be directed to support teachers.

Charter schools, some focused on science, technology, engineering, and mathematics (STEM) themes, have grown rapidly. One study estimates that in the 2012-2013 school year, there were more than 6,000 charter schools serving about 2.3 million students, and that more than 4 percent of the total public school population in the United States consisted of charter school students (Center for Research on Education Outcomes, 2009). These figures represent an 80 percent increase from 2009.

Some charter schools are taking innovative approaches to supporting teachers by investing in tools and models for professional growth that include instructional guidance, access to coaches and teacher leaders, and the use of data to improve teaching and learning (Education Resource Strategies, 2013). Within the growing literature on charter schools, however, few studies are subject-specific, so one can only cautiously infer implications for how to improve science teaching and learning and support the development of science teachers.

There also has been a recent proliferation of external vendors, funders, and providers of professional development in science. Some of them, such as science museums and industry, offer unique sources of expertise to support teachers' learning, but access to those resources is unevenly distributed. For example, far too few rural schools have access to nearby museums and other informal learning institutions, which makes establishing such partnerships especially challenging. In addition, the quality of these services and providers is highly variable. This variability promises to increase as vendors sell materials and services that are aligned only superficially with the NGSS. As the field grows increasingly crowded, it becomes more difficult for system leaders to identify high-quality resources and experiences that will offer the kinds of support science teachers need in this age of reform.

The Place of Science in the K-12 Curriculum

Science has always had a place in the K-12 curriculum, but as noted above, it receives less emphasis than mathematics and English language arts, especially at the elementary level. Separate science classes with teachers who specialize in science typically do not begin until middle and high school. Generally, there are fewer individuals with expertise in science and science pedagogy than individuals with comparable expertise in English language arts and mathematics available within the school or district, and many administrators do not have science backgrounds. Lack of science expertise among district and school leaders can have implications for selecting curriculum materials, observing classroom instruction, making hiring decisions, and allocating resources for professional learning opportunities in science (National Research Council, 2015).

There are also topics in science about which educators, parents, and community members may have conflicting views (National Academy of Sciences and Institute of Medicine, 2008). Navigating how to teach about controversial issues is not unique to science; however, some topics in science, such as evolution and climate change, have become highly politicized.

In sum, the committee determined that making relevant and actionable recommendations concerning science teachers' learning over time would require taking a broad view of trends in science education; shifting conceptions of how and when teachers learn; the broader educational system, which includes new arrangements for teachers and their students; and education policies that shape both directly and indirectly what teachers are able to learn and teach. The goal of this report is to focus on science teachers' learning, but to do so in ways that acknowledge the important role of this larger context.

SOURCES AND STANDARDS OF EVIDENCE

In carrying out its charge, the committee examined and synthesized research on science teaching and learning, science teacher induction and professional development, teacher induction and professional development more generally, and the teacher workforce. We focused primarily on studies of science teachers. In some areas, however, studies focused on science were scarce. For this reason, we also drew on studies in other subject areas, primarily mathematics given its centrality to arguments concerning STEM education. For some broad issues, such as the importance of collaboration and professional community, we consulted the broader literature on teacher learning to identify important factors for supporting learning and then considered how they might play out in the context of science specifically. Likewise, there was a notable lack of research on how policy and school context affect science and science teachers in particular. For this reason, we drew on a broader literature on education policy, school reform and improvement efforts that conceptualize professional learning as an integral part of a larger reform agenda that also includes attention to curriculum, assessment, leadership, and community connections. Throughout the report, we have noted where the evidence comes primarily from studies in science and where we drew on studies outside of science.

The bodies of research we reviewed comprise many types of studies, from qualitative case studies, ethnographic and field studies, and interview studies to large-scale surveys of teachers and randomized controlled trials. When weighing the evidence from this research, we adopted the stance of an earlier Academies committee that "a wide variety of legitimate scientific designs are available for education research" (National Research Council, 2002, p. 6). According to that report, to be scientific,

> . . . the design must allow direct, empirical investigation of an important question, [use methods that permit direct investigation of the question], account for the context in which the study is carried out, align with a conceptual framework, reflect careful and thorough reasoning, and disclose results to encourage debate in the scientific community.

We also relied heavily on the American Educational Research Association's standards for reporting on social science (American Educational Research Association, 2006) and on humanities-oriented (American Educational Research Association, 2009) research in identifying quality research to be included in our review.

Recognizing the value of many types of research, we used different types of evidence to achieve different aims related to our charge. We did not automatically exclude studies with certain designs from consideration; rather, we examined the appropriateness of the design to the questions posed, whether the research methods were sufficiently explicated, and whether conclusions were warranted based on the design and available evidence. To provide descriptive summaries and conclusions about such topics as available learning opportunities for science teachers and the nature of the K-12 science teaching workforce, we relied on all types of research and on state- and national-level survey and administrative data. Descriptive evidence often is essential for understanding current conditions, in preparation for contemplating change. Identifying what changes are needed, however, requires research that goes beyond description to indicate what new outcomes would be expected to emerge as a result of the changes being considered.

When making these kinds of causal claims about the impacts of professional learning on various student or teacher outcomes (e.g., teacher practice, knowledge, attitudes, or beliefs), our goal was to draw conclusions based on research evidence that rules out alternative explanations for the measured impacts or patterns of change. For these purposes, we considered findings to be *suggestive* if they identify conditions that were associated with success but could not be disentangled from other influences on the desired outcomes. Examples of designs that might provide such evidence include qualitative studies and correlational quantitative analyses. We considered findings to give *evidence of success* if they resulted from research studies that were designed to support causal conclusions by credibly ruling out alternative explanations. Examples of designs that provide this level of evidence include experiments and nonexperimental studies in which assignment to treatment and control groups was random or effectively random around a cut point with a known assignment rule (i.e., regression discontinuity design). We also considered findings to give evidence of success if the research employed other nonexperimental designs that meaningfully reduced the likelihood of alternative explanations and several such studies yielded a body of evidence with consistent findings. With nonexperimental designs, our confidence was greater in findings that were found repeatedly in a variety of contexts because such replication makes alternate explanations less likely (National Research Council, 2002). We also privileged consistent findings across a variety of contexts, which resulted from experimental and/or nonexperimental designs that spoke to the findings' broader applicability.

Regardless of the methods used, we considered the quality of the study design and the fidelity with which that design was carried out to be of paramount importance. For example, high-quality well-implemented studies designed to support causal inferences can support causal statements. In contrast, even the highest-quality studies without a causal design are unlikely to rule out competing alternatives—although, as noted, the findings from an accumulated body of those studies may be consistent with causal conditions. Likewise, studies that are intended to identify causes but are poorly designed or poorly conducted may be unreliable in ruling out competing alternative explanations.

The committee also was concerned with understanding the mechanisms through which teachers learn. To gain greater insight into such mechanisms, we sought out richly descriptive work. While case studies and other interpretive work did not lead us to draw causal conclusions, they did help us understand potential contextual factors that shape both what and how teachers learn across various settings.

To address the issue of quality, we relied heavily on studies published in peer-reviewed publications. We also relied on several technical reports that contain information unavailable through any other sources.

ORGANIZATION OF THE REPORT

Chapter 2 summarizes the new vision for K-12 science education described in the Framework and the NGSS. Chapter 3 contrasts this vision with current teaching and learning, illuminating the gap between the vision and the present reality. Chapter 4 provides an overview of the current K-12 science teaching workforce and Chapter 5 outlines a set of learning needs for science teachers to support them in achieving the vision.

Chapter 6 then begins to examine the existing research on how best to support teachers' learning. As reviewed in Chapter 6, much of the research base to date has focused on professional development programs that consist of sessions offered outside of the school building, combined with opportunities for teachers to meet a few times during the school year. Chapter 7 examines emerging models for supporting teachers' learning that are embedded in their workday. Research on these models generally is less well developed than that on more formal professional development but holds promise for enhancing teachers' learning across their careers.

Chapter 8 then considers the broader context for teaching learning—administrative support, use of time, allocation of resources and space, the place of science in the curriculum—and identifies some of the policies and practices likely to help catalyze and support effective strategies for furthering teachers' learning. Finally, Chapter 9 presents the committee's conclusions and recommendations and identifies key areas in which research is needed to advance understanding of how to best support science teachers' learning across their careers.

REFERENCES

American Association for the Advancement of Science. (1993). *Benchmarks for Science Literacy*. Project 2061. New York: Oxford University Press. Available: http://www.project2061. org/publications/bsl/online/index.php?txtRef=http%3A%2F%2Fwww%2Eproject20 61%2Eorg%2Fpublications%2Fbsl%2Fdefault%2Ehtm%3FtxtRef%3D%26txtURIOld% 3D%252Ftools%252Fbsl%252Fdefault%2Ehtm&txtURIOld=%2Fpublications%2Fbsl% 2Fonline%2Fbolintro%2Fhtm [June 2015].

American Educational Research Association. (2006). Standards for reporting empirical social science research in AERA publications. *Educational Researcher, 35*(6), 33-40. Available: http://www.sagepub.com/upm-data/13127_Standards_from_AERA.pdf [January 2015].

American Educational Research Association. (2009). Standards for reporting on humanities-oriented research in AERA publications. *Educational Researcher, 38*(6), 481-486.

Ball, D.L., and Cohen, D.K. (1999). Developing practice, developing practitioners: Toward a practice-based theory of professional education. In L. Darling-Hammond and G. Sykes (Eds.), *Teaching as the Learning Profession: Handbook of Policy and Practice* (pp. 3-23). San Francisco, CA: Jossey-Bass.

Ball, D.L., and Forzani, F.M. (2011). Building a common core for learning to teach and connecting professional learning to practice. *American Educator, 35*(2), 17-21, 38-39.

Banilower, E.R., Smith, P.S., Weiss, I.R., Malzahn, K.A., Campbell, K.M., and Weis, A.M. (2013). *Report of the 2012 National Survey of Science and Mathematics Education*. Chapel Hill, NC: Horizon Research.

Blank, R.K. (2013). Science instructional time is declining in elementary schools: What are the implications for student achievement and closing the gap? *Science Education, 97*(6), 830-847.

Britton, E., Paine, L., Pimm, D., and Raizen, S. (2003). *Comprehensive Teacher Induction: Systems for Early Career Learning*. Dordrecht, The Netherlands: Springer.

Bryk, A., Sebring, P., Allensworth, E., Suppescu, S., and Easton, J. (2010). *Organizing Schools for Improvement: Lessons from Chicago*. Chicago, IL: University of Chicago Press.

Carroll, T., and Foster, E. (2010). *Who Will Teach? Experience Matters*. Washington, DC: National Commission on Teaching and America's Future. Available: http://nctaf.org/wp-content/uploads/2012/01/NCTAF-Who-Will-Teach-Experience-Matters-2010-Report. pdf [January 2015].

Center for Research on Education Outcomes. (2009). *Multiple Choice: Charter School Performance in 16 States*. Available: http://credo.stanford.edu/reports/MULTIPLE_CHOICE_CREDO.pdf [June 2015].

Center on Education Policy. (2007). *Choices, Changes, and Challenges: Curriculum and Instruction in the NCLB Era*. Washington, DC: Center on Education Policy.

Cohen, D., Raudenbush, S., and Ball, D. (2003). Resources, instruction, and research. *Educational Evaluation and Policy Analysis, 25*(2), 1-24.

Cuban, L. (2010). *As Good as it Gets: What School Reform Brought Austin*. Cambridge, MA: Harvard University Press.

Cusick, P.A. (2014). The logic of the U.S. educational system and teaching. *Theory into Practice, 53*(3), 176-182.

Dorph, R., Goldstein, D., Lee, S., Lepori, K., Schneider, S., and Venkatesan, S. (2007). *The Status of Science Education in the Bay Area: Research Brief*. Berkeley: Lawrence Hall of Science, University of California. Available: http://lawrencehallofscience.org/rea/bayareastudy/pdf/final_to_print_research_brief.pdf [January 2015].

Dorph, R., Shields, P., Tiffany-Morales, J., Hartray, A., and McCaffrey, T. (2011). *High Hopes, Few Opportunities: The Status of Elementary Science Education in California*. Sacramento, CA: The Center for the Future of Teaching and Learning at WestEd. Available: http://www.wested.org/resources/high-hopes-mdash-few-opportunities-full-report-the-status-of-elementary-science-education-in-california [January 2015].

Education Resource Strategies. (2013). *A New Vision for Teacher Professional Growth and Support: Six Steps to a More Powerful School System Strategy*. Available: http://www.erstrategies.org/cms/files/1800-gates-pgs-white-paper.pdf [September 2014].

Feuer, M.J., Floden, R.E., Chudowsky, N., and Ahn, J. (2013). *Evaluation of Teacher Preparation Programs: Purposes, Methods, and Policy Options*. Washington, DC: National Academy of Education.

Gamoran, A., Anderson, C.W., Quiroz, P.A., Secada, W.G., Williams, T., and Ashmann, S. (2003). *Transforming Teaching in Math and Science: How Schools and Districts Can Support Change*. New York: Teachers College Press.

Hartry, A., Dorph, R., Shields, P., Tiffany-Morales, J., and Romero, V. (2012). *The Status of Middle School Science Education in California*. Sacramento, CA: The Center for the Future of Teaching and Learning at WestEd.

Institute for Education Sciences. (2014). *State Requirements for Teacher Evaluation Policies Promoted by Race to the Top*. Washington, DC: Institute for Education Sciences. Available: http://ies.ed.gov/ncee/pubs/20144016/pdf/20144016.pdf [January 2015].

Johnson, S.M., Kraft, M.A., and Papay, J.P. (2012). How context matters in high-need schools: The effects of teachers' working conditions on their professional satisfaction and their students' achievement [special issue]. *Teachers College Record, 114*(10), 1-39.

Kraft, M.A., and Papay, J.P. (2014). *Can Professional Environments in Schools Promote Teacher Development?* Available: http://scholar.harvard.edu/files/mkraft/files/kraft_papay_2014_can_professional_environments_in_schools_promote_teacher_development.pdf [June 2015].

Martin, M.O., Mullis, I.V.S., Foy, P., and Stanco, G.M. (2012). *TIMSS 2011 International Results in Science*. Chestnut Hill, MA: TIMSS and PIRLS International Study Center, Boston College.

McLaughlin, M.W., and Talbert, J.E. (2001). *Professional Communities and the Work of High School Teaching*. Chicago, IL: University of Chicago Press.

Miller, J.D. (2010). The conceptualization and measurement of civic scientific literacy for the 21st century. In J. Meinwald and J.G. Hildebrand (Eds.), *Science and the Educated American: A Core Component of Liberal Education* (pp. 241-255). Cambridge, MA: American Academy of Arts and Sciences.

Miller, L. (2013). *A Descriptive Analysis of New York's Science Teacher Labor Market, 1999-2009*. Paper commissioned by the Committee on Strengthening Science Education through a Teacher Learning Continuum, Board on Science Education, National Research Council, Washington, DC. Available: http://sites.nationalacademies.org/cs/groups/dbassesite/documents/webpage/dbasse_084574.pdf [October 2015].

National Academy of Sciences and Institute of Medicine. (2008). *Science, Evolution, and Creationism*. Washington, DC: The National Academies Press.

National Research Council. (1996). *National Science Education Standards*. National Committee for Science Education Standards and Assessment. Board on Science Education, Division of Behavioral and Social Sciences and Education. Washington, DC: National Academy Press.

National Research Council. (2000). *Educating Teachers of Science, Mathematics, and Technology: New Practices for the New Millennium*. Committee on Science and Mathematics Teacher Preparation. Center for Education, Division of Behavioral and Social Sciences and Education. Washington, DC: National Academy Press.

National Research Council. (2002). *Scientific Research in Education*. Committee on Scientific Principles for Education Research. R.J. Shavelson, and L. Towne, (Eds.). Center for Education, Division of Behavioral and Social Sciences and Education. Washington, DC: National Academy Press.

National Research Council. (2007). *Enhancing Professional Development for Teachers: Potential Uses of Information Technology*. Committee on Enhancing Professional Development for Teachers, National Academies Teacher Advisory Council. Center for Education, Division of Behavioral and Social Sciences and Education. Washington, DC: The National Academies Press.

National Research Council. (2010). *Preparing Teachers: Building Evidence for Sound Policy*. Committee on the Study of Teacher Preparation Programs in the United States. Center for Education, Division of Behavioral and Social Sciences and Education. Washington, DC: The National Academies Press.

National Research Council. (2012). *A Framework for K-12 Science Education: Practices, Crosscutting Concepts, and Core Ideas*. Committee on a Conceptual Framework for New K-12 Science Standards. Board on Science Education, Division of Behavioral and Social Sciences and Education. Washington, DC: The National Academies Press.

National Research Council. (2015). *Guide to Implementing the Next Generation Science Standards*. Committee on Guidance on Implementing the Next Generation Science Standards. Board on Science Education, Division of Behavioral and Social Sciences and Education. Washington, DC: The National Academies Press.

Next Generation Science Standards Lead States. (2013). *Next Generation Science Standards: For States, By State*s. Washington, DC: The National Academies Press.

OECD. (2014). *PISA 2012 Results: What Students Know and Can Do, Student Performance in Mathematics, Reading, and Science* (vol. I, revised ed.). Available: http://www.keepeek.com/Digital-Asset-Management/oecd/education/pisa-2012-results-what-students-know-and-can-do-volume-i-revised-edition-february-2014_9789264208780-en#page1 [January 2015].

Sass, T. (2013). *The Market for New Science Teachers in Florida*. Paper commissioned by the Committee on Strengthening Science Education through a Teacher Learning Continuum, Board on Science Education, National Research Council, Washington, DC.

Smith, P.S., Banilower, E.R., McMahon, K.C., and Weiss, I.R. (2002). *The National Survey of Science and Mathematics Education: Trends from 1977 to 2000*. Chapel Hill, NC: Horizon Research.

Vescio, V., Ross, D., and Adams, A. (2008). A review of research on the impact of professional learning communities on teaching practice and student learning. *Teaching and Teacher Education*, 24(1), 80-91.

Wilson, S.M., Rozelle, J.J., and Mikeska, J.N. (2011). Cacophony or embarrassment of riches: Building a system of support for teacher quality. *Journal of Teacher Education*, *62*(4), 383-394.

2

A New Vision of Science Teaching and Learning

A discussion of how and what science teachers need to learn over the course of their careers must be anchored in an explicit vision of quality science teaching, which itself needs to be grounded in aspirations for students' learning. *A Framework for K-12 Science Education* (hereafter referred to as the Framework) (National Research Council, 2012) and the *Next Generation Science Standards* (hereafter referred to as the NGSS) (Next Generation Science Standards Lead States, 2013) describe aspirations for students' learning in science that are based on key insights from research:

- that science learning involves the integration of knowing and doing (Knorr-Cetina, 1999; Latour, 1990; Nersessian, 2012; Pickering, 1992);
- that developing conceptual understanding through engaging in the practices of science is more productive for future learning than simply memorizing lists of facts (Bruer, 1993; Clark, 2006; Cognition and Technology Group at Vanderbilt, 1993; Driver et al., 1996); and
- that science learning is best supported when learning experiences are designed to build and revise understanding over time (Carey, 1985; Gelman and Lucariello, 2002; Lehrer and Schauble, 2006; Smith et al., 2006).

These are not new ideas. The Framework and NGSS build on previous documents that lay out expectations for K-12 students in science (e.g., *National Science Education Standards* [National Research Council, 1996], *Benchmarks for Science Literacy* [American Association for the Advancement of Science, 1993], *Science Framework for the 2009 National Assessment of Educational Progress* [National Assessment of Educational Progress, 2009], and *Science College Board Standards for College Success* [College Board, 2009]). Yet despite a long history of efforts to improve K-12 science education, rigorous and science-rich learning experiences are not standard fare in U.S. public schools. Too often, local curricular guidance takes the form of long lists of detailed and disconnected facts that teachers must cover in limited time, often leading to instruction focused on memorization instead of deep understanding. As a result, students are left with fragmented knowledge, little sense of the inherent logic and consistency of science, and virtually no experience engaging in genuine scientific investigations and discovery. The current round of reform, catalyzed in large part by the Framework and NGSS, is intended to address these issues. In this chapter, the committee briefly discusses what students need to learn about science and the implications for science instruction, with an emphasis on the Framework and NGSS.

WHAT STUDENTS NEED TO LEARN ABOUT SCIENCE

Science educators have struggled with how to characterize school science, wishing to highlight not only the *content* of science—facts and concepts, for example—but also the *doing* of science—the habits of mind, skills, and practices that bring science to life and make it a compelling enterprise. The Framework and NGSS articulate three dimensions of science learning: scientific and engineering practices, crosscutting concepts, and disciplinary core ideas. But they also go beyond prior standards by urging the integration of these three dimensions into standards, curricula, instruction, and assessment and emphasizing that no single dimension adequately characterizes what it means to know science; taught alone, each can seem empty or irrelevant.

As noted, educators have long argued for an approach to science education that allows students to engage in investigations and teaches fewer topics in greater depth. But these ideals have not been realized in many U.S. classrooms. Instead, students often engage in lock-step, prescribed experiments, and the number of scientific facts they must memorize has continued to expand. As a result, teachers must teach more in less time, and what students are expected to learn has widened instead of deepening. The Framework and NGSS are designed to combat those trends. A major goal of the Framework and NGSS is to shift the emphasis in science education from teaching detailed facts to immersing students in doing science and understanding the big-picture ideas.

Scientific Practices[1]

Research has shown that students best understand scientific ideas when they actively apply their knowledge while engaging in the *practices* of science—for example, modeling, developing explanations or solutions, and arguing about evidence (Bamberger and Davis, 2013; Berland and Reiser, 2009; McNeill, 2011; McNeill et al., 2006; Smith et al., 2000). Without personally engaging in these activities, students cannot come to understand the nature of scientific discovery; instead, they see science as abstract and far removed from the real world. It is difficult for students to understand scientific investigations without opportunities to design and carry them out firsthand. It is also difficult for students to see the relevance of scientific ideas and concepts unless they learn how to use them in building their own arguments and explanations. Thus, a major goal associated with the current vision for science education involves greater emphasis on immersing students in *doing* science rather than simply *learning about* science.

Learning through practice helps students of all ages understand how scientific knowledge develops and gives them an appreciation of the wide range of approaches that are used by scientists to investigate, model, and explain the world. Engaging in the practices of science also pushes students to use their knowledge and reflect on their own understanding of scientific ideas. They thereby gain a more flexible understanding of scientific explanations of natural phenomena and can take a critical perspective on scientific claims (Chinn et al., 2008; Duschl and Duncan, 2009; Herrenkohl and Guerra, 1998; Radinsky et al., 2010; Rosebery et al., 1992; Sandoval and Millwood, 2005). Indeed, research demonstrates that in-depth participation in scientific practices can support the development of students' science content knowledge (Lehrer and Schauble, 2000, 2003, 2005; National Research Council, 2007). The shift toward a tighter coupling of scientific and engineering practices, disciplinary core ideas, and crosscutting concepts acknowledges that knowledge is used, reinforced, or reshaped in practice, and that the practices by their nature involve learning from and communicating with others. Moreover, this coupling guards against the tendency to have students either memorize

---

[1]The NGSS describe science and engineering practices, emphasizing how the two complement one another. Here, in accordance with the committee's charge (Box 1-1 in Chapter 1), the focus is on science practices.

BOX 2-1
Practices for K-12 Science Classrooms Described in the Framework and NGSS

Practices include

- asking questions (for science) and defining problems (for engineering);
- developing and using models;
- planning and carrying out investigations;
- analyzing and interpreting data;
- using mathematics, information and computer technology, and computational thinking;
- constructing explanations (for science) and designing solutions (for engineering);
- engaging in argument from evidence; and
- obtaining, evaluating, and communicating information.

---

disconnected facts or engage in "the scientific method" as a rote set of scripted steps.

Engagement in the practices of science may look different in 2nd, 8th, and 10th grades, but students at all levels have the capacity to think scientifically and engage in science practices (see Box 2-1). It is especially important to note that, under carefully constructed conditions of support, elementary-age students can reason in ways and participate in activities previously considered beyond their developmental capabilities (Metz, 1995; National Research Council, 2007), an observation with significant implications for science instruction in grades K-5.

Disciplinary Core Ideas

Scientific knowledge is constantly evolving. New fields are created, new models are proposed, and new intricacies of the natural world are revealed. Science textbooks have been enlarged accordingly to reflect this new knowledge, making it challenging for teachers to explore any topic in depth or to decide how to prioritize what should be taught—"coverage" has marginalized exploration and discovery. The Framework and NGSS authors confronted this age-old problem by focusing on disciplinary core ideas in four major areas: physical sciences; life sciences; earth and space sciences; and engineering, technology, and the applications of science (National Research Council, 2012; Next Generation Science Standards

---

BOX 2-2
Disciplinary Core Ideas

Physical Sciences
PS 1: Matter and Its Interactions
PS 2: Motion and Stability: Forces and Interactions
PS 3: Energy
PS 4: Waves and Their Applications in Technologies for Information Transfer

Life Sciences
LS 1: From Molecules to Organisms: Structures and Processes
LS 2: Ecosystems: Interactions, Energy, and Dynamics
LS 3: Heredity: Inheritance and Variation of Traits
LS 4: Biological Evolution: Unity and Diversity

Earth and Space Sciences
ESS 1: Earth's Place in the Universe
ESS 2: Earth's Systems
ESS 3: Earth and Human Activity

Engineering, Technology, and the Applications of Science
ETS 1: Engineering Design
ETS 2: Links among Engineering, Technology, Science, and Society

SOURCE: National Research Council (2012).

Lead States, 2013) (see Box 2-2). In the life sciences, for example, the first core idea is "From Molecules to Organisms: Structures and Processes," which addresses how individual organisms are configured and how these structures function to support life, growth, behavior, and reproduction. This core idea hinges on the unifying principle that cells are the basic unit of life.

This emphasis on a focused set of core ideas is designed to allow sufficient time for teachers and students to use science practices to explore ideas in depth so as to develop understanding. It is assumed that teachers and students will circle back to ideas to address misunderstandings, to slow down when things are particularly challenging, and to constantly make new connections as students' understanding grows. The goal is to avoid superficial coverage of multiple disconnected topics. The College Board has adopted a similar approach in its recent efforts to restructure Advanced Placement science courses in biology, chemistry, and physics based on recommendations in a National Research Council (2002) report. The Framework and NGSS also articulate how disciplinary core ideas

---

BOX 2-3
Crosscutting Concepts

The Framework and NGSS describe the following crosscutting concepts:

- patterns;
- cause and effect: mechanism and explanation;
- scale, proportion, and quantity;
- systems and system models;
- energy and matter: flows, cycles, and conservation;
- structure and function; and
- stability and change.

---

should build coherently through multiple grades and connect across the life, physical, earth, and space sciences and engineering.

Crosscutting Concepts

In science, ideas do not exist in isolation but are part of complex webs of meaning. Thus, learning science also involves linking specific disciplinary core ideas to crosscutting concepts that lead to a coherent, scientific view of the world. For example, the concept of "cause and effect" could be discussed in the context of plant growth in a biology class or in the context of the motion of objects in a physics class. The emphasis on understanding the interconnectedness of scientific ideas is not new, as it is reflected in the unifying concepts and processes of the *National Science Education Standards* (National Research Council, 1996) and the common themes highlighted in the *Benchmarks for Science Literacy* (American Association for the Advancement of Science, 1993). The Framework and NGSS draw on these earlier documents to describe a set of seven crosscutting concepts (see Box 2-3). Here, too, the emphasis in the current vision of science education is on explicitly attending to the integration of these crosscutting concepts with practices and disciplinary core ideas.

Support for Learning over Time

The design of the Framework and NGSS is intended to support coherent sequences for learning over multiple grades. Research on learning clearly shows that to develop a thorough understanding of scientific explanations of the world, students need sustained opportunities to engage in the practices of science and work with its underlying ideas, and to appreciate the interconnections among those ideas over a period of years rather than weeks or months (National Research Council, 2007). This notion of a systematic sequence for learning over time often is referred to as a learning progression (Corcoran et al., 2009; National Research Council, 2007; Smith et al., 2006). Learning progressions are descriptions of both how students' understanding of an idea matures over time and the instructional supports and experiences that are needed for them to make this progress. Progressions are empirically grounded, hypothetical trajectories for learning across multiple grades. They are shaped by students' instructional and curricular experiences and are not developmentally inevitable. Also, because students bring different personal and cultural resources to the process of learning science, there are likely to be variations in the paths of individual students that need to be taken into account in instruction (Duncan and Hmelo-Silver, 2009; National Research Council, 2007).

Importantly, these progressions begin in the earliest grades of school. Therefore, the building of progressively more sophisticated explanations of natural phenomena should be central throughout grades K-5, as opposed to a focus only on description in the early grades, with explanation deferred to the later grades. Similarly, students can engage in scientific and engineering practices beginning in the earliest grades.

An Illustration

The Framework offers a concrete illustration of how students might investigate the same core ideas over multiple years through instruction that integrates the three dimensions of scientific and engineering practices, crosscutting concepts, and disciplinary core ideas. The following are examples from this illustration—focused on developing an understanding of "Structure and Properties of Matter" (a component of the physical sciences core idea "Matter and Its Interactions")—in the early elementary grades and at the high school level.

Grades K-2 Students investigate a wide variety of substances (e.g., wood, metal, water, clay) in multiple contexts and engage in discussion about the substances' observable characteristics and uses. These experiences begin to elicit students' questions about matter, which they answer by planning and conducting their own investigations and by making observations. Throughout such experiences, the teacher has students offer explanations of their observations and data. After students observe and measure a variety of solid and liquid substances, for instance, the teacher uses intentional and appropriate questions and prompts during class discussion to make students' thinking visible, crafting meaningful opportunities for students to focus on identifying and characterizing the materials from which objects are made and the reasons why particular materials are chosen for particular tasks. The teacher then asks students to use evidence to generate claims about different kinds of matter and their uses, as well as interrogate those claims.

Starting in kindergarten (or before), teachers invite students to manipulate a variety of building toys, such as wooden blocks, interlocking objects, or other construction sets, leading them to recognize that although what one can build depends on the things from which one is building, many different objects can be constructed with multiple copies of a small set of different components. Students' progress in their building efforts advances from free play to solving design problems, and teachers facilitate this progression by asking appropriate questions about the objects that students build, by having them draw diagrams of what they have built, and by directing their attention to built objects outside the classroom.

Teacher-guided student experiences and investigations also help students gain awareness of another important concept about matter—that some materials (not just water but also chocolate, wax, and ice cream, for example) can be either liquid or solid depending on the temperature and that there is a characteristic temperature for each substance at which this transition occurs. The transition from liquid to gas is not stressed in this grade band, however, because the concept of gases other than air, or even the fact that air is matter, cannot readily be developed on the basis of students' observations and experiences.

Grades 3-5 Students begin to explore matter with greater emphasis on detailed measurements and exploration of changes to matter such as melting, freezing, or dissolving. Through investigations, they come to understand that weight is an additive property of matter; that is, the weight of a set of objects is the sum of the weights of the component objects. They might investigate whether the amount of material remains the same when water or other fluids are frozen and then melted again by recording the material's weight at each stage.

Through guided investigations and use of simulations, students develop two important ideas: that gas is a form of matter and that it is modeled as a collection of particles moving around. Students need multiple learning experiences to shift their concept of matter to include the gaseous state. These experiences might begin with investigations of air, which is a familiar yet invisible material. Investigations, such as weighing a deflated balloon and comparing its weight with that of an inflated balloon, provide contexts for students to explore whether gases take up space and have weight.

Students' understanding of the categories, properties, and uses of matter are refined and expanded over this grade band. Students investigate the properties of different materials and consider how those properties can be used to categorize materials or identify which materials are best suited for particular purposes (such as building a skyscraper or protecting an object from breaking). Across this grade band, students develop increasingly sophisticated models of matter and become more sophisticated in their ability to relate their models to evidence and inferences drawn from observations of actual phenomena.

Grades 6-8 In this grade band, students carry out investigations and develop explanations and models that help them deepen and apply their understanding of the particle model of matter. In grade 6, representations of the states of matter include the concept that the particles are in motion in each state, but the spacing and degree of motion vary among them. The role of forces between particles is also explored. Over 7th and 8th grades, students refine their understanding by comparing their models of matter with empirical observations of such phenomena as transmission of smells or changes of state.

Students also need opportunities to connect their knowledge to crosscutting concepts such as energy and apply their emerging understanding of matter in the context of life and earth science. Ultimately, using evidence collected and analyzed from their own investigations, evidence from outside sources (e.g., atomic images), and the results of simulations, students confirm a model that matter consists of atoms in motion with forces between them, and that the motion of the atoms is dependent on temperature. Students can use this model to defend such claims as that all substances are made from approximately 100 different types of atoms, that atoms form molecules, and that gases and liquids are made up of molecules that are moving about relative to each other.

Grades 9-12 Teachers introduce students to the structures *within* atoms and their relationships to the forces *between* atoms. Students' understanding of the particle model of matter is developed and refined as teachers engage them in investigations and analyses of data, both their own and those from experiments that cannot be undertaken in the science classroom. Teachers support students as they develop increased sophistication—both in their model-based explanations and in the argumentation by which evidence and explanation are linked—by using mathematical and language skills appropriate to their grade level.

Note that for every grade band, the teacher is essential to instruction, intentionally creating and orchestrating experiences that are carefully structured to engage students actively with practices, disciplinary core ideas, and crosscutting concepts and discussing the phenomena at hand and related science ideas. To enact this kind of teaching, teachers need to understand all three dimensions (science practices, disciplinary core ideas, and crosscutting concepts), and to have a sense of the goals for students' learning in a particular grade and across the grade band. Working in this kind of an environment requires considerable intellectual and pedagogical proficiency; turning hands-on work into minds-on work requires that teachers be able to hear what students are trying to understand, point students' attention to critical moments and issues that arise, interject powerful examples and ideas, and manage the unpredictable nature of experience. Moreover, teachers must be fluent in shifting class discussions from rigid question-answer routines to rich opportunities for students to negotiate meaning through productive disciplinary talk—the antithesis of "teacher telling" (e.g., Engle and Conant, 2002; Engle et al., 2014).

Equity and Diversity

One of the guiding principles of the Framework is promoting equity, which means that *all* students must have access to high-quality learning opportunities in science (National Research Council, 2012). The U.S. student population is increasingly diverse along a range of characteristics, including socioeconomic status, race, English language fluency, and learning disabilities (Kena et al., 2014):

- In 2012, approximately 21 percent of school-age children were living in poverty, compared with 17 percent two decades earlier (1990).
- In the decade from 2001 to 2011, the percentage of white students enrolled in public schools fell from 60 to 52 percent, while the percentage of Hispanic students increased from 17 to 24 percent; the share of black students declined slightly, from 17 to 16 percent.
- The percentage of English language learners in school year 2011-2012 was higher (9.1 percent) than in 2002-2003 (8.7 percent). Among school-age children nationally, more than one in five speak a foreign language at home; the proportion is 44 percent in California and roughly one in three in Texas, Nevada, and New York (Zielger and Camarota, 2014). Among students who speak another language at home, 44 percent (27.2 million) were born in the United States (Zielger and Camarota, 2014).

In school year 2011-2012, 13 percent of all public school students received special education services, and of these, about 36 percent had specific learning disabilities. The current percentage represents a decline from 14 percent in 2004-2005. Prior to that time, the percentage had increased from about 11 percent in 1990-1991.

While there are differences among specific demographic groups in their science achievement and patterns of science learning, robust evidence indicates that all students are capable of learning science when supportive conditions for learning are in place (National Research Council, 2012). There are many challenges, however, to providing all students with equitable opportunities to learn science. Some of these challenges stem from inequities in resources and expertise across schools, districts, and communities. At the same time, instruction can also be more or less responsive to the needs of diverse students. It is increasingly recognized that diverse customs and experiences can be valuable assets in the science classroom and that instruction needs to build on students' interests and backgrounds to engage them meaningfully. Teachers also need to be aware that students may have different ways of engaging in classroom discussion or expressing their knowledge. The adaptation of instruction in rigorous and meaningful ways is dependent on contexts that are not treated in detail in the brief scenarios offered here; further discussion of contextual issues is contained in Chapter 5.

IMPLICATIONS FOR SCIENCE TEACHING

. As this report addresses the learning needs of teachers, the ambitious, challenging, and dynamic vision of science learning presented above—which integrates ideas with concepts and practices and allows students to see the connectedness of scientific knowledge and its relevance to their own lives—serves as a guide.

A major animating idea of this new vision of science learning is that students' understanding of any idea or concept is intimately related to their having engaged with phenomena through practices. The vision also emphasizes students' understanding that scientific knowledge is generated by scientists who engage in experiments, field work, and archival research; that the knowledge derived from this work is the result of hypothesizing, testing, and arguing; and that scientists' explanations of the natural world are revised as new evidence is generated. It follows, then, that science instruction needs to engage all students with a broad array of natural phenomena, support rigorous intellectual work, and facilitate full immersion in scientific and engineering practices over long periods of time. However, such practices include a broad range of intellectual habits—asking questions, developing and using models, analyzing data, and constructing explanations from data. Thus science practices are not synonymous simply with "hands-on" activity.

The new vision for science learning does not specify the universal use of a particular pedagogy. Rather, multiple instructional approaches are likely to be required. While student learning outcomes (i.e., what students should know and be able to do) are made clear in both the Framework and the NGSS, the requisite teaching practices for helping them achieve those outcomes are not spelled out. The learning goals for students do suggest that particular shifts in instructional practices will be needed (see Table 2-1); given the situated nature of teaching, however, it also is likely that teachers will always need to adapt their instructional approaches to the specific needs of their students. That said, many science educators have explored the nature of good science teaching, a literature that also informed the committee's deliberations.

In a review of the literature on science learning and teaching, Windschitl and Calabrese Barton (forthcoming) identify three common patterns of what they call "ambitious" science teaching, or teaching that "aims to support all students in engaging deeply with science" (p. 3).

The first pattern involves carefully framing the students' relationship with the intellectual work at hand, including

- teachers having high expectations of students and supporting these expectations in a range of ways;
- students engaging in scientific practices; and
- teachers giving students increasing responsibility for assessing their own understanding and evaluating progress toward important goals.

Metz (2004, 2011), for example, worked with teachers who had high expectations for the ability of elementary students to design and execute independent forms of scientific investigation. These teachers immersed children in a single domain, such as ornithology or animal behavior, for a year or longer. The children developed domain-specific knowledge that, in turn, supported further learning as they engaged in scientific practices. In the early stages of the children's participation in the study, teachers carefully scaffolded their investigations; as the children learned to pose and answer scientific questions, they were able to understand and apply tools, representations, and forms of data analysis that were particular to the domain (e.g., animal behavior). Later, teachers gave the children increasing responsibility for the design and evaluation of scientific investigations. An analysis of pre- and post-structured interviews and students' written work demonstrated that the children's understanding

TABLE 2-1 Implications of the Framework and NGSS for Instruction

Science Instruction Will Involve Less	Science Instruction Will Involve More
Rote memorization of facts and terminology	Learning facts and terminology as needed while developing explanations and designing solutions supported by evidence-based arguments and reasoning
Learning ideas disconnected from questions about phenomena	Using systems thinking and modeling to explain phenomena and to provide a context for the ideas to be learned
Teachers providing information to the whole class	Students conducting investigations, solving problems, and engaging in discussions with teachers' guidance
Teachers posing questions with only one right answer	Students discussing open-ended questions that focus on the strength of the evidence used to generate claims
Students reading textbooks and answering questions at the end of the chapter	Students reading multiple sources, including science-related magazine and journal articles and web-based resources; students developing summaries of information
Having preplanned outcomes for "cookbook" laboratories or hands-on activities	Conducting multiple investigations driven by students' questions, with a range of possible outcomes that collectively lead to a deep understanding of established core scientific ideas
Using worksheets	Students' producing journals, reports, posters, and media presentations that explain and argue
Oversimplifying activities for students who are perceived to have less capability in science and engineering	Providing supports so that all students can engage in sophisticated science and engineering practices

SOURCE: National Research Council (2015).

of science practices had grown. In one study, all student teams in a 2nd-grade classroom and in a mixed 4th- and 5th-grade classroom were able to formulate both research questions and methods for investigating their questions. Some teams even proposed methods for controlling extraneous variables (Metz, 2000).

The second pattern involves anchoring teaching and learning activities around specific concepts and topics by:

- focusing instructional units on subject matter relevant to students' lives, interests, or curiosity;
- coupling important science ideas with extended investigations of complex phenomena;
- making the explanation of the "hows" and "whys" of scientific phenomena a priority as a learning goal;
- building coherence across learning activities and among the bigger science ideas featured in the unit of instruction; and
- interweaving the development of science skills with the development of conceptual knowledge.

Lehrer and Schauble (2003, 2005, 2012), for example, explored elementary students' learning of biological ideas related to growth and change in living systems. Participating teachers built on children's interests by inviting them to represent living things in a variety of ways—through language, drawings, physical models, maps, and patterns. They engaged the children in scientific practices such as quantifying or visualizing biological phenomena and applying concepts of measurement and ideas about data and uncertainty. Through this interweaving of science concepts and practices, the children gained an understanding of biological growth and change and how to represent these concepts mathematically. Early-elementary students learned to use their own representations of plant growth to ask questions about how much more rapidly one specimen grew than another, turning their attention from comparing final heights to noting successive differences in change itself from the day-to-day measurements. In later grades, students used progressively more symbolic and mathematically powerful representations. The investigators document substantial learning effects, with students in grades 1 through 5 outperforming much older students on nationally benchmarked assessment items (Lehrer and Schauble, 2005).

In another example, Roth and colleagues (2006, 2009) posit that effective teachers identify clear and reasonable goals for student learning and craft coherent sequences of lessons related to these goals; the authors refer to these sequences as "coherent science content storylines." A science content storyline focuses on integrating and sequencing science ideas and learning activities within a science lesson or unit to help students construct a coherent "story" that makes sense to them.

The third pattern involves teachers carefully mediating students' learning activity by

- identifying clear learning/participation goals and designing individual activities through which to reach these goals;

- adapting the progression of experiences to learners' current needs;
- designing instruction that uses the diversity of students' ideas and everyday experiences as resources to further all students' understanding;
- using supports and symbols to engage students in scientific reasoning, discourse, and other interactions; and
- using classroom discourse for a variety of purposes—for example, to make students' thinking visible, reinforce the norms of science talk, prompt sense making and reasoning, "seed" conversations with new ideas, make confusion public, and position young learners as competent knowers of science.

In an early example of this pattern, Brown and Campione (1994) pioneered an approach to coupling investigations with other activities so as to cultivate deep content knowledge of targeted science ideas. In their research project with K-8 students in the 1980s and 1990s, the investigators viewed learning and teaching as a social process facilitated by the use of talk, gesture, drawing, computers, and text. Teachers mediated students' learning activities, introducing a set of science ideas through a compelling and scientifically rich story or video. They encouraged students to ask questions while also guiding the ensuing discussion to ensure that important science ideas related to the learning goals were presented and were later investigated. A primary support used by teachers to engage students in scientific reasoning and discourse was the "research-share-perform" cycle. Students first read and analyzed texts about scientific studies relevant to the domain under study and then divided into small groups to investigate questions or ideas emerging from these texts, such as food chains or food webs. Over the course of their investigations, they were encouraged to develop specialized expertise and to share that expertise with others, as well as to reflect on their own learning and how to support it. Students in these classroom communities routinely outscored learners in control groups in both literacy and science.

It is important to note that much of the research on which Windschitl and Calabrese Barton (forthcoming) draw involved sustained opportunities for teachers and students to engage with scientific ideas and practices over periods of months and years, rather than days and weeks. While the Framework and the NGSS were designed to compel and support this kind of coherence (beginning in the earliest grades), it is not typical of current science teaching and learning in the United States (see Chapter 3 for detailed discussion of current science instruction). Furthermore, the instructional approaches that have been researched were heavily resourced. Quality instruction is not due simply to a well-prepared teacher with good intentions; it requires ongoing support from others, a solid understanding of the content, well-tested materials, and time. Cohen and colleagues (2003) and Bryk and colleagues (2010), among others, posit that these resources are embedded in a supportive culture for teaching that enables their strategic use.

If the Framework and NGSS are clear on student learning outcomes and less so on specifics of the instruction needed to realize those outcomes, they are virtually silent on other aspects of the larger ecology in which individual teachers might engage in these science practices with their students. For example, they say little about the nature of the school cultures in which these teachers would need to work, or how expertise in science would be distributed across and among the teachers in a school or district. While these standards have emerged from the larger standards movement, which presumes that systems of levers or supports—assessment, curriculum, teacher training—are necessary for instructional reform, the documents themselves do not describe the range of material, human, and social resources that schools and districts would need to enact this vision, or how school, district, and state policies might be used to create the receptive conditions and environments in which all of this innovation would need to unfold. Yet policies on what is taught, how students are assessed, how teachers are evaluated, how schools are judged, how schools are staffed, how the school day and year are organized, how schools are run, and how leaders are supported can have crucial implications for what and how science is taught in schools. These contexts matter to ambitious teaching, a point to which the discussion returns later in this report.

CONCLUSION

Any decisions made about science teaching ought to be anchored in a well-explicated, empirically informed vision of science learning for all students. Educators, scientists, and education researchers have been working on such a vision—through instructional guidance materials such as standards and through research on students' science learning—for decades. The current vision, articulated in such documents as the Framework and the NGSS, both build on and extend past efforts, which have yielded important understanding and learning for all students. This vision—one that acknowledges science as fundamental to human understanding and driven by complex, relevant problems—involves learning about scientific practices, crosscutting concepts, and disciplinary core ideas in an integrated manner. This conception of science learning reflects the nature of scientists' work: geologists, physicists, chemists, and biologists explore and extend scientific understanding by calling on their deep knowledge of fundamental scientific ideas while posing questions, building models, conducting a range of investigations, testing hypotheses, and interpreting evidence. In the sciences, as in all fields, the doing of science goes hand in hand with mastering and using knowledge.

While some might think such an ambitious view of learning is beyond the reach of all students, careful research has demonstrated that challenging instruction is possible if teachers have a clear vision of their goals, well-designed lessons and materials, and—most important—the professional knowledge and skill required to teach to these high standards. But ambitious instruction is not yet standard fare in American classrooms, and the following chapter describes the current conditions that thwart efforts to guarantee that every child learns science in intellectually substantive and exciting ways.

REFERENCES

American Association for the Advancement of Science. (1993). *Benchmarks for Science Literacy.* Project 2061. New York: Oxford University Press. Available:http://www.project2061. org/publications/bsl/online/index.php [June 2015].

Bamberger, Y.M., and Davis, E.A. (2013). Middle school science students' scientific modelling performances across content areas and within a learning progression. *International Journal of Science Education, 35*(2), 213-238.

Berland, L.K., and Reiser, B.J. (2009). Making sense of argumentation and explanation. *Science Education, 93*(1), 26-55.

Brown, A.L., and Campione, J.C. (1994). Guided discovery in a community of learners. In K. McGilly (Ed.), *Classroom Lessons: Integrating Cognitive Theory and Classroom Practice* (pp. 229-270). Cambridge, MA: MIT Press/Bradford Books.

Bruer, J. (1993). *Schools for Thought.* Cambridge, MA: MIT Press.

Bryk, A., Sebring, P., Allensworth, E., Suppescu, S., and Easton, J. (2010). *Organizing Schools for Improvement: Lessons from Chicago.* Chicago, IL: University of Chicago Press.

Carey, S. (1985). *Conceptual Change in Childhood.* Cambridge, MA: MIT Press/Bradford Books.

Chinn, C., Duschl, R., Duncan, R., Pluta, W., Buckland, L., Ruppert, J., Bausch, A., and Freidenreich, H. (2008, March). *Promoting Growth in Scientific Reasoning: A Year-Long Microgenetic Study of Middle School Students Learning through Model-Based Inquiry.* Paper presented at the Annual Meeting of the American Educational Research Association, New York.

Clark, D.B. (2006). Longitudinal conceptual change in students' understanding of thermal equilibrium: An examination of the process of conceptual restructuring. *Journal of the Learning Sciences, 24*(4), 467-563.

Cognition and Technology Group at Vanderbilt. (1993). Anchored instruction and situated cognition revisited. *Educational Technology, 33*(3), 52-93.

Cohen, D.K., Raudenbush, S.W., and Ball, D.L. (2003). Resources, instruction, and research. *Educational Evaluation and Policy Analysis, 25*(2), 1-24.

College Board. (2009). *Science College Board Standards for College Success.* Available: http:// professionals.collegeboard.com/profdownload/cbscs-science-standards-2009.pdf [June 2015].

Corcoran, T., Mosher, F.A., and Rogat, A. (2009). *Learning Progressions in Science: An Evidence-based Approach to Reform.* New York: Center on Continuous Instructional Improvement, Teachers College, Columbia University and Consortium for Policy Research on Education. Available: http://www.cpre.org/images/stories/cpre_pdfs/lp_science_rr63.pdf [June 2015].

Driver, R., Leach, J., Millar, R., and Scott, P. (1996). *Young People's Images of Science.* Buckingham, UK: Open University Press.

Duncan, R.G., and Hmelo-Silver, C.E. (2009). Learning progressions: Aligning curriculum, instruction, and assessment. *Journal of Research on Science Teaching, 46*(6), 606-609.

Duschl, R., and Duncan, R.G. (2009). Beyond the fringe: Building and evaluating scientific knowledge systems. In T. Duffy and S. Tobias (Eds.), *Constructivist Theory Applied to Instruction: Success or Failure?* (pp. 311-332). London, UK: Taylor and Francis.

Engle, R.A., and Conant, F.R. (2002). Guiding principles for fostering productive disciplinary engagement: Explaining an emergent argument in a community of learners' classroom. *Cognition and Instruction, 20*(4), 399-483.

Engle, R.A., Langer-Osuna, J.M., and de Royston, M.M. (2014). Toward a model of influence in persuasive discussions: Negotiating quality, authority, privilege, and access within a student-led argument. *The Journal of Learning Sciences, 23*(2), 245-268.

Gelman, R., and Lucariello, J. (2002). Learning in cognitive development. In H. Pashler (Series Ed.) and R. Gallistel (Vol. Ed.), *Stevens' Handbook of Experimental Psychology: Learning, Motivation, and Emotion* (vol. 3, 3rd ed.) (pp. 395-443). New York: Wiley.

Herrenkohl, L.R., and Guerra, M.R. (1998). Participant structures, scientific discourse, and student engagement in fourth grade. *Cognition and Instruction, 16,* 433-475.

Kena, G., Aud, S., Johnson, F., Wang, X., Zhang, J., Rathbun, A., Wilkinson-Flicker, S., and Krstapovich, P. (2014). *The Condition of Education 2014.* NCES 2014-083. Washington, DC: U.S. Department of Education, National Center for Education Statistics.

Knorr-Cetina, K. (1999). *Epistemic Cultures: How the Sciences Make Knowledge.* Cambridge, MA: Harvard University Press.

Latour, B. (1990). Postmodern? No modern. Steps toward an anthropology of science. *Studies in History and Philosophy of Science, 21,* 165-171.

Lehrer, R., and Schauble, L. (2000). Modeling in mathematics and science. In R. Glaser (Ed.), *Advances in Instructional Psychology* (vol. 5, pp. 101-159). Mahwah, NJ: Lawrence Erlbaum Associates.

Lehrer, R., and Schauble, L. (2003). Origins and evolution of model-based reasoning in mathematics and science. In R. Lesh (Ed.), *Beyond Constructivism: Models and Modeling Perspectives on Mathematics Problem Solving, Teaching and Learning* (pp. 59-70). Mahwah, NJ: Lawrence Erlbaum Associates.

Lehrer, R., and Schauble, L. (2005). Developing modeling and argument in elementary grades. In T.A. Romberg, T.P. Carpenter, and F. Dremock (Eds.), *Understanding Mathematics and Science Matters* (pp. 29-53). Mahwah, NJ: Lawrence Erlbaum Associates.

Lehrer, R., and Schauble, L. (2006). Scientific thinking and science literacy. In W. Damon, R. Lerner, K.A. Renninger, and I.E. Sigel (Eds.), *Handbook of Child Psychology* (vol. 4, 6th ed., pp. 153-196). Hoboken, NJ: Wiley.

Lehrer, R., and Schauble, L. (2012). Seeding evolutionary thinking by engaging children in modeling its foundations. *Science Education, 96*(4), 701-724.

McNeill, K.L. (2011). Elementary students' views of explanation, argumentation and evidence and abilities to construct arguments over the school year. *Journal of Research in Science Teaching, 48*(7), 793-823.

McNeill, K.L., Lizotte, D.J, Krajcik, J., and Marx, R.W. (2006). Supporting students' construction of scientific explanations by fading scaffolds in instructional materials. *The Journal of the Learning Sciences, 15*(2), 153-191.

Metz, K.E. (1995). Reassessment of developmental constraints on children's science instruction. *Review of Educational Research, 65*(2), 93-127.

Metz, K.E. (2000). Young children's inquiry in biology: Building the knowledge bases to empower independent inquiry. In J. Minstrell and E. van Zee (Eds.), *Inquiring into Inquiry in Science Learning and Teaching* (pp. 371-404). Washington, DC: American Association for the Advancement of Science.

Metz, K.E. (2004). Children's understanding of scientific inquiry: Their conceptualizations of uncertainty in investigations of their own design. *Cognition and Instruction, 22*(2), 219-290.

Metz, K.E. (2011). Disentangling robust developmental constraints from the instructionally mutable: Young children's reasoning about a study of their own design. *Journal of the Learning Sciences, 20*(1), 50-110.

National Assessment of Educational Progress. (2009). *Science Framework for the 2009 National Assessment of Educational Progress.* Washington, DC: U.S. Government Printing Office. Available: http://www.nagb.org/publications/frameworks/science-09.pdf [June 2015].

National Research Council. (1996). *National Science Education Standards.* National Committee for Science Education Standards and Assessment. Board on Science Education, Division of Behavioral and Social Sciences and Education. Washington, DC: National Academy Press.

National Research Council. (2002). *Learning and Understanding: Improving Advanced Study of Mathematics and Science in U.S. High Schools.* Committee on Programs for Advanced Study of Mathematics and Science in American High Schools. J.P. Gollub, M.W. Bertenthal, J.B. Labov, and P.C. Curtis (Eds). Center for Education, Division of Behavioral and Social Sciences and Education. Washington, DC: National Academy Press.

National Research Council. (2007). *Taking Science to School: Learning and Teaching Science in Grades K-8.* Committee on Science Learning, Kindergarten through Eighth Grade. R.A. Duschl, H.A. Schweingruber, and A.W. Shouse (Eds.). Board on Science Education, Division of Behavioral and Social Sciences and Education. Washington, DC: The National Academies Press.

National Research Council. (2012). *A Framework for K-12 Science Education: Practices, Crosscutting Concepts, and Core Ideas.* Committee on a Conceptual Framework for New K-12 Science Standards. Board on Science Education, Division of Behavioral and Social Sciences and Education. Washington, DC: The National Academies Press.

National Research Council. (2015). *Guide to Implementing the Next Generation Science Standards.* Committee on Guidance on Implementing the Next Generation Science Standards. Board on Science Education, Division of Behavioral and Social Sciences and Education, Washington, DC: The National Academies Press.

Nersessian, N.J. (2012). Engineering concepts: The interplay between concept formation and modeling practices in bioengineering sciences. *Mind, Culture, and Activity, 19*(3), 222-239.

Next Generation Science Standards Lead States. (2013). *Next Generation Science Standards: For States, By States.* Washington, DC: The National Academies Press.

Pickering, A. (1992). *Science as Practice and Culture.* Chicago, IL: University of Chicago Press.

Radinsky, J., Oliva S., and Alamar, K. (2010). Camila, the earth, and the sun: Constructing an idea as shared intellectual property. *Journal of Research in Science Teaching, 47*(6), 619-642.

Rosebery, A.S., Warren, B., and Conant, F.R. (1992). Appropriating scientific discourse: Findings from language minority classrooms. *Journal of the Learning Sciences, 2*(1), 61-94.

Roth, K.J., Druker, S.L., Garnier, H.E., Lemmens, M., Chen, C., Kawanaka, T., Rasmussen, D., Trubacova, S., Warvi, D., Okamoto, Y., Gonzales, P., Stigler, J., and Gallimore, R. (2006). *Teaching Science in Five Countries: Results from the TIMSS 1999 Video Study.* (NCES 2006-011). U.S. Department of Education, National Center for Education Statistics. Washington, DC: U.S. Government Printing Office.

Roth, K.J., Chen, C., Lemmens, M., Garnier, H., Wickler, N., Atkins, L., Calabrese Barton, A., Roseman, J.E., Shouse, A., and Zembal-Saul, C. (2009, April). *Coherence and Science Content Storylines in Science Teaching: Evidence of Neglect? Evidence of Effect?* Colloquium and paper presented at the Annual Meeting of the National Association for Research in Science Teaching, Garden Grove, CA.

Sandoval, W.A., and Millwood, K.A. (2005). The quality of students' use of evidence in written scientific explanations. *Cognition and Instruction, 23*(1), 23-55.

Smith, C.L., Maclin, D., Houghton, C., and Hennessey, M.G. (2000). Sixth-grade students' epistemologies of science: The impact of school science experiences on epistemological development. *Cognition and Instruction, 18*(3), 349-422.

Smith, C.L., Wiser, M., Anderson, C.W., and Krajcik, J. (2006). Implications of research on children's learning for standards and assessment: A proposed learning progression for matter and the atomic molecular theory. *Measurement: Interdisciplinary Research and Perspectives, 4*(1-2), 1-98.

Windschitl, M., and Calabrese Barton, A. (forthcoming). Rigor and equity by design: Seeking a core of practices for the science education community. In *AERA Handbook of Research on Teaching* (5th ed.).

Zielger, K., and Camarota, S. (2014). *One in Five U.S. Residents Speaks Foreign Language at Home, Record 61.8 Million.* Center for Immigration Studies backgrounder. Available: http://cis.org/record-one-in-five-us-residents-speaks-language-other-than-english-at-home [January 2015].

3

The Current Status of
Science Instruction

The vision of quality science instruction described in Chapter 2 is not standard fare in U.S. classrooms. Answering the question, "How do we achieve these rigorous and ambitious goals for students' science learning?" requires exploring the associated questions, "Where are we starting from?" and "How might we get from here to there?"

This chapter concerns what answers research provides to the question, "Where are we starting from?" To develop a broad picture of current science instruction in the United States, the committee reviewed four surveys that gather national-level data on teachers' beliefs about teaching and learning and their instructional practices (see Box 3-1). First, the 2012 National Survey of Science and Mathematics Education (NSSME) documents both teachers' beliefs and self-reports about their instruction from a representative national sample in the United States. Second, the 2011 National Assessment of Educational Progress (NAEP) included a teacher questionnaire that asked about teachers' perceptions of effective instructional practices and their own practices, and asked students to report on instruction they had received. This survey was administered to 4th- and 8th-grade students and teachers only. The other two surveys capture characteristics of science teachers' perceptions and classroom instruction across countries that include the United States. The Teaching and Learning International Survey (TALIS) 2013 describes teachers' beliefs about the nature of teaching and learning and self-reported instructional practices across 23 OECD countries. However, the United States did not meet the international standards for participation rates; therefore, it is not appro-

---

BOX 3-1
Surveys Reviewed

National Survey of Science and Mathematics Education (NSSME)—2012
- Conducted by Horizon Research, Inc.
- U.S. nationally representative sample at all grade levels (1,504 schools; $N = 7,700$ teachers)
- Response rate = 77 percent
- Teachers' perceptions of objectives, classroom activities, and assessment
- Self-reported classroom practices

National Assessment of Educational Progress (NAEP)—2011
- Conducted by the National Center for Education Statistics
- Nationally representative sample of 4th- and 8th-grade students and other teachers
- Teachers' beliefs about teaching
- Self-reported classroom practices

Teaching and Learning International Survey (TALIS)—2013
- Conducted by OECD
- 23 OECD countries
- Teachers' beliefs about teaching
- School principals report on school climate, leadership, teacher evaluation and induction
- Teachers' reports of preparation, professional development opportunities and needs, classroom practices

Trends in International Mathematics and Science Study (TIMSS)—2011
- More than 60 countries
- 4th- and 8th-grade students (more than 20,000 students in 1,000 schools in the United States)
- Self-reported classroom practices, school resources, interaction with colleagues, and perception of preparation to teach

---

priate to use these data in establishing an accurate picture of national trends. The 2011 Trends in International Mathematics and Science Study (TIMSS) included survey items about instructional practices in 4th- and 8th-grade classrooms.

The committee focused primarily on results of the NSSME, the only survey that included a representative national sample at all grade levels. We examined results of the other surveys when possible to confirm whether similar trends were observed. We note also that *A Framework for K-12 Science Education* (hereafter referred to as the Framework) and the *Next Generation Science Standards* (hereafter referred to as NGSS) had not been published at the time these four surveys were conducted, so the available evidence does not align completely with the vision of science teaching and learning laid out in those documents. However, because the Framework and NGSS build upon and evolved from earlier efforts to articulate a similar vision of science instruction, much can be learned from this existing research.

Although there are many individual classrooms in which children are routinely engaged in challenging and well-supported science learning (e.g., Gallas, 1995; Lemke, 1990; Nemirovsky et al., 2009), the national-level picture is sobering. We begin with a big-picture view of instruction before turning to more fine-grained analyses of practice at the elementary, middle, and high school levels.

CURRENT SCIENCE INSTRUCTION:
A GAP BETWEEN VISION AND REALITY

The NSSME documents what science teachers report about their instruction with respect to objectives, classroom activities, and assessment; it helps paint an overall portrait of contemporary science instruction. As noted earlier, the survey is not explicitly aligned with the Framework and NGSS as it was developed before the standards were available; however, some of the survey items reflect instructional approaches that are consistent with the goals outlined in the two documents.

Overall, the survey indicates that there is a gap between current science teaching and learning and the vision embodied in the Framework and NGSS (see Chapter 2). About 60 percent of science teachers in the United States indicate that they are using "reform-oriented science teaching practices," such as "have students do hands-on/laboratory activities," "require students to supply evidence in support of their claims," and "have students represent and/or analyze data using tables, charts, or graphs" (Banilower et al., 2013). While these kinds of practices are not fully aligned with the Framework and NGSS, they are in keeping with the broad learning goals outlined in the two documents. At the same time, teachers' self-reports of the classroom activities in their most recently taught lesson confirm that teachers typically engage in more traditional instructional practices, such as "teacher explaining a science idea to the whole class," "whole-class discussion," and "students completing textbook/worksheet problems" (Banilower et al., 2013). Specifically,

- Seventy to 80 percent of teachers said they "have students work in small groups" at least once a week.
- About 17 percent of teachers said they "require students to supply evidence in support of their claims" during all or almost all

lessons; about 60 percent of teachers do so at least once a week. Few teachers said they never do so.

- About half of teachers (44 to 58 percent) said they "have students represent and/or analyze data using tables, charts, or graphs" at least once a week, and 8 percent said they do so during all or almost all lessons. Again, few teachers said they never do so.
- Three to 9 percent of teachers said they "have students practice for standardized tests" during all or almost all lessons. Interestingly, the percentages decrease from elementary to high school (9 percent of elementary, 6 percent of middle, and 3 percent of high school teachers). About one-fifth of teachers (19-23 percent) said they do this activity at least once a week.

Although teachers' estimates of the frequency of different instructional practices offer some insight into what is happening in science classrooms, they do not provide information about the quality of implementation of those practices. Few large-scale observational studies of science classrooms provide assessments of the quality of instruction. The few that are available suggest that science lessons are often inadequate.

One such study, conducted by Weiss and colleagues (2003) included classrooms sampled from elementary, middle, and high schools clustered by feeder pattern in 31 sites involving 93 U.S. schools.[1] The researchers focused on two primary goals of science and mathematics instruction: helping students develop conceptual understanding and deepening their ability to engage in processes of science and mathematics. With these goals in mind, the investigators developed a five-level scale of lesson quality:

- ineffective instruction (Level 1), characterized by "passive learning" or by "activity for activity's sake";
- partial presence of elements of effective instruction (Level 2);
- beginning stages of effective instruction (Level 3);
- accomplished instruction (Level 4); and
- exemplary instruction (Level 5).

---

[1]Weiss and colleagues (2003) selected a nationally representative set of 40 middle schools and then randomly selected an elementary school and a high school in the feeder pattern for each of these middle schools. Each set of three schools constituted a site. Two randomly selected science teachers/classes were selected for observation in each school in a given site. Observations were completed in 31 sites (93 schools) and form the basis of the reported findings. Observations were carried out in 2001 prior to full implementation of the No Child Left Behind Act and may not reflect the impact on science instruction of this legislation and the required large-scale assessments in mathematics and reading.

In Level 5 lessons, the teacher clearly articulated the instructional objectives; engaged students intellectually with science or mathematics content; portrayed the disciplines as dynamic bodies of knowledge; and provided a climate that encouraged students to generate ideas, questions, and conjectures. Teachers often invited students to interact with the content through multiple pathways, including direct experience with natural phenomena and real-world examples. These lessons were characterized by intellectual rigor, constructive criticism, and challenging of ideas. Teachers frequently used questioning strategies to elicit students' level of understanding of the targeted concepts and adjusted instruction accordingly, building on what students knew to advance their thinking. They probed students for elaboration, explanation, justification, or generation of new questions or conjectures. These effective teachers also presented relevant and accessible examples and demonstrations and engaged students in laboratory activities, coupled with discussion of or writing about their observations or ideas to promote sense making (see Boxes 3-2 and 3-3). Because the study predates the Framework and NGSS, the characteristics of high-quality lessons do not exactly match what one would expect to see in lessons aligned with the NGSS. For example, they do not consistently integrate all three dimensions discussed in Chapter 2: science practices, crosscutting concepts, and core disciplinary ideas. Nonetheless, these prototypes provide importance guidance for considering what teachers need to know and be able to do to implement high-quality science instruction.

Accomplishing this kind of instruction entails considerable knowledge and skill. Not only would the teacher in this example need to be deft at managing a classroom in which students were engaged in laboratory activities, but she would also need to be able to anticipate the likely predictions that students would generate and what those predictions would signify with respect to students' understanding. Leading a discussion is not a natural act, but instead takes considerable experience with hearing what students say, capitalizing on their emergent ideas, and selecting some comments for further collective discussion while being respectful of the broad array of student contributions (Brookfield and Preskill, 2005; Engle and Conant, 2002; Engle et al., 2014). We return to a discussion of the knowledge required for this kind of teaching in Chapter 5.

In contrast to high-quality instruction, lessons categorized as Level 1 (ineffective) included "passive learning" and "activities for activity's sake." Ineffective or less effective lessons tended to portray science as a static body of factual knowledge, and procedures in which the students engaged were not intellectually rigorous (Weiss et al., 2003). Teacher questioning tended to evoke only yes/no or fill-in-the-blank responses from students that failed to promote conceptual engagement or the develop-

BOX 3-2
An Exemplary Science Lesson

In an example lesson classified by Weiss and colleagues (2003) as Level 5, "High-Quality, Reform-Oriented Instruction," a high school biology class was in the middle of a unit on cells. In the previous lesson, students had conducted a membrane lab using starch or sugar solutions and dialysis tubing, and the goal of this lesson was to help them learn about molecule size and transport across cell membranes. The teacher opened the lesson by asking the students, in their lab groups, to predict what they expected to happen with their lab and to use the concept of particle size to explain why. After they had made their predictions, the groups examined their data and discussed whether their predictions were right or wrong. The teacher then led the entire class in a discussion about what had happened in the experiment. Students suggested hypotheses, and the class discussed methods for testing them. As needed, the teacher chimed in with suggestions about lab techniques that would enable the students to test their ideas and prodded the groups to make sure that they conducted enough tests to explain fully what had happened. The teacher skillfully guided the students as they finished making observations and analyzing the data, asking questions that pushed students to examine their results and to provide evidence for their conclusions.

After the groups had finished all of their tests, the teacher assigned them to write a story about a paramecium living in the local freshwater river that traveled to the ocean. In their stories, the groups were instructed to use a list of eight vocabulary words related to transport across a membrane. The students spent the remainder of the class period working on their stories, an activity that allowed them to reflect on what they had learned about transport across a membrane and apply it to organisms living in their local river. This was a critical component of the lesson as it allowed the students to make sense of the lab results. Throughout the lesson, all of the students were engaged in meaningful investigation of important science content, and the teacher did a masterful job of guiding the class. Students were generating and debating hypotheses, and were given the tools they needed to test their ideas. Writing their stories allowed the students to make sense of the data and conclusions drawn from the lab investigation. The students had clearly taken ownership of their learning, and the teacher pushed and challenged all students to engage with the content.

ment of understanding. In some classrooms, the teacher both asked and answered the questions. These lessons did not provide sufficient time or support for students to discuss, reflect on, and make sense of laboratory activities, lectures, or demonstrations or to connect new information to existing knowledge (see Box 3-3).

Weiss and colleagues (2003) categorized only 15 percent of the science and mathematics lessons they observed as high quality (Levels high 3 through 5), 27 percent as medium quality (Levels low 3 and solid 3), and

---

BOX 3-3
An Ineffective Science Lesson

In an example lesson classified by Weiss and colleagues (2003) as Level 1, a 9th-grade biology class was near the end of a unit on evolution. The teacher opened the class by asking the students to complete a worksheet that referred to facts from their textbook. Without looking in the book, students had to decide whether the statements were true or false and correct the false ones. Then, the teacher asked them to check their work against the book, working in small groups to reach consensus on the answers, and to document where in the book (what page and paragraph) they found each answer. However, about half the students did not try to answer the questions. When they had finished the worksheet, the students copied from the board a timeline of evolution that focused on bacteria. Then the teacher announced the answers to the worksheet questions. Some students raised their hands and asked about items they did not understand, in which case the teacher asked the class to explain the answer, but he rarely gave students the time to speak before answering himself. The teacher then read through each worksheet problem one more time and asked students to identify the page and paragraph where they had found the answer.

Next, the teacher gave a lecture based on the chapter students had just read. He began by asking students to look at the inside of the textbook's back cover, which showed a chart of the evolution of all life and when each life form was found, explaining that this chart summarized the material they were about to cover. The rest of the lecture consisted of a series of names of organisms and time frames of their existence. The focus was on lists of facts taken from the book; at several points, the teacher read straight out of the textbook or asked students to do so. The teacher instructed students to take notes in a two-column format in which one column was titled "Main Themes" and the other "Detail." Only a few students adhered to this format, and the teacher never followed through or helped identify the main themes. The teacher's questions rarely required higher-order thinking and never drew on previous knowledge or real-world connections, and the teacher never offered enough wait time for students to consider an answer.

---

59 percent as low quality (Levels 1 and 2). These findings are echoed in the TIMSS 1999 video study, which compared 8th-grade science lessons in the United States with those in four other countries that outperformed the United States on the 1999 TIMSS assessment. In 44 percent of U.S. lessons, there were weak or no connections between learning activities and science ideas. Perhaps more worrisome, 27 percent of U.S. lessons included no science ideas at all (Roth and Garnier, 2007). Results such as these highlight the urgency of creating substantial learning opportunities for teachers.

One aspect of classroom instruction that is important for supporting the learning goals in the Framework and NGSS is providing students with opportunities to make sense of investigations and discuss their emerging ideas. This kind of systematic sense making is supported by verbal prompts from teachers or varied opportunities for student talk. In the Weiss et al. (2003) study, the authors examined teacher questioning and discourse in general. In their analyses, fewer than one in five lessons incorporated questioning that was likely to move student understanding forward (i.e., finding out what students know, pressing for reasoning, encouraging self-monitoring of one's thinking)—even when the rest of the lesson was otherwise well designed. Many incidents were cited of teachers asking low-cognitive-demand, "fill-in-the-blank" questions in rapid-fire sequence, with the focus on correct responses (often single words or phrases) rather than on student understanding. The authors conclude that questioning was "among the weakest elements of [science] instruction" (p. 71). These findings are similar to those of Bowes and Banilower (2004), who analyzed lessons from classrooms where teachers had been supported for years through well-funded professional development initiatives. Their data showed that fewer than half of the lessons, even those of teachers who had received the most professional development, were likely to be rated as adequate in the areas of questioning and sense-making opportunities.

In a study of classrooms in a large school district in the eastern United States that included data from observations of 55 elementary classrooms, 37 middle school science classrooms, and 29 high school science classrooms (Corcoran and Gerry, 2011), fewer than one-third of these observations showed students engaged in any type of higher-order thinking. Qualitative reports on these classrooms indicated that although the lessons appeared to be well organized, students were often disengaged, and didacticism dominated instruction.

Disparities in Instruction

Differences are seen across different student groups and communities in the type and quality of instruction available to students. In the survey conducted by Banilower and colleagues (2013), classes with high-achieving students were more likely than classes consisting mainly of low-achieving students to stress reform-oriented objectives and instructional practices.

In the observational study conducted by Weiss and colleagues (2003), the quality of lessons varied across different communities and student populations. Lessons in rural schools were less likely than those in suburban and urban communities to receive high ratings, and lessons in classes that were "majority minority" scored lower than lessons in other classes.

TABLE 3-1 Science Classes in Which Teachers Report Engaging in Various Activities at Least Once a Week, by Grade Level

| Activity | Percentage of Classes | | | | |
| | Elementary | | | Middle | High |
	K-2	3-5	K-5		
Explain science ideas to the whole class	87	89	88	96	95
Engage the whole class in discussion	90	91	90	92	83
Have students work in small groups	65	79	72	79	83
Require students to supply evidence in support of their claims	46	62	54	64	61
Do hands-on laboratory activities	54	55	55	62	70
Have students represent and/or analyze data using tables, charts, or graphs	42	46	54	54	58
Have students read from a science textbook or other material in class, either aloud or to themselves	39	55	48	56	37
Have students write their reflections in class or for homework	38	48	44	44	21
Focus on literacy skills (e.g., informational reading or writing strategies)	45	51	48	44	25

SOURCES: Banilower et al. (2013, Table 5.12, p. 76), Trygstad (2013, Table 18, p. 12).

Finally, science lessons in classes comprising low- and middle-ability students were less likely to receive high ratings than lessons in classes comprising students of high or heterogeneous ability. Again, these results clearly point to the need to create learning opportunities for all teachers. Table 3-1 provides an overview of teachers' reported practices in elementary, middle, and high school science classrooms from the NSSME.

Elementary Science Instruction

Most elementary students do not receive daily science instruction: only 19 percent of grades K-2 classes and 30 percent of grades 3-5 classes receive science instruction on all or most days every week of the school year (Banilower et al., 2013; Trygstad, 2013). Elementary students receive less instruction in science than in reading or mathematics and less than students at higher grade levels (Banilower et al., 2013; Dorph et al., 2007; Smith et al., 2002). On the days when science instruction is provided, on average it accounts for only 19 minutes per day at the K-3 level, compared with 54 minutes per day in mathematics and 89 minutes per day in language arts. Although the average rises to 24 minutes per day in grades 4-6—compared with 61 minutes in mathematics and 83 minutes in language arts per day (Banilower et al., 2013, p. 54)—this is still less than a half hour for science learning on those days when science instruction is offered. No differences were reported by teachers in time spent on science across different student groups or different schools in the Banilower et al. (2013) study. However, a study in California found further that science was most likely to be sacrificed in elementary schools struggling to remedy weak performance results in mathematics and English language arts—the same schools most likely to enroll low-income students, African American and Latino students, and English language learners (Dorph et al., 2007). The California study encompassed surveys of elementary school teachers, together with interviews with district and county officials and surveys of and interviews with science program staff and professional development providers.

In the limited time accorded to science in the elementary grades, what is the nature of instruction that students experience? Teachers' self-reports on the 2012 NSSME indicate that the instructional activities most frequently used in elementary school science lessons are conducting whole-class discussion, the teacher explaining science ideas to the class, and having students work in small groups (see Table 3-1). Teachers also reported employing three activities that are consistent with the Framework and NGSS—having students perform hands-on/laboratory investigations, requiring them to supply evidence in support of their claims, and having them write reflections on their science learning—but with somewhat less frequency. In addition, there were some notable differences in class activities between the upper- and lower-elementary school grade bands. Grades 3-5 classes were more likely than grades K-2 classes to engage in reading about science (55 versus 39 percent). They also had more opportunity than lower-elementary students to engage in the science practice of supporting their claims with evidence (62 versus 46 percent) and to write their reflections (48 versus 38 percent). Formal assessment also receives more emphasis at the upper-elementary level, where students are more likely to be given tests and quizzes as well as to practice for standardized tests. Table 3-1 compares the frequency of various instructional activities within the elementary grade bands and the middle and high school levels.

Other studies indicate that elementary science instruction tends to focus on activities that are connected only loosely (if at all) to science ideas and are selected primarily to be fun and motivating for students (Dorph et al., 2011; Roth et al., 2006). Often, activities progress from topic to topic, with few attempts to help students make connections between them; the goal is to sustain students' attention rather than to engage them deeply in scientific practices or model building. The observational study by Weiss and colleagues (2003) discussed above lends support to this lack of focus on disciplinary core ideas, as the investigators judged that only one-third of the lessons they observed were likely to have a positive impact on students' understanding of science concepts. In addition, the researchers found that the greatest weakness of elementary science lessons was in the area of giving students the time and structure needed for sense making and wrap-up.

In addition to the lack of adequate time in the school week and day for elementary school science instruction to achieve the vision of the Framework and NGSS, elementary school teachers lack appropriate technology, curriculum, and instructional materials to support instruction aligned with the vision. As reported in the 2012 NSSME (Banilower et al., 2013), median per pupil spending per year for scientific equipment (e.g., microscopes), consumable supplies (e.g., chemicals), and science instructional software was $1.55 in elementary schools, compared with $3.13 in middle schools, and $6.11 in high schools. Reflecting these low budgets, elementary science teachers are less likely than their middle and high school counterparts to have access to various instructional resources. Although most have access to the Internet, nongraphing calculators, and personal computers, fewer than half have access to other scientific resources (e.g., microscopes, probes for collecting data, and classroom response systems or "clickers"). Perhaps more important, only about one-third of elementary science teachers reported having adequate facilities, equipment, consumable supplies, and instructional technology for science instruction (see Table 3-2). Perhaps because only one-third of the elementary teachers view the available instructional technology as adequate, only 22 percent indicated that they had used it in their most recent science lesson (Banilower et al., 2013).

Curriculum materials are an important source of support for science teachers, and nearly 70 percent of elementary teachers responding to the NSSME reported that their classes use commercially published textbooks or modules as the basis for instruction (Banilower et al., 2013). Of these classes, more than half use these instructional materials for 50 percent or more of their science instructional time. However, much elementary science instruction appears to be pulled together from multiple sources, with 40 percent of grades K-2 classes and 23 percent of grades 3-5 classes

TABLE 3-2 Classes with Adequate Resources for Science Instruction by Grade Range

Resources	Percentage of Classes Where Adequate		
	Elementary	Middle	High
Facilities (e.g., lab tables, electrical outlets, faucets, sinks)	31	57	71
Equipment (e.g., microscopes, beakers, photogate timers, Bunsen burners)	37	47	60
Consumable supplies (e.g., chemicals, living organisms, batteries)	34	39	59
Instructional technology (e.g., calculators, computers, probes/sensors)	34	37	48

SOURCE: Banilower et al. (2013, Table 6-23, p. 106).

using noncommercially published materials most of the time. Additionally, teachers in elementary classes using commercially published materials frequently supplement them with other materials, and do not always use the commercially published materials as designed. As professionals, it is important that teachers use their professional discretion in selecting and adapting curriculum. However, given the fact that many elementary teachers have not had an opportunity for substantial engagement in science content and practices, this finding suggests the need for significant opportunities for elementary teachers to enhance their content knowledge as well as their pedagogical content knowledge.

Middle School Science Instruction

Most middle schools have dedicated science teachers, and students participate in science class daily or every other day. About a third (31 percent) of middle schools use block scheduling, allowing time for laboratory investigations to extend beyond the 50-minute class period that is typical of daily scheduling in U.S. middle schools (Banilower et al., 2013). As at the elementary level, the most frequent instructional techniques reported by teachers are the teacher explaining science ideas, whole-class discussions, and students working in small groups (Banilower et al., 2013; see Table 3-1). However, middle school science teachers were more likely than elementary teachers to report that at least once a week their students were asked to (1) supply evidence in support of their claims (64 versus 54 percent); (2) engage in hands-on/laboratory activities (62 versus 55 percent); (3) represent and/or analyze data using tables, charts, or graphs

(54 versus 44 percent); and (4) read from a science textbook or other material (56 versus 48 percent). Reflecting the increasing emphasis on testing and accountability at higher grade levels, middle school science teachers also are more likely than elementary teachers to give tests and quizzes, including short-answer tests and tests requiring constructed responses.

Differences in self-reported instructional activity are nonetheless insufficient indicators of enhanced instructional quality at the middle school level, or more specifically, of the degree to which middle school science instruction is consistent with the vision expressed by the Framework and NGSS. Two observational studies of science classrooms conducted since 2000, although predating the release of the current standards, suggest that middle school students may have limited experience of high-quality science instruction.

In their observational study of schools in 31 nationally representative sites, Weiss and colleagues (2003) found that middle school science lessons were weaker than those at the elementary and high school levels. Specifically, 78 percent of lessons were rated as Level 1 or 2 (ineffective or incorporating only some elements of effective instruction), 16 percent were rated of medium quality, and only 7 percent were rated of high quality. A common weakness across the observed lessons was a lack of time and structure for sense making.

Similar observations about a lack of support for making sense of natural phenomena come from TIMSS video analyses of recordings from 8th-grade classrooms in five countries (Roth et al., 2006). During "practical" (i.e., laboratory) activities, students in all countries, including the United States, were more likely to observe phenomena than to construct models or conduct controlled experiments. In four other high-achieving countries, students typically concluded practical activities by discussing the results and drawing conclusions, but in U.S. science lessons, this was the rare exception.

In all four higher-achieving countries, science lessons focused on high content standards and expectations for student learning, but each country used a slightly different instructional approach. In the Czech Republic, for instance, instruction was dominated by regular discussion of science content among students and their teachers. Teachers engaged students in whole-class discussions, presentations, and oral quizzes, focusing on rigorous science content. In contrast, students in the Netherlands tended to learn science independently, both when reading and writing answers at their seats and when conducting individual practical activities. Whole-class discussions often focused on homework review. In Japan, students were regularly pressed to draw connections between ideas and evidence. They conducted practical activities and collected and interpreted the resulting data to reach a main idea or conclusion. And in Australia, students regularly drew connections among ideas, evidence, and real-life issues. As in Japan, they conducted practical activities and collected and interpreted the resulting data to reach a main idea or conclusion, but they also discussed real-life issues to support the development of science ideas (Roth et al., 2006).

In contrast to these approaches, U.S. science lessons were dominated by activities with less attention to the science content, and even less attention to the links between the activities and science ideas. Relative to the other nations, important ideas in science played a less central role and sometimes no role at all. In fact, in 27 percent of U.S. lessons, students engaged in activities and followed procedures with no mention of even a single science idea (e.g., "A complete circuit is needed to light the light bulb."). Instead, instruction involved students in such activities as games, puzzles, dramatic demonstrations, and outdoor excursions without explicit connections to science ideas. The American tendency to teach science through "activity without understanding" has been identified in other studies as well (see, for example, Corcoran and Gerry, 2011).

Roth and colleagues (2006) found that in higher-achieving countries, teachers more commonly used activities to develop science ideas and organized lessons in coherent ways. The contrast between U.S. lessons and those in higher-achieving countries highlights the need for teachers to develop the knowledge required to organize specific science content so that students can see and make the links between science ideas and lesson activities. The knowledge demands of teaching are examined in Chapter 5.

As noted above, compared with elementary schools, middle schools provide more time for science learning and spend about twice as much per pupil for science equipment and supplies (Banilower et al., 2013). Reflecting this higher spending, middle school teachers' access to instructional resources for science teaching is greater than that of elementary teachers, although less than that of high school teachers (Banilower et al., 2013). As shown in Table 3-2, the majority (57 percent) of middle school teachers indicated that their facilities were adequate, and about half viewed their equipment as adequate, while only about 40 percent viewed their consumable supplies and instructional technology as adequate.

As at other levels, middle school science classes do not incorporate instructional technology to a great extent (Banilower et al., 2013). Only 30 percent of middle school teachers reported that they had used instructional technology in their most recent lesson. This limited usage may be linked to teachers' perceptions, as captured by the survey, that the available instructional technology is inadequate. It is possible that the use of instructional technology would increase if better technology were available. However, research on technology integration in middle school science classrooms suggests that robust outcomes for lesson design, instruction, and student learning are more likely where teachers experience extended professional learning opportunities and other supports (Penuel et al., 2009; Yerrick and Johnson, 2009). In a review of 43 studies of technology integration across all levels of K-12 schooling, Gerard and colleagues (2011) found that outcomes were strongest (with a few exceptions) where supports extended over more than one school year. They report, "The studies suggest teachers needed support to distinguish effective ways to use new technologies, especially when the goal was to support inquiry learning" (p. 434).

Most middle school teachers (80 percent) use commercially published textbooks or modules as the basis for instruction (Banilower et al., 2013), and about half use these texts or modules for 50 percent or more of their science instructional time. However, middle school teachers are more likely than elementary teachers to supplement these materials with other resources or to skip parts they deem unimportant.

High School Science Instruction

Like middle schools, high schools provide more time for science learning than elementary schools, and about one-third (34 percent) offer block scheduling, allowing extended time for laboratory investigations (Banilower et al., 2013). All states and districts require high school students to participate in at least 1 year of science classes, and 64 percent require students to complete 3 years of high school science (Banilower et al., 2013).

As at the elementary and middle school levels, the most frequent instructional approaches in high school are the teacher explaining science ideas to the whole class, students working in small groups, and whole-class discussions (see Table 3-1). Relative to elementary and middle school teachers, however, high school teachers are more likely to ask students, at least once a week, to do hands-on laboratory investigations (70 versus 62 percent in middle school and 55 percent in elementary school) and to represent or analyze data using tables, charts, or graphs (58 versus 53 percent in middle school and 44 percent in elementary school) (see Table 3-1).

Relative to the middle and elementary levels, high school teachers less often ask students to read from a science textbook or other material (see Table 3-1). Only half as many high school teachers as middle and elementary school teachers ask students to write their reflections (see Table 3-1). In addition, high school classes are slightly less likely than middle school classes to require students to support their claims with evidence. These data suggest that the weaknesses identified at the elementary and middle school levels, including limited use of science practices to support conceptual understanding and lack of time and support for sense making, are present as well at the high school level.

In their observational study, Weiss and colleagues (2013) found that high school science lessons were weaker than those in elementary school, although stronger than those in middle school. Specifically, 66 percent of high school science lessons were rated as ineffective or marginally effective (Levels 1 and 2 on the 5-point scale), compared with 54 percent of elementary and 78 percent of middle school lessons (see Boxes 3-1 and 3-2 for examples of exemplary and ineffective lessons, respectively).

High schools invest more heavily than middle and elementary schools in resources for science instruction—twice as much as middle and about four times as much as elementary schools (see Table 3-2). As at the middle and elementary school levels, most high school teachers report that their classes have access to the Internet, personal computers, and nongraphing calculators. However, high school teachers have greater access to more sophisticated scientific equipment, including microscopes, probes for collecting data, and graphing calculators (Banilower et al., 2013). This greater access to scientific equipment is reflected in higher percentages of high school teachers, relative to elementary and middle school teachers, who rate their facilities, equipment, consumable supplies, and instructional technology as adequate (see Table 3-2). Although the 48 percent of high school teachers rating their instructional technology as adequate is greater than the corresponding percentage of middle school teachers (37 percent), it is still less than half, and this may explain, in part, why only about a third of high school teachers reported using instructional technology in their most recent lesson.

Most high school teachers (77 percent) use commercially published textbooks or modules as the basis for instruction, relying more than teachers at lower levels on textbooks rather than modules (Banilower et al., 2013). During their science classes, high school teachers use textbooks and modules less extensively than teachers at lower levels: fewer than one-third use them for 50 percent or more of their science instructional time. Like middle school teachers, high school teachers often supplement textbooks and modules with other resources or skip parts they deem unimportant.

Summary of Science Instruction across Levels of Schooling

The vision of science teaching and learning portrayed by the Framework and NGSS will likely present a substantial challenge for many teachers, especially at the elementary level, but also at the middle and high school levels. Although the available research suggests that the classroom environment for learning is moderately well organized and characterized by a climate that is generally positive and respectful toward students, other common themes point to potential priorities for teacher learning and support:

- Although students frequently engage in "active work," it is often procedural and does not involve authentic forms of scientific practice or reasoning.
- Far too few teachers in American classrooms help students link activity to substantive science ideas.
- Teacher questioning and tasks in general do not demand much from students intellectually; instruction is frequently aimed at the recall and reproduction of textbook explanations.
- Big-picture science ideas for students to develop understandings of or for teachers to organize units around are rare.

The committee does not wish to imply that instructional excellence and innovation do not exist in U.S. schools. Recall that in their observations of science classrooms, Weiss and colleagues (2003) found compelling examples of excellent instruction, albeit in only 15 percent of the classroom sample. Furthermore, an extensive descriptive literature portrays quality science instruction. For example, some elementary teachers integrate science into their curriculum, support meaningful science learning, and find ways to engage in their own professional learning—all despite working in teaching contexts and with curricula that rarely support such integration (Banilower et al., 2013; Dorph et al., 2011; Gallas, 1995; National Research Council, 2007). Similarly, some middle and high school teachers focus on fewer topics, exploring them with their students through investigations and providing time and structure for sense making (see Box 3-1). While excellence in science teaching is not yet widespread, then, it is important to remember that there are teachers in today's schools who engage students in meaningful science learning. Indeed, their instruction inspired the committee's notion of what Shulman (1986) has called the "images of the possible." Yet even for these teachers, integrating the three dimensions described in the Framework (science practices, crosscutting concepts, and disciplinary core ideas) and creating coherent progressions that support students' learning over months and years may represent a large change.

Certain factors exacerbate the disparity between vision and reality. At the elementary level, science is not taught much. With double periods of mathematics and language arts, there simply is not room in the school day for teaching science. At the middle and elementary school levels, teachers are underprepared to teach deep content and to focus on core ideas—they may not understand these ideas themselves. In high school, teachers too often are siloed in their own classrooms and certainly in their own departments—an arrangement that again is antithetical to the notion of core ideas and of one learning experience serving as the basis for the next. In addition, high school science teachers often are uncomfortable supporting students in writing about science—or even reading work outside of texts. All of these problems are more pronounced and more challenging in schools that serve English language learners, students from underresourced homes, and students with disabilities. Finally, elementary, middle, and high school teachers have infrequent opportunities to interact with and learn from one another with respect to articulating students' experiences across grade levels.

TEACHERS' PERCEPTIONS OF EFFECTIVE INSTRUCTION

It is important to understand not only the characteristics of current dominant instructional practice but also science teachers' perceptions of effective teaching and learning (i.e., what they think they should do to best help students learn science in their classrooms). Efforts to reform science instruction will depend on working closely with educators to alter or expand their current perceptions and aspirations.

Responses to the NSSME suggest that teachers regard organizing information, making clear presentations, and organizing for effective delivery as more important than student-oriented activity to effective science teaching (Banilower et al., 2013). More than 85 percent of teachers agreed that (1) students should be told the purpose for a lesson as it begins, (2) most class periods should include review of previously covered material, (3) most class periods should give students the opportunities to share their thinking/reasoning, and (4) most class periods should conclude with a summary of the key ideas addressed in that lesson. Three of these four statements (1, 2, and 4) appear to indicate that teachers view clear and well-organized representation of information as important to effective science instruction. Yet while this is an essential aspect of effective instruction, this view does not begin to include features of instruction that are more student oriented, including attention to the quality of student engagement and discourse.

Teachers' opinions about ability grouping vary considerably by grade range, with 65 percent of high school science teachers, 48 percent of those in the middle grades, and 32 percent at the elementary level indicating that students learn science best in classes with other students of similar ability. On other statements in the survey, teachers' opinions are largely consistent across grade ranges (Banilower et al., 2013, p. 21). For example:

- More than 75 percent of teachers at each grade range agreed that it is better to focus on ideas in depth, even if doing so means covering fewer topics; this is one of the central tenets of calls for reform in science instruction. Although current practice does not reflect this emphasis on depth over coverage, it appears that teachers are ready to embrace this aspect of the new vision.

- Roughly 40 percent of science teachers at each grade level agreed that teachers should explain an idea to students before having them consider evidence for that idea.
- More than 50 percent indicated that laboratory activities should be used primarily to reinforce ideas that students have already learned. It is heartening that teachers appear to appreciate the importance of laboratory activities. However, this finding suggests that teachers need to consider the advantages of integrating scientific practices throughout all aspects of instruction, not merely as part of reinforcement.
- From 70 to 85 percent of science teachers at the various grade ranges indicated that students should be given definitions for new vocabulary at the beginning of instruction on a science idea. Taken together with using laboratory activities to illustrate or reinforce ideas, this view of instruction is aligned more with the conventional view of effective teaching focused on conveying final forms of knowledge to students than with the vision embodied in the Framework and NGSS. Those perceptions accord with instructional practices that are reported by many researchers.

In short, most U.S. teachers think of organizing information, making clear presentations, and organizing for effective delivery as important aspects of teaching that support student learning. A significant number of U.S. science teachers hold pedagogical perceptions that are aligned with a conventional view of teaching. Equally important, however, is that many teachers appreciate the importance of covering a smaller number of ideas in depth and the valuable role that laboratory activities can play.

CONCLUSION

A notable gap exists between the reality of current teaching practices and the vision of science learning that emerges from research on learning and teaching, as crystalized in the Framework and NGSS. Current science instruction places greater emphasis on ensuring that the learning environment is organized than on students' sense-making activities (Weiss et al., 2003). Although teachers across grade levels report some use of such practices as "having students do hands-on/laboratory activities," "requiring students to supply evidence in support of their claims," and "having students represent and/or analyze data using tables, charts, or graphs," they spend most class time explaining science ideas or leading whole-class discussions (Banilower et al., 2013).

Activities for students sometimes include science practices but are rarely sequenced and integrated in ways that support focused learning of key science ideas (Roth et al., 2006; Weiss et al., 2003). Students rarely have time to make sense of the findings of their investigations or to engage in reflection on and revision of their understanding (Banilower et al., 2013; Weiss et al., 2003). In some cases, science lessons include no science ideas at all (Roth et al., 2006)—for example, a lesson on electric circuits in which students focus on lighting a light bulb with no mention of the idea of complete and incomplete circuits. Scientific investigations often involve performing iterative, dynamic, and inefficient activities, and the theorizing and interpretive work involved in moving from data to explanations and claims too often is missing from science classrooms (Windschitl et al., 2008).

> **Conclusion 1:** *An evolving understanding of how best to teach science, including the NGSS, represents a significant transition in the way science is currently taught in most classrooms and will require most science teachers to alter the way they teach.*

It is critical, however, to resist the temptation to blame teachers for the current state of science teaching practices, which reflect the varied and underconceptualized support teachers receive from schools and districts. In addition to being prepared as generalists, elementary teachers have very limited time to plan and deliver science instruction, while teachers at all levels receive little time, structure, and support for their own learning, whether through traditional professional workshops or through teacher study groups or one-on-one coaching. Finally, resources for science are limited, and many teachers, especially at the elementary level, view the available equipment, supplies, facilities, and instructional technology as inadequate. These issues related to supports for high-quality science teaching are taken up in detail in the next three chapters.

REFERENCES

Banilower, E.R., Smith, P.S., Weiss, I.R., Malzahn, K.A., Campbell, K.M., and Weis, A.M. (2013). *Report of the 2012 National Survey of Science and Mathematics Education*. Chapel Hill, NC: Horizon Research.

Bowes, A.S., and Banilower, E.R. (2004*). LSC Classroom Observation Study: An Analysis of Data Collected Between 1998 and 2003*. Chapel Hill, NC: Horizon Research.

Brookfield, S.D., and Preskill, S. (2005). *Discussion as a Way of Teaching: Tools and Techniques for Democratic Classrooms* (2nd ed.). San Francisco, CA: Jossey Bass.

Corcoran, T., and Gerry, G. (2011). *Science Instruction in Newark Public Schools.* Consortium for Policy Research in Education Research Report RR-71. New York: Teachers College, Columbia University.

Dorph, R., Goldstein, D., Lee, S., Lepori, K., Schneider, S., and Venkatesan, S. (2007). *The Status of Science Education in the Bay Area: Research Brief.* Berkeley: Lawrence Hall of Science, University of California. Available: http://lawrencehallofscience.org/rea/bayareastudy/pdf/final_to_print_research_brief.pdf [January 2015].

Dorph, R., Shields, P., Tiffany-Morales, J., Hartry, A., and McCaffrey, T. (2011). *High Hopes-Few Opportunities: The Status of Elementary Science Education in California.* Sacramento, CA: The Center for the Future of Teaching and Learning at WestEd. Available: http://www.wested.org/resources/high-hopes-mdash-few-opportunities-full-report-the-status-of-elementary-science-education-in-california [January 2015].

Engle, R.A., and Conant, F.R. (2002). Guiding principles for fostering productive disciplinary engagement: Explaining an emergent argument in a community of learners' classroom. *Cognition and Instruction, 20*(4), 399-483.

Engle, R.A., Langer-Osuna, J.M., and de Royston, M.M. (2014). Toward a model of influence in persuasive discussions: Negotiating quality, authority, privilege, and access within a student-led argument. *The Journal of Learning Sciences, 23*(2), 245-268.

Gallas, K. (1995). *Talking Their Way into Science: Hearing Children's Questions and Theories, Responding with Curricula.* New York: Teachers College Press.

Gerard, L.F., Varma, K., Corliss, S.B., and Linn, M.C. (2011). Professional development for technology-enhanced inquiry science. *Review of Educational Research, 81*(3), 408-448.

Lemke, J. (1990). *Talking Science: Language, Learning, and Values.* New York: Praeger.

National Research Council. (2007). *Taking Science to School: Learning and Teaching Science in Grades K-8.* Committee on Science Learning, Kindergarten through Eighth Grade. R.A. Duschl, H.A. Schweingruber, and A.W. Shouse (Eds.). Board on Science Education, Division of Behavioral and Social Sciences and Education. Washington, DC: The National Academies Press.

Nemirovsky, R., Rosebery, A.S., Solomon, J., and Warren, B. (2009). *Everyday Matters in Science and Mathematics: Studies of Complex Classroom Events.* Mahwah, NJ: Lawrence Erlbaum Associates.

Penuel, W.R., McWilliams, H., McAuliffe, C., Benbow, A., Mably, C., and Hayden, M. (2009). Teaching for understanding in Earth science: Comparing impacts on planning and instruction in three professional development designs for middle school science. *Journal of Science Teacher Education, 20*(5), 415-436.

Roth, K.J., and Garnier, H.G. (2007). What science teaching looks like: An international perspective. *Educational Leadership, 64*(4), 16-23.

Roth, K.J., Druker, S.L., Garnier, H.E., Lemmens, M., Chen, C., Kawanaka, T., Rasmussen, D., Trubacova, S., Warvi, D., Okamoto, Y., Gonzales, P., Stigler, J., and Gallimore, R. (2006). *Teaching Science in Five Countries: Results from the TIMSS 1999 Video Study.* NCES 2006-011. U.S. Department of Education, National Center for Education Statistics. Washington, DC: U.S. Government Printing Office.

Shulman, L.S. (1986). Paradigms and research programs in the study of teaching. In M.C. Wittrock (Ed.), *Handbook of Research on Teaching* (3rd ed., pp. 3-36). New York: MacMillan.

Smith, P.S., Banilower, E.R., McMahon, K.C., and Weiss, I.R. (2002). *The National Survey of Science and Mathematics Education: Trends from 1977 to 2000.* Available: http://2000survey.horizon-research.com/reports/trends.php [June 2015].

Trygstad, P.J. (2013). *2012 National Survey of Science and Mathematics Education: Status of Elementary School Science.* Chapel Hill, NC: Horizon Research.

Weiss, I., Pasley, J., Smith, S., Banilower, E., and Heck, D. (2003). *Looking Inside the Classroom: A Study of K-12 Mathematics and Science Education in the United States*. Chapel Hill, NC: Horizon Research.

Windschitl, M., Thompson, J., and Braaten, M. (2008). How novice science teachers appropriate epistemic discourses around model-based inquiry for use in classrooms. *Cognition and Instruction*, 26(3), 310-378.

Yerrick, R., and Johnson, J. (2009). Meeting the needs of middle grade science learners through pedagogical and technological intervention. *Contemporary Issues in Technology and Teacher Education*, 9(3), 280-315.

4

The K-12 Science Teaching Workforce

Creating new and productive ways to support science teachers depends on understanding not only current instructional practice but also the current science teaching workforce—specifically, its capacity to meet new curricular and instructional demands in science education. Just as Chapter 3 describes both the current state of science instruction and the gap between that state and the new vision embodied in *A Framework for K-12 Science Education* (hereafter referred to as the Framework) and the *Next Generation Science Standards* (hereafter referred to as NGSS), this chapter reviews the composition and qualifications of the current science teacher workforce. Chapter 5 then describes what learning needs that workforce will have given the new vision. Because this study focuses on teachers' learning over a continuum, this chapter looks at preparation pathways; patterns of retention, attrition, and career advancement; professional development opportunities; and the changing student population.

CHARACTERISTICS OF THE K-12 SCIENCE TEACHING WORKFORCE

It is surprisingly difficult to obtain basic information about who teaches science to the nation's children. Although states regularly collect information on teacher certification and employment, infrastructure and tools for readily synthesizing or comparing this information across states are lacking (Feuer et al., 2013; National Research Council, 2010). Some general information is available about science teachers' demographic characteristics, education, certification, and experience, especially for grades 7-12. The discussion below draws on three complementary analyses commissioned by the committee to examine existing databases and describe science teachers, their preparation to teach, and their retention in their initial teaching placements. One of these analyses examined the National Center for Education Statistics' 2007-2008 Schools and Staffing Survey (SASS), a census of teachers in that school year (Bird, 2013); the other two examined administrative databases in Florida (Sass, 2013) and New York (Miller, 2013). The discussion here also draws on the 2012 National Survey of Science and Mathematics Education (NSSME) (Banilower et al., 2013), which includes a nationally representative sample of mathematics and science teachers.[1]

There are about 211,000 middle and high school science teachers in the United States (National Science Foundation, 2013). Although most middle school science teachers are women (70 percent), the teaching population at the high school level is more evenly split between women and men (54 and 46 percent, respectively). At both levels, most science teachers are white (90 percent or more) and over 40 years old; about half have more than 10 years of teaching experience. At the middle school level, 41 percent have at least a bachelor's degree in a science or engineering field or in science education, a proportion that doubles to 82 percent at the high school level (see Box 4-1).

Relative to their peers who teach other subjects, middle and high school science teachers are more likely to have entered teaching through an alternative to traditional university-based teacher preparation.[2] In New York, for example, 35 percent of first-year science teachers were alternatively certified in 2009, an increase from 5 percent in 2002 (Miller, 2013). This trend is not surprising, as many alternative routes were created to fill shortages in certain fields, including science and mathematics.

---

[1] The advantage of the NSSME is its in-depth focus on science teachers and the recency of the data collection. The advantage of the 2007-2008 SASS is that it enables comparison of science teachers with other middle and high school teachers. The administrative databases provide a level of geographic and trend detail not found in the other sources. The SASS and the NSSME provide some overlapping statistics that differ only in small ways for the results presented here.

[2] Some alternative pathways for certification target midcareer individuals; others target applicants who are not interested in traditional preparation. Many such programs are structured to allow participants to move into classrooms quickly. Instead of requiring participants to follow the traditional teacher preparation pattern of academic coursework and supervised student teaching before taking charge of a classroom, many alternative programs move candidates into their own classrooms after a short period of training. Candidates continue their studies at night and on weekends and often receive structured mentoring and support while they teach.

BOX 4-1
The Science Teaching Workforce at a Glance

Number, grades 7-12	211,000
Gender	96% female (elementary school)
	70% female (middle school)
	54% female (high school)
Race/ethnicity	90% or more white
More than 10 years of teaching science	45% (elementary school)
	42% (middle school)
	49% (high school)
Bachelor's degree in science, engineering, or science education	5% (elementary school)
	41% (middle school)
	82% (high school)
Certification (grades 7-12)	35% more likely to have alternative certification than the average teacher

SOURCE: Created by the committee based on Banilower et al. (2013), Bird (2013), and Miller (2013).

For example, one national survey (Birman et al., 2007) found that the majority of school districts (65 percent) experienced difficulty attracting highly qualified teachers in science, mathematics, and special education, and the problem was exacerbated in high-poverty, high-minority, and urban districts. These districts are more likely than more affluent districts to offer financial incentives and alternative certification as a way to recruit qualified candidates—strategies that appear to have paid off in some contexts, but not in others (e.g., Liu et al., 2004).

The 1,726,000 elementary school teachers who work in U.S. public schools often are responsible for teaching all academic subjects, including science, although some schools and districts have a dedicated science teacher, especially for grades 3-5 (Jones and Edmunds, 2006). Accordingly, the National Science Teachers Association (NSTA) has recommended that elementary science teachers be prepared to teach life, earth, and physical sciences. Unfortunately, most elementary teachers are not prepared in these subjects: 36 percent of elementary science teachers reported having completed courses in all three of those areas, 38 percent had completed courses in two of the three areas, and 20 percent had completed courses in one area. At the other end of the spectrum, 6 percent of elementary science teachers indicated that they had taken no college science courses (Banilower et al., 2013).

Even when teachers have completed one course in a topic, they are underprepared for teaching to the new standards reflected in the Framework and NGSS, and these data do not reveal whether science teachers have deep knowledge of or experience with the core concepts of a science field and its scientific practices. Although most high school science teachers have completed a science major, fewer than half of middle school science teachers and only 5 percent of elementary science teachers have done so. Elementary and middle school teachers without science majors likely have had limited opportunities to engage in scientific investigations and may thus be unprepared to engage their students in science practices in ways that build conceptual understanding. However, even high school teachers who have majored in science are unlikely to have experienced authentic investigations that were closely integrated with core science ideas and crosscutting concepts as envisioned in the NGSS (see Chapter 2) (National Research Council, 2006, 2012).

Science Teachers' Preparation to Teach Science

Although there have always been multiple paths into the teaching profession, the range of pathways has recently grown (Grossman and Loeb, 2008; National Research Council, 2010; Wilson, 2009). These pathways and programs are typically grouped into the shorthand categories "traditional," which refers to those that are housed in colleges and universities and lead to a bachelor's or master's degree, and "alternative," a catch-all phrase that encompasses other pathways (Grossman and Loeb, 2008, 2010; National Research Council, 2010). Within each category, state requirements for teacher certification vary widely. Detail about teacher preparation programs is beyond the scope of the current study; these programs are discussed in depth in a recent National Research Council (2010) report *Preparing Teachers* (see Box 4-2 for a summary of the report's major findings).

An emerging body of research suggests that teacher certification in school subjects positively affects student learning. For example, Goldhaber and Brewer (2000) found that mathematics teachers who had standard state certification had a statistically significant positive impact on student test scores relative to teachers who either held private school certification or were uncertified in their subject area. Darling-Hammond and

BOX 4-2
Preparation Programs for Science Teachers

The report *Preparing Teachers: Building Evidence for Sound Policy* (National Research Council, 2010) discusses teacher preparation in reading, mathematics and science. According to the report, teacher preparation programs are extremely diverse along almost any dimension of interest: the selectivity of programs, the quantity and content of what they require, and the duration and timing of coursework and fieldwork. However, there is very little systematic research regarding the specific ways teachers of reading, mathematics, and science are currently being prepared. The limited information the committee found did not support conclusions about the current nature and content of teacher preparation programs.

It is clear from the available data that aspiring teachers in the United States are prepared in many different kinds of programs. Between 70 and 80 percent are enrolled in "traditional" programs housed in postsecondary institutions; the rest enter the profession through one of the approximately 130 "alternative" routes. However, the distinctions among pathways and programs are not clear-cut and there is more variation within the "traditional" and "alternative" categories than there is between these categories. The committee that authored the report found no evidence that any one pathway into teaching is the best way to attract and prepare desirable candidates and guide them into the teaching force. The committee cautioned that this finding does not mean that the characteristics of pathways do not matter; rather, it reflects the lack of research in this area.

The report points out that it is difficult to determine whether a particular teacher preparation program is more or less effective in part because it is difficult to measure teacher effectiveness in valid and reliable ways. The most readily available assessments of student learning in K-12 are quantitative and do not adequately measure all aspects of the curriculum in a given subject area. Also, establishing clear causal links between aspects of teacher preparation and outcomes for students is extremely difficult. The effects of teacher preparation are hard to disentangle from other factors, such as school, curriculum, community, and family influences.

In general, the evidence base supports conclusions about the characteristics it is valuable for teachers to have, but not conclusions about how teacher preparation programs can most effectively develop those characteristics. In science, these characteristics include: a grounding in college-level study of the science disciplines suitable to the age groups and subjects the teacher intends to teach; understanding of the objectives for students' science learning; understanding of the way students develop science proficiency; and command of an array of instructional approaches designed to develop students' learning of the content, intellectual conventions, and other attributes essential to science proficiency. Much of the available research on science teacher preparation focuses on teachers of grades K-8. Overall, there are numerous questions about the preparation of science teachers that remain unanswered.

colleagues (2005) examined 4th- and 5th-grade student achievement gains as measured by six different reading and mathematics tests over a 6-year period, finding that certified teachers (including those recruited through Teach for America) consistently produced stronger student achievement gains relative to uncertified teachers. More recently, Nield and colleagues (2009) found that students of middle school teachers certified in science at the secondary level (inclusive of grades 6-12) showed larger increases in learning than students of uncertified teachers or teachers with elementary certification.

Information about state certification requirements, as well as teacher preparation programs, is limited (National Research Council, 2010). According to available data, 33 of 50 states and the District of Columbia require that to be certified, high school teachers must have majored in the subject they plan to teach, but only 3 states have that requirement for middle school teachers (Editorial Projects in Education, 2006, 2008, cited in National Research Council, 2010). In 42 states, prospective teachers must pass some kind of written test for certification.

Certification of middle school teachers varies considerably across states. Most states offer middle-grades certification as an option (Association for Middle Level Education, 2013). Many offer teachers the option of pursuing certification for elementary education (K-6), secondary education (7-12), or some variation on these grade-level breakdowns (Nield et al., 2009). Compared with elementary and high school teachers, middle-grade teachers also are more likely to enter the field through alternative licensing programs (such as receiving a bachelor's degree in a field other than education and pursuing certification through a program outside of the university setting) (Feistritzer, 2011).

A recent analysis of representative national data from the 2011-2012 SASS compares science teachers' fields of certification with the fields they are assigned to teach (Hill and Stearns, 2015). This analysis, together with analyses of state-level data (Bird, 2013; Miller, 2013; Sass, 2013), show that some teachers are teaching outside their fields (see Table 4-1). At the high school level, about one-fifth to one-quarter of teachers assigned to teach biology are not certified in this subject. The fraction of high school teachers not certified in their subjects rises to 30-40 percent in chemistry and from 40 to more than 50 percent in physics. The lack of preparation is worse at the middle school level, where certification in particular subjects is less common (Baldi et al., 2015). Overall, fewer than half of departmentalized middle-grades science teachers hold both a major and certification in science. One-half to two-thirds of biology teachers, two-thirds of chemistry teachers, and more than 90 percent of physics teachers are not certified to teach those subjects.

These certification data provide general information about trends in

TABLE 4-1 Percentage of Teachers Certified to Teach Science

	Grades 6-8	Grades 9-12
Any Science Certification	56.8-60.0	85.7-85.9
In Science Subject They Teach:		
Science, general	42.7	38.5
Biology/life sciences	33.2-47.5	75.0-80.0
Chemistry	32.4	59.3-69.8
Physics	9.2	47.8-60.8
Physical sciences	16.2-21.2	36.8-67.4
Earth sciences	20.2-22.6	35.0-62.5

SOURCES: Created by the committee based on Baldi et al. (2015), Bird (2013), Hill and Stearns (2015), Miller (2013), and Sass (2013).

science teachers' preparation and certification. However, the committee was unable to locate research on the depth, breadth, or extent of such initial preparation because the field lacks a cumulative, systematic research base on core programmatic issues in science teacher preparation. For example, information is lacking on the extent of prospective teachers' field experiences (in terms of length, timing, content, or structure), how well graduates of science teacher preparation programs integrate their content knowledge with their instructional practice, and whether and how they were prepared to teach diverse learners (including but not limited to English language learners; children with special needs; and children from cultural, ethnic, and racial backgrounds different from their own).

Although the science preparation of teachers across all grades is inadequate to help them realize the vision of the Framework and NGSS, the problem affects particular schools and students disproportionately. Teachers with strong science backgrounds are not evenly distributed across schools. Schools in the highest quartile of student poverty are 30 percent more likely than schools in the lowest poverty quartile to have a teacher without a science degree (Banilower et al., 2013). Similarly, teachers who identify their students as mostly low achievers are less likely have a substantial background in the science subject they teach (57 percent) relative to teachers who identify their students as mostly high achievers (69 percent) (Banilower et al., 2013). These trends in science echo more general disparities in the distribution of well-prepared teachers. In a national survey, Birman and colleagues (2009) found that the percentage of teachers who were not "highly qualified" as defined by the No Child Left Behind Act was higher in high-poverty and high-minority schools than in other schools. Among teachers who were considered highly qualified, those in high-poverty schools had less experience and were less likely to have a degree in the subject they taught than teachers in more affluent schools.

The Birman et al. (2007) study builds on earlier research showing that schools with large proportions of nonwhite and/or low-income students tend to have teachers with far weaker qualifications relative to teachers in schools serving large portions of white and/or more affluent students (Betts et al., 2000; Clotfelter et al., 2006, 2007; Lankford et al., 2002). Most recently, an analysis of data from Washington State found that in elementary, middle, and high school classrooms, the quality of teachers—as measured by experience, licensure exam scores, and value added—was distributed inequitably across every indicator of student disadvantage, including free/reduced-price lunch status, underrepresented minority, and low prior academic performance (Goldhaber et al., 2015). This uneven distribution of qualified teachers has implications for the learning needs of science teachers in higher-poverty schools and for the availability of expertise with which to continue building the collective capacity in those schools.

Teachers' Perceptions of Their Science Preparation

These patterns of uneven science preparation accord with teachers' own perceptions. According to the NSSME, middle and high school teachers' sense of feeling prepared varied by the types of students they taught. Compared with teachers of classes of "mostly low achievers," teachers of classes with "mostly high achievers" were more likely to feel well prepared to teach science content, encourage students' interest in science, teach students from diverse backgrounds, and implement instruction in a particular unit. In addition, teachers of classes with a higher proportion of minority students and in higher-poverty schools indicated they felt less well prepared compared with teachers of classes with a lower proportion of minority students and in more affluent schools (Banilower et al., 2013).

Only 39 percent of elementary teachers felt very well prepared to teach science, while 43 percent felt fairly well prepared. By comparison, 77 percent and 81 percent of elementary teachers, respectively, felt very well prepared to teach mathematics and reading. These perceptions may reflect the reality that while elementary teachers are prepared as generalists, the greatest emphasis is placed on their literacy and mathematics preparation, and they receive minimal preparation in science content and methods courses and have few opportunities to learn through practice in their field placements. Elementary teachers responding to the NSSME felt more prepared to teach life or earth science than physical science (Banilower et al., 2013).

When middle and high school teachers were asked how prepared they felt to teach specific topics in the courses for which they were responsible, high school chemistry teachers were more likely than teachers of any other science subject or grade range to report a high level of preparedness. Physics teachers' responses varied widely depending on the topic; only 19 percent of high school physics teachers reported feeling very well prepared to teach modern physics (e.g., relativity), compared with 43-71 percent for the other topics (force and motion, waves, energy, electricity, and magnetism). High school biology, chemistry, and physics teachers were more likely than their counterparts in the middle grades to report feeling very well prepared to teach topics within those disciplines, with no differences seen in earth, space, and environmental sciences (Banilower et al., 2013).

Patterns of Retention and Attrition

The development of science teachers' expertise over time is influenced by their teaching experiences, initial preparation, and ongoing opportunities to learn. Research shows that second-year teachers generally are more effective than first-year teachers, and third-year teachers, are more successful than second-year teachers (Wilson, 2009). On average, teachers improve steadily for up to 5 (or more) years, after which their rate of improvement typically levels off (Boyd et al., 2006; Kane et al., 2008; Rice, 2003; Wilson, 2009). At the same time, recent data show that many teachers' careers do not last long enough for them to fully develop this expertise. This observation led the committee to investigate patterns of retention and attrition among science teachers.

As shown in Box 4-1, nearly half of all high school science teachers and 42 percent of middle school science teachers have more than 10 years of science teaching experience (Banilower et al., 2013). As is the case with teachers generally, however, schools with greater proportions of students who are eligible for free and reduced-price lunches are less likely than schools with fewer poor students to have an experienced science teacher. In schools in the highest poverty quartile, 45 percent of science teachers have 5 or fewer years of science teaching experience, compared with just 25 percent of those in the lowest poverty quartile (Banilower et al., 2013).

It is interesting to note that when Murnane and colleagues (1989) analyzed attrition data for a sample of new teachers in North Carolina, they found that among those who left within the first 5 years, 30 percent returned to teaching.[3] They found similar patterns in a study of new

---

[3]At the high school level, 17 percent of teachers left after the first year, another 9 percent left after 2 years, and fewer than half (46 percent) remained in the profession after 8 years. Elementary teachers were far less likely to leave: 8 percent left after the first year, 6 percent

teachers in Michigan (Murnane et al., 1988), observing that these trends were consistent with national data showing that 84 percent of new hires in schools came from a "reserve" pool of certified teachers who had not been teaching the previous year. Historically, the phenomenon of teachers returning to the profession was due in part to women leaving teaching to have and raise children; other reasons include poor preparation, misaligned expectations of the nature of the work, the ebb and flow of the marketplace for teachers, and the desire to try other professions before committing to a lifetime of teaching.

In both studies by these authors, chemistry and physics teachers were particularly likely to leave teaching after only 1 or 2 years in the classroom. In Michigan, chemistry and physics teachers were less likely than teachers of other subjects to return to teaching. It is unknown whether this bimodal distribution of teachers still exists, nor are comprehensive data available on how science teachers compare with other reentering teachers.

Although the committee could not locate national data on retention and attrition among first-time science teachers, we offer illustrative data from New York and Florida (see Table 4-2). These data indicate that a considerable portion of new entrants continue to leave within their first 5 years of teaching. In Florida, for example, only 38 percent of new science teachers are still teaching in that state by the end of their fourth year of teaching. In New York, slightly fewer than half of science teachers are still teaching by the end of their fifth year. National trends for all teachers reported by Ingersoll (2003) are similar. He found that after 5 years, 40-50 percent of teachers had left the profession. In addition, he found that teacher turnover—when a teacher leaves his or her current position—was highest in science and mathematics (Ingersoll, 2003).

In both Florida and New York, retention of science teachers varies substantially across the preparation pathways through which teachers entered teaching. In New York, teachers who entered through a traditional pathway are more likely to be teaching in the state after 5 years than those who entered through an alternative pathway, while this trend is reversed in Florida. Differences in the retention of teachers who entered the profession through alternative certification pathways may be explained in part by how these pathways are designed and implemented. In some alternative certification programs, teachers begin their teaching career before completing all phases of preparation. Some programs recruit young people who may not intend to teach for a lifetime—for example, by providing appropriate assignments for newly certified teachers and preparing them with mentors and other supports. Some provide intensive

---

more left after each of the following 4 years, and 60 percent remained in the profession after 8 years.

TABLE 4-2 Retention of New Science Teachers by Preparation Pathway, New York and Florida (percentage of teachers remaining in a science teaching position at any school in the state)

Years of Teaching	All Paths	Traditional Preparation	Alternative Certification	Interstate Reciprocity
New York (entering teachers 2003-2008) (Miller, 2013)				
1	78.4	89.1	87.8	81.2
2	65.5	83.3	67.5	67.6
3	57.6	77.4	54.6	57.2
4	52.2	72.9	47.4	52.4
5	48.3	67.9	41.4	46.3
Florida (entering teachers 1999-2005) (Sass, 2013)				
1	71.6	72.0	90.4	71.7
2	56.2	57.5	81.2	57.7
3	45.1	46.6	69.3	46.0
4	37.5	37.5	57.9	37.9

NOTE: Two pathways to teaching, individual evaluation and unknown, are not shown as separate columns but are included in the percentage for all paths. Teachers whose pathway into science teaching was unknown tended to have low-retention rates, which lowers the overall retention rates for all paths.
SOURCES: Created by the committee based on Miller (2013) and Sass (2013).

ongoing support, encouraging teachers to stay in the profession, while others do not. Some are well aligned with school policies on teaching and learning, curriculum and assessment, and teacher evaluation.

The data and research on teacher attrition suggest that the level of experience in science is the lowest in schools that most need teachers with deep expertise in teaching science to diverse students in challenging circumstances. The data also suggest that many science teachers are not staying in the profession long enough to develop expertise in science teaching, a situation that requires rethinking how to support early-career teachers so that they develop as much expertise as possible, as quickly as possible. Not only will this benefit students, but if some teachers leave the profession because they feel unprepared, increasing their ability may also stem some of the observed attrition.

INVESTING IN SCIENCE TEACHERS' ONGOING LEARNING

All professionals need opportunities to keep pace with advances in their field, and this is true for science teachers. Just as doctors must constantly refresh their knowledge of new treatments, technologies, and research, science teachers need to refresh their understanding of science;

new scientific methods and discoveries; new research on student learning; and new research on how best to support student engagement, motivation, scientific literacy, and scientific understanding.

Across the United States, schools and districts invest considerable human and material resources in professional learning opportunities. In one recent study, The New Teacher Project (2015) reports that one district offered more than 1,000 professional learning courses during the 2013-2014 school year. Teachers in three large urban districts reported spending approximately 150 hours a year on professional learning, one-third to one- half of which was mandated.

Science teachers have many opportunities for learning. In their early years, "induction" (early-career support) programs are offered. Overlapping with and extending those experiences are countless structured professional development opportunities offered by schools, cultural institutions, and universities; advanced degree programs at institutions of higher education; teacher-led teams and study groups; and meetings, seminars, and workshops offered by professional organizations. Learning also occurs through online courses and webinars, research and development projects, and intermediate school district workshops. In the best of circumstances, teachers' schools are carefully sustained learning organizations in which teachers and leaders collaborate regularly on improving instruction.

Of course, every learning opportunity is not equally useful, relevant, or high quality. Historically, teachers have largely been left on their own to negotiate and use this panoply of opportunities. Some teachers, eager to keep honing their skills, jump at new chances to learn science or how to teach science. Others do little, utilizing only those opportunities that are mandatory. Despite growing awareness that school districts would benefit from a more coherent approach to managing district-based learning opportunities (e.g., Elmore and Burney, 1997; Miles, 2003) and that schools themselves benefit from leadership that creates a learning culture (Bryk et al., 2010), most teachers in the United States are left on their own to decide how much professional development to pursue. The available evidence suggests that most science teachers spend limited time in formally organized, science-focused professional development activities—on average, less than 35 hours over a 3-year period (Banilower et al., 2013, p. 50).

Staying up to date is particularly challenging for teachers at the elementary level, as they typically teach multiple subjects. Results from the NSSME (Banilower et al., 2013) indicate that 41 percent of responding elementary teachers had participated in no science-focused professional development in the prior 3 years, and only 12 percent had participated for 16 or more hours (the equivalent of approximately 1 day per year) over the same period. In comparison, just 18 percent of middle school teachers had participated in no science-focused professional development, and 47 percent had participated for at least 16 hours. Similarly, only 15 percent of high school teachers had participated in no science-focused professional development in the prior 3 years, and 57 percent had participated for more than 16 hours.

Teachers responding to the NSSME who had participated in professional development in the last 3 years were asked a series of additional questions about the nature of those experiences. As can be seen in Table 4-3, 84-91 percent of these teachers had attended a workshop, the most common form of professional development. Roughly three-fourths of middle and high school teachers and more than half of their elementary school colleagues reported participating in professional learning communities or teacher study groups focused on science or science teaching. Middle and high school teachers also attended science teacher association meetings at a higher rate than elementary teachers, reflecting the fact that elementary teachers are responsible for teaching multiple subjects and are less likely than those teaching at higher levels to belong to science teacher associations. Roughly one-third of secondary science and mathematics teachers reported attending a professional association meeting; a similar percentage reported taking a formal course for college credit in science or science teaching in the last 3 years. Finally, not only are elementary science teachers less likely to have participated recently

TABLE 4-3 Types of Activities among Science Teachers Who Participated in Professional Development in the Past 3 Years

Activity	Percentage of Teachers		
	Elementary	Middle	High
Attended a workshop on science or science teaching	84	91	90
Participated in a professional learning community/lesson study or teacher study group focused on science or science teaching	55	75	73
Received feedback on science teaching from a mentor/coach	24	47	54
Attended a national, state, or regional science teacher association meeting	8	35	44

NOTE: Does not include teachers who reported that they had participated in no science-related professional development over the past 3 years.
SOURCE: Banilower et al. (2013, p. 35, Table 3.5).

in professional development in science, but they also are far less likely to have received feedback on their teaching from a mentor/coach relative to any other group.

Although these data describe the duration of—and venues for—teacher learning opportunities, they reveal little about the content and quality of those experiences. Did these science teachers have opportunities to work with teacher colleagues who face similar challenges, reflect on student work, test new teaching approaches in their classrooms, or engage in their own scientific investigations? Accordingly, teachers were asked about these characteristics of their professional development experiences in science. The characteristics included in the NSSME reflect current consensus on what constitutes effective professional development (see Chapter 6 for further discussion of characteristics of effective professional development). As shown in Table 4-4, at the elementary school level, only about a third of elementary teachers who had participated in professional development in science, compared with more than half of middle and high school teachers, had substantial opportunities to work with other science teachers and to apply and then talk about what they had learned. Such opportunities were provided in teacher study groups, which tended to focus on analyzing student assessment results or instructional materials and/or on jointly planning lessons, with less emphasis on analyzing stu-

TABLE 4-4 Teachers Whose Professional Development in Science Had Each of a Number of Characteristics

Characteristic	Percentage of Teachers		
	Elementary	Middle	High
Worked closely with other science teachers from your school	34	61	62
Worked closely with other science teachers, whether or not they were from your school	37	54	58
Had opportunities to try out what was learned in the classroom and then talk about it	34	51	47
Had opportunities to engage in science investigations	48	52	45
Had opportunities to examine student work	31	40	33
The professional development was a waste of time	8	5	8

NOTE: Percentages shown include teachers indicating 4 or 5 on a 5-point scale ranging from 1 (not at all) to 5 (to a great extent).
SOURCE: Banilower et al. (2013, p. 35, Table 3.5).

dent work. Across all levels, about half of teachers' professional development experiences in science included substantial opportunities to engage in science investigations.

Another series of items on the NSSME asked teachers about the focus of their recent professional development or formal higher education coursework. For teachers across all levels, these learning opportunities largely emphasized planning instruction to meet the needs of students at different achievement levels, monitoring student understanding during instruction, and assessing student understanding at the end of instruction. Deepening science content knowledge was emphasized less for elementary than for secondary teachers.

The NSSME also asked school science program representatives about locally offered professional development opportunities. Their responses indicate that in-service workshops were the most prevalent form of professional development offered, and that these workshops often focused on state science standards, science content, and/or use of instructional materials. In addition, about 20 percent of schools at all levels offered one-on-one coaching to teachers, focused on improving their science instruction. The survey does not shed light on how that coaching was structured and whether coaches were trained in that role.

Responses on the NSSME reveal some differences in the learning opportunities for teachers by type of school and community. Teachers in smaller schools reported lower-quality professional development experiences relative to teachers in larger schools. There were no significant differences in the reported quality of professional development by school type or proportion of students eligible for free or reduced-price lunch. Schools with different proportions of students eligible for free or reduced-price lunch were about equally likely to provide assistance for science teachers who needed it. In contrast, the largest schools were significantly more likely than the smallest schools to offer science-focused teacher-study groups. One-on-one coaching was more likely to be offered in schools in the highest quartile of proportion of students eligible for free and reduced-price lunch than in schools in the lowest quartile. Also, the largest were more likely than the smallest schools and urban more likely than rural schools to offer coaching.

In summary, no centralized system for collecting data on teachers' professional learning opportunities exists, and thus the committee relied heavily for such data on teachers' responses to the NSSME. On average, no more than half of the teachers responding reported participating in opportunities to collaborate with other science educators (these opportunities are more common among high school teachers), to try out and reflect on new instructional approaches or curricula, or to have a colleague or school leader observe and discuss their performance. No substantial, large-scale evidence is available to shed light on the quality of those experiences. Thus there is no way to know the extent to which teachers are encouraged to engage in rigorous study of the sciences and scientific practices, and when they do, whether their content knowledge or pedagogical content knowledge is enhanced, whether their instruction improves, and whether students benefit. Given that surveys collect information at a high level of abstraction, the quality of the limited experiences teachers reported is likely quite varied, with some teachers experiencing rich opportunities for learning and others encountering offerings of limited depth and utility. A similar observation results from analyses of professional development for mathematics teachers. Hill (2007), for example, presents evidence that while most mathematics teachers report participating in professional development, those experiences are typically "one-shot" workshops. She concludes that "by all accounts, professional development in the United States consists of a hodgepodge of providers, formats, philosophies, and content" (p. 114). Many authors have drawn similar conclusions (e.g., Ball and Cohen, 1999; The New Teacher Project, 2015; Wilson, 2009).

Chapters 6 and 7 present available evidence from studies of particular programs that reach targeted populations. Nonetheless, there remains a gap in understanding of how the science teacher workforce in general is supported in its ongoing learning. The evidence that is available is sobering.

MOVEMENT INTO DIFFERENT ROLES

As emphasized throughout this report, teachers have many opportunities for learning outside of formal professional development activities, and the committee sought any data that would help in portraying these opportunities. Some of these opportunities relate to the potential for teachers to move into new roles. Historically, teachers had few opportunities for career advancement unless they were willing to become school principals. However, school reform efforts and the implementation of more rigorous national standards have led to the creation of new roles for accomplished teachers, shifting traditional career paths and offering new opportunities for states and districts to retain and develop skilled teachers. For example, the National Science Foundation (NSF), which has supported teacher leaders with Presidential Awards for Excellence in Mathematics and Science Teaching, the Master Teacher Fellowship of the Robert Noyce Teacher Scholarship Program, and the Math and Science Partnership Program, recently announced a new effort—the STEM Teacher Leader Initiative—whose goal is to explore effective programs for the development and support of science, technology, engineering, and mathematics teacher leaders. In the same vein, NSTA sponsors a Leadership Institute designed to keep experienced teachers current in developments in science, science education practice and policy, and research on teaching and learning.

The committee was interested in the expansion of teacher roles for several reasons. First, it reflects changes in how schools organize instruction and teacher learning opportunities. For example, the introduction of instructional coaches in the process of comprehensive school reform gave some teachers opportunities to interact with an accomplished colleague who observed their instruction and provided concrete, focused feedback. This activity veers sharply away from the historically isolated teacher who might be observed by her principal once a year for 15 minutes.

Second, these new roles themselves offer new learning opportunities for those teachers who become leaders. The various new roles of teacher leaders—lead teacher, curriculum specialist, mentor, collaborating teacher, instructional coach, professional development leader—often emphasize helping fellow teachers learn. For example, the NSSME asked teachers whether they had served in such roles as leading a teacher study group or serving as a formally assigned mentor or coach (see Table 4-5). At the elementary school level, about 40 percent of science teachers indicated that they had supervised a student teacher, but only 5 percent or fewer had served as a mentor/coach for other science teachers, led a teacher study group for science teachers, or taught in-service workshops focused on science. At the secondary level, teachers had served more frequently in these leadership roles. In addition, the survey found that 56 percent of science teacher study groups offered by the local school or district had designated leaders, and 87 percent of these leaders came from within the school (Banilower et al., 2013).

A summary of research on teacher leaders' instructional support practices across grade levels and subject areas (Schiavo et al., 2010) found that

TABLE 4-5 Science Teachers' Participation in Leadership Roles

Role	Percentage of Teachers		
	Elementary	Middle	High
Led a teacher study group focused on science teaching	4	19	26
Served as a formally assigned mentor/ coach for science teaching	5	17	24
Supervised a student teacher	38	24	23
Taught in-service workshops on science or science teaching	3	15	17

teacher leaders frequently support teacher learning and instruction, but they also carry out administrative tasks (e.g., selecting instructional materials, working directly with the principal), communicate information (e.g., sharing information with teachers or acting as a liaison for an initiative), and manage materials or resources. When supporting their colleagues' instruction and learning, teacher leaders observe classroom teaching and give feedback, lead workshops, model lessons, engage in lesson planning, lead teacher study groups in analysis of student work, or co-teach. They carry out these activities both outside and within the classroom, and there is no one prevailing model for providing instructional support. The authors note that because most of the studies they reviewed focused on teacher leaders within systems undergoing significant change, their findings illuminate emerging practices by relatively new teacher leaders.

Depending on how teacher leader positions are defined, they can be either full- or part-time, with teachers spending portions of their day working with students. For example, when the NSSME asked school science representatives about individuals providing coaching to science teachers, 24 percent indicated that these individuals had no classroom teaching responsibilities (i.e., they were full-time teacher leaders), 17 percent that they had part-time classroom teaching responsibilities, and 34 percent that they had full-time classroom teaching responsibilities. In most cases, applicants are required to undergo a formal hiring process to ensure that they are qualified and receive subsequent specialized training. The NSSME, however, provides little insight into the learning opportunities for the leaders themselves. Leading teachers is different from leading children, and the pedagogies of professional development can be significantly different from those of K-12 science instruction.

In their summary of research on teacher leaders, Schiavo and colleagues (2010) note that professional development programs for teacher leaders often were extensive, lasting more than 100 hours over a 1- to 2-year period. Programs typically used summer institutes and/or regular meetings during the academic year to emphasize content knowledge, along with specialized knowledge of a specific curriculum or other skills (e.g., facilitation skills to lead teacher study groups or to analyze data). (One study [Oehrtman et al., 2009] found that teacher leaders with weak backgrounds in science were less able than those with stronger knowledge of science subject matter to facilitate effective discussions of classroom instruction in teacher workgroups.)

Related work focused on the selection, preparation, and use of coaches in mathematics (Coburn and Russell, 2008) found that the districts' own approach to selection, training, and role definition mattered, and that school leaders' decisions about how to allocate coaching resources influenced the connections, intensity, and quality of teachers' interactions with professional networks.

CONCLUSIONS

Within the current science teacher workforce, preparation in science, whether through a disciplinary major or coursework, is especially weak among elementary teachers and not strong among middle school teachers. At the high school level, more teachers have completed science majors, but there is some mismatch between teachers' preparation and the subjects they teach. The problems of insufficient content knowledge and misaligned certification are exacerbated in schools and classrooms serving low-income and low-achieving students. Across all grade levels, the emphasis on scientific practices in the vision laid out in the Framework and NGSS will challenge many teachers who themselves have had limited experience participating in investigations.

At the same time, on average, the science teaching workforce has fewer years of classroom experience than in previous decades, giving teachers less opportunity to develop an understanding of science and science teaching. Efforts to support science teachers' learning will need to take into account the issue of how to design successful learning opportunities for teachers when the cohort in a school may include few highly experienced teachers.

Conclusion 2: The available evidence suggests that many science teachers have not had sufficiently rich experiences with the content relevant to the science courses they currently teach, let alone a substantially redesigned science curriculum. Very few teachers have experience with the science and engineering practices described in the NGSS. This situation is especially pronounced both for elementary school teachers and in schools that serve high percentages of low-income students, where teachers are often newer and less qualified.

Following their initial preparation, science teachers currently participate in limited and sporadic professional development. Although most teachers participate in some form of professional development in science over a 3-year period, these learning opportunities are quite brief and seldom linked to one another. The NSSME reveals that this lack of sustained learning is especially problematic for elementary teachers, close to 90 percent of whom received only 15 hours or less of professional development in science over this period. Even at the secondary level, 54 percent of middle school and 43 percent of high school science teachers received only 15 hours or less of professional development in science over this period (Banilower et al., 2013). Professional development typically is provided in the form of brief workshops; however, about a third of elementary teachers responding to the NSSME and more than half of middle and high school teachers had opportunities to work with other science teachers, and to try out what they learned and then talk about it through teacher study groups. In addition, 20 to 25 percent of secondary teachers (but only 8 percent of elementary teachers) had taken a college-level course in science or science teaching over a 3-year period. On a positive note, the focus of these various professional development opportunities included planning instruction to enable students at different levels of achievement to enhance their understanding of the targeted science ideas, monitoring student understanding during instruction, eliciting students' ideas and prior knowledge prior to instruction on a topic, assessing students' understanding at the end of instruction on a topic, and deepening students' science content knowledge.

> **Conclusion 3:** *Typically, the selection of and participation in professional learning opportunities is up to individual teachers. There is often little attention to developing collective capacity for science teaching at the building and district levels or to offering teachers learning opportunities tailored to their specific needs and offered in ways that support cumulative learning over time.*

In summary, many science teachers have weak grounding in the subjects they teach and few opportunities to deepen their professional knowledge or extend their teaching practice. This situation is not the fault of the individual teachers who constitute the workforce. Rather, it is a result of the educational system, as embodied in both policies and practices that fail to support the initial and ongoing preparation of teachers in ways that lead to deep science knowledge for teaching or enhanced practice. Achieving the aspirations for a very different vision of science instruction in U.S. schools will require a systematic strategy that entails making changes in preparation and professional development programs, supporting changes in the culture of U.S. schools, and creating a policy system that is aligned in terms of curricular vision and educator expectations. It will depend heavily on leveraging partnerships with organizations that have established programs such as NSF, NSTA, and other institutions that have been exploring how to create and support cadres of knowledgeable and skillful science teachers and leaders. This is an ambitious agenda, but anything less will leave teachers where they long have been: trying their best to meet the needs of their students and the instructional mandates of their schools with little support in acquiring the knowledge and skills they need to do so or to transform their schools into cultures of learning for both students and themselves.

Any such changes will have to be grounded in a clear understanding of teacher learning needs that flows from the vision of science instruction set forth in the Framework and NGSS. The next chapter delineates these needs, set against the backdrop of the depiction of the current state of the workforce provided in this chapter.

RFEFERENCES

Association for Middle Level Education. (2013). *Certification/Licensure by State.* Available: http://www.amle.org/AboutAMLE/ProfessionalPreparation/Certification-Licensure byState/tabid/264/Default.aspx [November 2015].

Baldi, S., Warner-Griffin, C., and Tadler, C. (2015). *Education and Certification Qualifications of Public Middle Grades Teachers of Selected Subjects: Evidence from the 2011-12 Schools and Staffing Survey.* NCES 2015-815. U.S. Department of Education, National Center for Education Statistics. Washington, DC: U.S. Government Printing Office.

Ball, D.L., and Cohen, D.K. (1999). Developing practice, developing practitioners: Toward a practice-based theory of professional education. In G. Sykes and L. Darling-Hammond (Eds.), *Teaching as the Learning Profession: Handbook of Policy and Practice* (pp. 3-32). San Francisco, CA: Jossey-Bass.

Banilower, E.R., Smith, P.S., Weiss, I.R., Malzahn, K.A., Campbell, K.M., and Weis, A.M. (2013). *Report of the 2012 National Survey of Science and Mathematics Education.* Chapel Hill, NC: Horizon Research.

Betts, J.R., Rueben, K.S., and Danenberg, A. (2000). *Equal Resources, Equal Outcomes? The Distribution of School Resources and Student Achievement in California.* San Francisco: Public Policy Institute of California.

Bird, K. (2013). *Secondary Science Teachers and Professional Development: Descriptive Statistics from the Schools and Staffing Survey.* Presentation to the Committee on Strengthening Education through a Teacher Learning Continuum, Division of Behavioral and Social Sciences and Education, Washington, DC. Available: http://sites.nationalacademies.org/DBASSE/BOSE/DBASSE_081821 [January 2015].

Birman, B.F., Carlson Le Floch, K., Klekotka, A., Ludwig, M., Taylor, J., Walter, K., Wayne, A., and Yoon, K.S. (2007). *State and Local Implementation of the No Child Left Behind Act, Vol. II—Teacher Quality under NCLB, Interim Report.* Washington, DC: U.S. Department of Education. Available: http://www2.ed.gov/rschstat/eval/teaching/nclb/report07.pdf [February 2015].

Birman, B.F., Boyle, A., Carlson Le Floch, K., Elledge, A., Holtzman, D., Song, M., Thomsen, K., Walters, K., and Yoon, K.S. (2009). *State and Local Implementation of the No Child Left Behind Act, Vol. VIII—Teacher Quality under NCLB, Final Report.* Available: http://files.eric.ed.gov/fulltext/ED504212.pdf [February 2015].

Boyd, D., Grossman, P., Lankford, H., Loeb, S., and Wyckoff, J. (2006). How changes in entry requirements alter the teacher workforce and affect student achievement. *Education, 1*(2), 176-216.

Bryk, A., Sebring, P.B., Allensworth, E., Luppescu, S., and Easton, J.Q. (2010). *Organizing Schools for Improvement: Lessons from Chicago.* Chicago, IL: University of Chicago Press.

Clotfelter, C.T., Ladd, H.F., and Vigdor, J.L. (2006). Teacher-student matching and the assessment of teacher effectiveness. *Journal of Human Resources, 41*(4), 778-820.

Clotfelter, C.T., Ladd, H.F., and Vigdor, J.L. (2007). Teacher credentials and student achievement: Longitudinal analysis with student fixed effects. *Economics of Education Review, 26*(6), 673-682.

Coburn, C.E., and Russell, J.L. (2008). District policy and teachers' social networks. *Educational Evaluation and Policy Analysis, 30*(3), 203-235.

Darling-Hammond, L., Holzman, D.J., Gatlin, S.J., and Heilig, J.V. (2005). Does teacher preparation matter? Evidence about teacher certification, Teach for America, and teacher effectiveness. *Education Policy Analysis Archives, 13*(42). Available: http://epaa.asu.edu/ojs/article/view/147 [August 2015].

Editorial Projects in Education. (2006). *Quality Counts at 10: A Decade of Standards-based Education*. Bethesda, MD: Editorial Projects in Education.

Editorial Projects in Education. (2008). *Technology Counts 2008: STEM: The Push to Improve Science, Technology, Engineering, and Mathematics*. Bethesda, MD: Editorial Projects in Education.

Elmore, R., and Burney, D. (1997). *Investing in Teacher Learning: Staff Development and Instructional Improvement in Community School District #2, New York City*. New York: Consortium for Policy Research in Education, Teachers College, Columbia University.

Feistritzer, C.E. (2011). *Profile of Teachers in the U.S. 2011*. Washington, DC: National Center for Education Information.

Feuer, M.J., Floden, R.E., Chudowsky, N., and Ahn, J. (2013). *Evaluation of Teacher Preparation Programs: Purposes, Methods, and Policy Options*. Washington, DC: National Academy of Education. Available: http://www.naeducation.org/xpedio/groups/naedsite/documents/webpage/naed_085581.pdf [January 2015].

Goldhaber, D., Lavery, L., and Theobald, R. (2015). Uneven playing field? Assessing the quality gap between advantaged and disadvantaged students. *Educational Researcher, 44*(5), 293-307.

Goldhaber, D.D., and Brewer, D.J. (2000). Does teacher certification matter? High school teacher certification status and student achievement. *Education Evaluation and Policy Analysis, 22*(2), 129-145.

Grossman, P., and Loeb, S. (Eds.). (2008). *Alternative Routes to Teaching: Mapping the New Landscape of Teacher Education*. Cambridge, MA: Harvard Education Press.

Grossman, P., and Loeb, S. (2010). Learning from multiple routes: The variation in teacher preparation pathways can propel our understanding of how best to prepare teachers. *Educational Leadership, 67*(8), 22-27.

Hill, H.C. (2007). Learning in the teacher workforce. *The Future of Children, 17*(1), 111-127.

Hill, J., and Stearns, C. (2015). *Education and Certification Qualifications of Departmentalized Public High School-Level Teachers of Selected Subjects: Evidence from the 2011-2012 Schools and Staffing Survey*. NCES 2015-814. Washington, DC: National Center for Education Statistics. Available: https://nces.ed.gov/pubsearch/pubsinfo.asp?pubid=2015814 [August 2015].

Ingersoll, R. (2003). Is there a shortage among mathematics and science teachers? *Science Educator, 12*(1), 1-9.

Jones, M.G., and Edmunds, J. (2006). Models of elementary science instruction: Roles of specialist teachers. In K. Appleton (Ed.), *Elementary Science Teacher Education: International Perspectives on Contemporary Issues and Practice* (pp. 317-343). Mahwah, NJ: Lawrence Erlbaum Associates.

Kane, T.J., Rockoff, J.E., and Staiger, D.O. (2008). What does certification tell us about teacher effectiveness? Evidence from New York City. *Economics of Education Review, 27*(6), 615-631.

Lankford, H., Loeb, S., and Wyckoff, J. (2002). Teacher sorting and the plight of urban schools: A descriptive analysis. *Educational Evaluation and Policy Analysis, 24*(1), 37-62.

Liu, E., Johnson, S.M., and Peske, H.G. (2004). New teachers and the Massachusetts sign-ing bonus: The limits of inducements. *Educational Evaluation and Policy Analysis, 26*(3), 217-236.

Miller, L. (2013). *A Descriptive Analysis of New York's Science Teacher Labor Market 1999-2009.* Paper commissioned by the Committee on Strengthening Science Education through a Teacher Learning Continuum, Division of Behavioral and Social Sciences and Educa-tion, Washington, DC.

Murnane, R.E., Singer, J.D., and Willett, J.B. (1988). The career paths of teachers: Implica-tions for teacher supply and methodological lessons for research. *Educational Researcher, 17*(6), 22-30.

Murnane, R.E., Singer J.D., and Willett, J.B. (1989). The influences of salaries and opportunity costs on teachers' career choices: Evidence from North Carolina. *Harvard Educational Review, 59*(3), 325-346. Available: http://gseacademic.harvard.edu/~willetjo/pdf%20files/Murnane_Singer_Willett_HER89.pdf [January 2015].

National Research Council. (2006). *America's Lab Report: Investigations in High School Science.* Committee on High School Laboratories: Role and Vision. S.R. Singer, M.L. Hilton, and H.A. Schweingruber (Eds.). Board on Science Education, Center for Education, Divi-sion of Behavioral and Social Sciences and Education. Washington, DC: The National Academies Press.

National Research Council. (2010). *Preparing Teachers: Building Evidence for Sound Policy.* Committee on the Study of Teacher Preparation Programs in the United States, Center for Education. Division of Behavioral and Social Sciences and Education. Washington, DC: The National Academies Press.

National Research Council. (2012). *Discipline-based Education Research: Understanding and Improving Learning in Undergraduate Science and Engineering.* S.R. Singer, N.R. Nielsen, and H.A. Schweingruber (Eds.). Committee on the Status, Contributions, and Future Directions of Discipline-Based Education Research. Board on Science Education, Divi-sion of Behavioral and Social Sciences and Education. Washington, DC: The National Academies Press.

National Science Foundation. (2013). *Science and Engineering Indicators, 2012. Teachers of Mathematics and Science.* Available: http://www.nsf.gov/statistics/seind12/c1/c1s3.htm [January 2015].

The New Teacher Project. (2015). *The Mirage: Confronting the Hard Truth About Our Quest for Teacher Development.* Brooklyn, NY: The New Teacher Project.

Nield, R.C., Farley-Ripple, E.N., and Byrnes, V. (2009). The effect of teacher certification on middle grades achievement in an urban district. *Educational Policy, 23*(5), 732-760.

Oehrtman, M., Carlson, M., and Vasquez, J. A. (2009). *Attributes of Content-Focused Profes-sional Learning Communities That Lead to Meaningful Reflection and Collaboration among Math and Science Teachers.* Washington, DC: National Science Teachers Association.

Rice, J.K. (2003). *Teacher Quality: Understanding the Effectiveness of Teacher Attributes.* Wash-ington, DC: Economic Policy Institute.

Sass, T. (2013). *The Market for New Science Teachers in Florida.* Paper commissioned by the Committee on Strengthening Science Education through a Teacher Learning Con-tinuum, Division of Behavioral and Social Sciences and Education, Washington, DC.

Schiavo, N., Miller, B., Busey, A., and King, K. (2010). *Summary of Empirical Research on Teacher Leaders' Instructional Support Practices.* Prepared for the Math and Science Part-nership Knowledge Management and Dissemination Project, Education Development Center, Inc., Washington, DC. Available: http://www.mspkmd.net/pdfs/blast05/3c2.pdf [January 2015].

Wilson, S. (Ed.). (2009). *Teacher Quality, Education Policy White Paper.* Washington, DC: Na-tional Academy of Education. Available: http://www.naeducation.org/cs/groups/naedsite/documents/webpage/naed_080867.pdf [January 2015].

5

Science Teachers' Learning Needs

eachers' learning is a dynamic process. Science teachers do not
follow a uniform path through initial preparation, an early-career
program, and formal professional development activities, facing
predictable learning challenges along the way. Rather, they prepare for
varying lengths of time, in a variety of settings, following a growing number of alternative paths into teaching. Once they are in the classroom, their
learning is shaped not only by formal professional development opportunities but also by the demands of particular teaching contexts, the materials and human resources available to them, educational reform efforts,
and policy mandates from their schools and states. Teachers' learning also
is significantly affected by their students and by how much they need
to learn in order to to meet students' needs. Against this backdrop, this
chapter addresses the individual and collective learning needs of K-12 science teachers. Given that the new vision set forth in *A Framework for K-12
Science Education* (hereafter referred to as the Framework) and the *Next
Generation Science Standards* (hereafter referred to as NGSS) represents a
significant departure from current teaching approaches, all teachers—
regardless of their preparation or experience—will require some new
knowledge and skills.

The committee's charge was to consider what is known about
teachers' learning over the course of their careers and how that knowledge might bear on current efforts to improve science teaching and learning in schools. As noted earlier, the committee views teacher learning as
a long-term process: dynamic, iterative, ongoing, and contingent both on

the contexts in which it unfolds (e.g., formal and informal policies, practices, school cultures, and norms) and on the characteristics and needs of individual teachers.

The committee's view contrasts with ways of thinking about a learning continuum that are oriented only around teachers' years of experience in the classroom. While useful in some regards, focusing solely on time in the classroom fails to acknowledge teachers' varying strengths and needs, both throughout the course of their careers and as contextual factors shift and change. One first-year teacher, for example, may have substantial scientific knowledge but not the expertise needed to support her students in engaging in productive scientific conversations. Another, more experienced teacher may be expert at supporting productive academic talk—helping students attend carefully to one another's ideas and construct new knowledge together—but needs support in developing accessible representations of scientific ideas. An elementary teacher who has long used teacher-centered instructional methods can feel like a novice when presented with a reform that calls for problem-based, student-centered approaches. What teachers need to know about science, teaching, and students is always changing, and no one teacher will be expert in all relevant domains (e.g., National Research Council, 2002, 2007, 2010).

Further, the committee was persuaded by recent research suggesting that teacher quality is dependent not only on individual teachers but also on their communities (e.g., Bryk et al., 2010). Thus, instead of a sequential conception of teacher learning, the committee identified expertise essential for both individual teachers and the collective workforce. In contrast to the view of teacher learning as an individual accomplishment along a linear continuum, our view is that science teachers build this expertise as they teach in classrooms; engage in professional learning; and work in systems that can support, accelerate, or constrain learning. Central to our thinking is the observation that the quality of individual teachers' instruction is shaped not only by their own capabilities and experience, but also by the leadership of their school, the professional community of teachers with whom they work, and the instructional resources available to them. We understand practice as contextualized and situated work enabled or constrained by the ecology in which it is embedded. Thus we think of teacher expertise in individual, collective, and contextual terms.

EXPERTISE FOR TEACHING SCIENCE

To achieve the vision outlined in Chapter 2, science teachers will need to develop professional knowledge and practices that include but extend well beyond disciplinary content. While experts have identified varying comprehensive lists of such competencies, the committee highlights three foci, each of which is discussed in turn below:

- the knowledge, skill, and competencies that enable *all* students to learn next-generation science, including the development of practices that are responsive to a diverse range of students;
- the knowledge, skill, and competencies associated with scientific practices, disciplinary core ideas, and crosscutting concepts; and
- the pedagogical content knowledge and teaching practices that support students in rigorous and consequential learning of science.

Box 5-1 presents a hypothetical example of how these foci intersect in providing learning experiences for students.

Each of these foci involves an array of knowledge, skills, competencies, habits of mind, and beliefs; each is crucial for designing science teaching and learning for the 21st century. These foci also are not static. Rather, the committee conceptualizes the expertise required of teachers as "adaptive" (Ericsson, 2007; Ericsson et al., 2009); that is, teachers must learn how to adapt their methods and strategies to their learners and other features of the environment in which they are working. As opposed to "routine" or "classic" expertise, adaptive expertise involves flexibility and the ability to draw on knowledge to invent new procedures for solving unique or fresh problems, rather than simply applying already mastered procedures. Adaptive experts are continuously upgrading their competence through experience-based learning.

Supporting Diverse Student Populations in Learning Science

The committee anticipates that the vision of science education set forth in the Framework and NGSS—where implemented well—stands to be highly motivating to students. Because it is substantially different from the typical fare of U.S. classrooms, however, it may prove challenging for all students. Students who traditionally have been successful with memorizing facts and reciting formulas may find it challenging to work on investigations, collaborate with other students, and generate models and explanations for their developing understanding. The substantial language and intellectual demands of the new vision also are likely to be challenging for students who are learning English as a new language. Teachers will need not only to understand the new standards but also to have a fluid and robust understanding of how to adapt curricular content to meet the needs of an increasingly diverse student population.

The United States has always been a country of expanding differ-

---

BOX 5-1
Teaching Condensation:
An Illustration of the Expertise Needed to Teach Science

The following hypothetical example illustrates how expertise in support for diverse learners, knowledge of science and its practices, and pedagogical content knowledge and instructional practices work together as teachers create learning experiences for students.

An elementary teacher is planning to teach a lesson on the phenomenon of condensation (the change of state from water vapor to liquid water), in which students are to engage in the scientific practice of developing and using scientific models. To meet the needs of all of her students, she would need to know the students' history of involvement with this phenomenon. Do they have prior experiences with phase changes on which she could build? She would need to know what kinds of supports are needed to help students leverage their repertoires of practices toward new ends. For example, in what ways are the students' everyday experiences with modeling likely to connect to the scientific practice of modeling? In what ways are they likely to need careful bridging? (Children often, for example, think of a model car—a smaller replica—as a "model," and overgeneralize the idea of smallness as a key characteristic of a model, neglecting the more scientifically important idea of helping someone explain or predict.) The teacher would also need to understand the significant diversity among students from different cultural communities and their varying needs. For example, a range of decisions—from simple ones, such as what kind of container to use for illustrating the phenomenon of condensation forming, to much more complex ones, such as which analogies and representations to use to make the phenomenon meaningful—have cultural ramifications that the teacher would need to think through in light of her actual students.

In terms of her scientific knowledge, the teacher would need to understand the mechanism of the process of condensation (that when water vapor in the surrounding air cools, its molecules lose energy, and thus it forms liquid water on a cold surface). She also would need to be able to anticipate and recognize typical alternative ideas that students may have about condensation (such as thinking that water leaks through a can of ice water), an aspect of pedagogical content knowledge. She would need to be able to plan a set of experiences with the phenomenon that could help address specific alternative ideas (such as putting food coloring in the water or showing condensation forming on a cold mirror). She should be

---

ences, and the committee views difference and diversity not as a deficit in need of remediation but as the starting point for planning instruction. Unfortunately, results from the National Survey of Science and Mathematics Education (NSSME) (Banilower et al., 2013) show that teachers at all grade levels feel less prepared to engage students from low socioeconomic backgrounds and racial or ethnic minorities in science relative to students of higher socioeconomic status and white students (see

able to draw on existing lesson plans to help her devise these experiences. And because she would want to integrate the students' learning of this disciplinary core idea related to the nature of matter with the scientific practice of developing and using models, she also would need to have strong specialized content knowledge around the scientific practice of modeling. In addition, she would need to know typical problems her students are likely to encounter as they engage in scientific modeling, as well as techniques she can use to support them in developing and using models of this phenomenon.

What teaching practices would the teacher need to employ, informed by and building on her content knowledge? She would need to identify a lesson plan to use and adapt it to meet her students' needs. She might launch the lesson by eliciting students' ideas about the source(s) of the condensate; to do so, she would need to develop and ask appropriate questions.

The teacher might then have her students investigate the phenomenon; thus, she would need to employ teaching practices related to the management of small groups conducting an investigation. Toward the end of the lesson, she might engage the students in whole-class sense-making discussion, during which she would again need to elicit students' ideas, as well as compile the groups' data (perhaps recording the data in a public space in a way that would allow students to see patterns across the groups) and move toward supporting the students in constructing explanations and models. This sense-making discussion would be an opportunity to foster and/or reinforce the discourse norms of science, such as supporting claims with evidence and reasoning. The teacher might also draw on individual students' written work, including their written explanations and drawn models, in a meeting with the students' parents or guardians.

This hypothetical example illustrates how creating authentic science learning experiences for students requires the integration and application of multiple kinds of professional knowledge. The professional knowledge needed for teaching is expansive, and here we have highlighted three dimensions of that knowledge: understanding how to support diverse students, understanding the content and how to teach it, and being able to draw on those understandings to enact a set of powerful instructional practices. Each dimension interacts with the others: a teacher's content knowledge shapes and is shaped by her instruction, and her ability to use high-leverage practices depends on her understanding of both students and science. Drawing on this range of professional knowledge and practices is essential to ambitious teaching.

Chapter 4). In addition, few teachers feel well prepared to teach science to students with learning or physical disabilities or those who are English language learners (Banilower et al., 2013, p. 27).

This lack of confidence is a matter of preparation, for there is evidence that all students can master high-quality science curriculum and that professional development can be designed to help teachers adapt their practices to all learners (Heller et al., 2012; Lee et al., 2008). However, state-wide studies of elementary and middle school science education in California (Dorph et al., 2011; Hartry et al., 2012) indicate that students who are eligible for free and reduced-price lunches are substantially less likely than their more affluent counterparts to have well-qualified science teachers, although their schools generally enjoy access to basic science materials and equipment (see Chapter 4). Low-income students also are more likely to be enrolled in low-performing schools, where the allocation of time to mathematics and literacy instruction is most likely to compromise science instruction. The research base on differential opportunities and outcomes linked to student characteristics remains modest and focused mainly on English language learners, and to a lesser extent on low-income students. Less is known about the learning experiences and outcomes for other populations of students, such as those with learning disabilities. Nonetheless, student characteristics are likely to be a factor in teachers' perceptions of their needs for professional development and other supports.

Making science available to all students requires knowing how to provide access to meaningful science instruction, as well as a range of academic and social supports students may need. This integration of substance and supports is particularly important because the new vision of science teaching in the Framework and NGSS requires a new pedagogical conceptualization of how to support students' engagement with new scientific practices, disciplinary ideas, and discourse practices. Providing an equitable science education requires that teachers listen carefully to their students, crafting instruction that responds to their diversity in meaningful ways.

All students also come to school with experiences and knowledge that offer starting points for building science knowledge and skills (National Research Council, 2011; Next Generation Science Standards Lead States, 2013, Appendix D). While all have learning challenges, students from nondominant communities often have an additional set of developmental needs resulting from disparities in social and economic conditions, including health problems that may bear on school attendance and performance. Instead of focusing primarily on what students do not know, effective teachers focus on what they do know that is relevant to the content being taught. Louis Moll and colleagues (Gonzalez et al., 2005; Moll et al., 1992) have argued that students have "funds of knowledge"—experiences at home and in their community—that can be rich resources for teachers if they are supported in learning strategies for uncovering those experiences and integrating them into instruction in meaningful ways. The challenge for teachers is to acquire a full appreciation of how young people learn and the essential role of everyday knowledge in developing robust science understandings.

Understanding language is central to supporting diverse student populations in learning science. Classrooms are rich in writing, in talk, and in public speaking, challenging teachers to help students bridge the gap between their home languages and the language of science. The new vision of science teaching is language-rich: students read authentic scientific prose, and during investigations, they engage in such writing themselves. They also participate in small- and large-group discussions, hypothesizing about phenomena, investigating them, and debating alternative explanations for what they are learning. Research on the cultural dimensions of learning has shown that both regularity and variance characterize language practices within and across groups of learners, including those who share a common language or country of origin (Gutiérrez and Rogoff, 2003; Rogoff, 2003). Authors of language socialization studies (Ochs, 1993; Ochs and Schieffelin, 2008, 2011; Schieffelin and Ochs, 1986) have long argued that children are socialized to particular language practices through their participation in the valued practices of the home and community. Such studies help the education community challenge simplistic and overly general conceptions of young people and their linguistic practices. Teachers need to be able to recognize and be responsive to differences in how children use language and engage in discourse.

Often, educators fail to recognize that the linguistic demands of dual language learners' everyday practices are far more complex than is commonly acknowledged (Faulstich Orellana, 2009). As an example, children who are learning English or who have bilingual capacities often serve as language and sociocultural brokers for their non-English-speaking family members across a range of financial, medical, and educational institutions. Yet these children's classroom experiences neither recognize nor make use of such important cognitive literacy activities and sociocultural accomplishments. The economic and educational consequences of failing to leverage these accomplishments are considerable.

The implication of these observations is that teachers need to develop classroom discourse practices that socialize students to new science practices and understandings. Research has shown that good curriculum materials and sound professional development opportunities can help teachers improve learning for diverse learners, including English language learners and low-performing students (e.g., Cuevas et al., 2005; Geier et al., 2008).

Knowledge of Science

Teaching science as envisioned by the Framework and NGSS requires that teachers have a strong and robust understanding of the science practices, disciplinary core ideas, and crosscutting concepts they are expected to teach, including an appreciation of how scientists collaborate to develop new theories, models, and explanations of natural phenomena. Science teachers need rich understandings of these ideas and concepts. Perhaps equally important, they need to be able to engage in the practices of science themselves and know how to situate this new knowledge in learning settings with a range of students.

Such opportunities for working as scientists do require very different approaches to and emphases in undergraduate study of the sciences, teacher preparation, and ongoing opportunities for teacher learning. For example, fluency in scientific practices develops from continuing and extensive research experiences. Recognition of this fact has led to many calls for reform of undergraduate science education (e.g., Boyer Commission on Educating Undergraduates in the Research University, 1998; National Research Council, 1999, 2003; National Science Board, 1986; Project Kaleidoscope, 2006), all of which emphasize the need for more active engagement of students in research activities.

Complicating matters more is the fact that the content knowledge one needs to understand and teach K-12 school science is not necessarily the same as content identified as central to undergraduate majors in various sciences. Some scholars have called the former "content knowledge for teaching" (e.g., Ball et al., 2008) in an attempt to distinguish between content knowledge for liberal arts education or a disciplinary major from the content knowledge needed to deeply understand the crosscutting concepts, disciplinary core ideas, and scientific practices that are central to the new vision of science teaching and learning.[1] Recently, educators at TeachingWorks have begun identifying what they call "high-leverage content," which they define as "the particular topics, practices, and texts that are foundational to the K-12 curriculum and vital for beginning teachers to be able to teach skillfully." As they note, "even when adults know this content themselves, they often lack the specialized understanding needed to unpack and help others learn it."[2]

---

[1]The concept of content knowledge for teaching combines content knowledge with pedagogical content knowledge (discussed below). Science education researchers have not yet widely adopted this frame, so here we use the distinction between content knowledge (which includes crosscutting concepts, disciplinary core ideas, and scientific practices) and pedagogical content knowledge and teaching practices).

[2]See http://www.teachingworks.org/work-of-teaching/high-leverage-content [November 2015].

Disciplinary majors in higher education are not designed with teacher preparation in mind. Rather, they prepare students for a wide array of careers. In most universities, for example, multiple biology majors now exist. Consider Cornell University, where one can concentrate in animal physiology, biochemistry, computational biology, ecology and evolutionary biology, general biology, genetics, genomics and development, human nutrition, insect biology, marine biology, microbiology, molecular and cell biology, neurobiology and behavior, plant biology, or systematics and biotic diversity. Multiple units—Biological Statistics and Computational Biology, Ecology and Evolutionary Biology, Entomology, Microbiology, Molecular Biology and Genetics, Neurobiology and Behavior, Plant Biology, Biomedical Sciences, and the Division of Nutritional Sciences—participate in these majors. At universities where future science teachers are prepared, advisors from teacher preparation programs often work closely with disciplinary departments to identify courses that are aligned with state teacher certification requirements and the content of state teacher tests. Teacher preparation and certification programs that work with prospective teachers who already have undergraduate degrees conduct transcript analyses to ensure that prospective teachers have studied the content of the K-12 school curriculum.

In the case of elementary teacher preparation, a small number of science content courses usually are required for all prospective teachers. In some universities, these are specialized courses designed to expose elementary teachers to the content of the K-6 curriculum. In other cases, elementary teachers satisfy their science requirements by taking one or two general education courses in the sciences. In some states, elementary teachers can elect to have an elementary teacher science major, which entails taking more courses in the sciences. There is no centralized source of information on how much content preparation the average elementary teacher has, save for the information summarized in Chapter 4.

Pedagogical Content Knowledge and Science Teaching Practices

The concept of pedagogical content knowledge (e.g., Shulman, 1986, 1987) has been widely adopted and elaborated by numerous science educators and teacher educators (e.g., Berry, Friedrichsen, and Loughran, 2015; Gess-Newsome and Lederman, 1999; Lederman and Gess-Newsome, 1992; Pardhan and Wheeler, 1998, 2000; van Driel et al., 1998). Pedagogical content knowledge encompasses three domains: knowledge of content and students, knowledge of content and instruction, and knowledge of content and curriculum.

Knowledge of content and students includes how likely students are to understand particular concepts during instruction and how integrated their everyday knowledge and practices are with their science learning. Many concepts in science are difficult for students to understand, and students often bring ideas to the classroom that are not consistent with scientific explanations and can pose obstacles to learning (diSessa, 2006). Teachers need to be aware of such ideas and which of them may be productive starting points for building scientific understanding. They also need to consider the kinds of questions students may ask during the course of an investigation or discussion and what the most challenging ideas or practices may be. In a diverse classroom, this includes being aware of the range of experiences students may have had outside of school that are relevant to the science classroom.

Knowledge of content and instruction includes the strengths and limitations of instructional representations or strategies that are likely to support students in understanding particular ideas and concepts or their engagement in science practices. Recent years have seen growing interest in identifying a core set of instructional practices—based on criteria distilled from research and careful examination of teaching practice—to emphasize in teacher preparation and for which teachers would be held accountable in educator evaluations. Ball and Forzani (2009) use the term "high-leverage practices" for this core set of teaching skills. Key criteria for high-leverage practices are that they support student work that is fundamental to the discipline, and that they improve the learning of *all* students (Ball and Forzani, 2009; Grossman et al., 2009). Examples include choosing and modifying tasks and materials for a specific learning goal, orchestrating a productive whole-class discussion, and recognizing patterns of student thinking (Davis and Boerst, 2014).

As discussed in Chapter 2, research on science teaching suggests a set of instructional strategies that are most effective for supporting students' science learning and might be considered high-leverage practices. These include carefully framing students' relationship with the intellectual work of science, anchoring teaching and learning activities around specific concepts and topics, and carefully mediating students' learning activity (Windschitl and Calabrese-Barton, forthcoming; see also Chapter 2). Windschitl and colleagues (2012) have further specified these strategies in a proposed a set of core practices for beginning secondary science teachers, including selecting big ideas to teach and treating them as models, attending to students' ideas, choosing activities and framing intellectual work, and pressing students for explanations. Identifying such core practices could enable precision in conceptualizing teachers' learning needs in moving toward the new vision for science education.

Identifying these core instructional practices is especially important in light of the limited experience of the current science teaching workforce and the expectations embodied in the new vision of science teaching. To teach to these new standards, all teachers need to know how to create learning opportunities that engage students in scientific practices while at the same time imparting crosscutting concepts and disciplinary core ideas. They need to know how to support students' discourse, both in small-group investigations and in whole-class discussions. For example, elementary and secondary science teachers need to be able to use their pedagogical content knowledge to lead whole-class discussions that help students make sense of data collected by different small groups as part of their investigations. They need to be able to use a range of instructional representations to illustrate, for example, the flow of electric current in a circuit and help students recognize the strengths and limitations of each representation (e.g., water flowing through pipes, teeming crowds, passing hand squeezes). They also need to employ strategies for connecting science to mathematics and literacy in meaningful ways. Finally, given the central role of ongoing assessments in informing instruction, teachers need to master a range of formative and summative assessment strategies.

Knowledge of content and curriculum includes awareness of the instructional materials teachers can use to support student learning and how existing curriculum materials can be adapted to students' historical involvement with science. Teachers need to be able to use existing textbooks or curriculum materials for support in working with their students on developing rich understandings; indeed, a key teaching practice is being able to use one's own resources and those in extant curriculum materials to make productive adaptations to the curriculum materials for use in one's classroom (Brown, 2009). Similarly, teachers need to be able to identify, select, and employ effective technologies, such as visualization or data collection or analysis tools, in their teaching (for examples, see Ryoo and Linn, 2012; Shen and Linn, 2011; Zhang and Linn, 2013). This capability encompasses computer-based learning environments for science investigations (Donnelly et al., 2014). Teachers need targeted support to use these tools and environments effectively (Gerard et al., 2011, 2013).

This list of knowledge and skills is daunting, even more so when one considers the fact that the above are but three domains of professional teaching knowledge and do not encompass all the knowledge, skills, and competencies that inform effective teaching. This observation serves as evidence for the need for ongoing, continuous professional learning. It also illuminates why support for and improvement of quality science teaching are best understood as a collective enterprise. Teachers are stronger for the professional communities to which they belong, and good schools strategically cultivate varied expertise across individual teachers so that the school can meet the learning needs of a diverse student population in an age in which the vision of science teaching and learning is increasingly ambitious, and knowledge of content and of pedagogy continues to expand.

CONTEXTUAL INFLUENCES ON TEACHERS' LEARNING NEEDS

Although no single set of learning needs defines every teacher, certain groups of science teachers are likely to have overlapping learning needs. For example, teachers with similar backgrounds—regardless of whether those backgrounds include science—or who teach the same grades or subject areas, or whose student populations share similar characteristics likely will share some of the same learning needs. But just as certain features of context facilitate or impede science teachers' effectiveness, so, too, does context affect their learning needs. In the discussion that follows, we pay particular attention to aspects of context that are likely to bear directly on the classroom and shape the nature and intensity of teachers' professional learning needs. Some of these contextual conditions affect teachers at all grade levels; others apply specifically or mainly to teachers at particular levels.

Special Issues for Beginning Teachers

As already noted, the K-12 science teaching workforce comprises many beginners. These beginners have varying needs for professional learning opportunities. In terms of content knowledge, beginning secondary teachers may need to learn disciplinary core ideas, crosscutting concepts, or practices that were not part of their disciplinary preparation. Teachers who may not have a strong science background or the confidence to teach science will need to learn the content and how to teach it in ways that lead to increased self-efficacy. Given their very limited opportunities for studying science in initial preparation, beginning elementary teachers likely have extensive needs for learning science content and practices (e.g., Davis et al., 2006). As Feiman-Nemser (2001) notes, beginning teachers have much to learn about practice-based knowledge, including knowledge of students' needs and interests and students' learning of science, as well as pedagogical content knowledge (e.g., Luft, 2009; Luft et al., 2011). Across the board, many new K-12 teachers have themselves never participated in the kinds of K-12 classrooms they are expected to lead, nor have they had extensive immersion in doing science. These general trends present significant challenges in designing professional learning opportunities for teachers as they are asked to teach to new, more challenging standards.

In addition, experienced teachers who are new to teaching a different discipline of science or to a new grade level can feel like beginning teachers. They may need support in learning the core ideas of the discipline, as well as how students learn in this content area (e.g., Watson et al., 2007).

Special Issues in the Elementary Grades

As noted in previous chapters, elementary teachers may have more limited content knowledge in science relative to teachers at higher levels (Davis et al., 2006), and they may have had limited opportunities to focus on science teaching and learning (Banilower et al., 2013; Dorph et al., 2007, 2011; Hartry et al., 2012; Smith et al., 2002) and improve their instructional practices in science. Thus, they will likely need to bolster their content knowledge in addition to their teaching practices. This is neither a simple nor straightforward task: in learning instructional practices that enhance students' learning of disciplinary core ideas, crosscutting concepts, and scientific practices, elementary teachers will need to continuously adapt instruction in ways that support all students' learning, including students will special needs, those for whom English is a second language, and those with diverse cultural backgrounds. Finally, as teachers of multiple subjects, elementary teachers need to balance the demands of developing expertise in English language arts, mathematics, and science, and often in other areas as well. Taken together, these conditions create a particularly challenging set of needs for elementary teachers in science.

By all accounts, then, elementary teachers will need considerable support to develop the expertise needed to achieve the new vision for science education. However, supports and resources for elementary teachers in science are currently lacking (Banilower et al., 2013; Dorph et al., 2007).

Special Issues in Middle Schools

As discussed earlier, middle schools are more likely than elementary schools to dedicate daily time to science instruction and to employ teachers who have majored in and/or have some additional training in science. However, the challenges for middle schools should not be underestimated. Middle school teachers experience several constraints on more ambitious and authentic science teaching. Science teachers' content knowledge may be matched only weakly to the array of science fields and topics in the middle school curriculum. Teachers may be asked to teach a discipline-specific class for which they have little preparation or an integrated science class that spans fields beyond those they have studied. Many middle school teachers likely will need extensive learning opportunities in disciplinary core ideas, crosscutting concepts, and scientific practices if the new vision for science education is to be realized.

Teachers often report that students currently arrive at middle school having had little experience of science in elementary school, and the lack of prior scientific knowledge or experience with scientific inquiry is particularly pronounced for students coming from low-performing elementary schools in which instruction is focused heavily on mathematics and English language arts. Once in middle school, those same students may be required to enroll in extra classes of remedial mathematics or language, further limiting their opportunities to learn science. Given these circumstances, as discussed earlier, teachers need to learn a great deal about the background, experiences, and interests of their students and to acquire considerable pedagogical content knowledge to support students' learning of science, sometimes for the first time in any kind of depth.

Here, too, supports are lacking. In the NSSME (Banilower et al., 2013), more than half of middle school teachers surveyed reported that access to professional development was a moderate or major problem—perhaps not surprising when only about half of the districts surveyed employed staff dedicated to supporting science instruction in the middle schools. In addition, Hartry and colleagues (2012) note an overall erosion of the professional development infrastructure over the last decade as county offices of education also have lost science specialists, while at the state level, funding for the state-wide California Science Project declined from more than $9 million in 2002 to $1.2 million in 2011. The findings of a study by Learning Forward echo this trend: the authors found that there were fewer professional development resources (and policies) than in the past to support quality long-term professional development.

Special Issues in High Schools

Science enjoys a relatively secure and valued place in the high school curriculum, with 85 percent of high schools requiring a minimum of 3 years of science for graduation (Banilower et al., 2013). Nonetheless, the push toward greater depth on core ideas and topics, understanding of crosscutting concepts (such as cause and effect), and experience with authentic science practices presents special challenges for high school teachers. Apart from sufficient access to well-qualified science teachers, achieving the new vision for science education will likely require high schools to examine current course configurations, and to consider integrated courses or resequencing and both the time and resources needed for investigation-centered instruction. The new vision of science curriculum and instruction will call for a kind of articulation across grades and disciplines that teachers generally describe as uncommon and for which they have little time, support, and resources.

Banilower and colleagues (2013) found that nearly all high schools surveyed for the NSSME offer at least introductory courses in biology (98 percent), chemistry (94 percent), and (to a somewhat lesser degree) physics (85 percent), but fewer than half (48 percent) offer courses in environmental science or in earth and space science. Fewer than one-quarter of high schools offer courses in engineering, and only 5 percent offer a second year of more advanced study in that discipline. Approximately two-thirds of high schools offer a second year of advanced study in biology and life sciences, but fewer than half offer advanced study in chemistry (44 percent), physics (34 percent), environmental science (18 percent), or earth and space science (4 percent). Overall, high school course offerings appear to be inadequately reflective of contemporary problems and advances in the sciences and engineering. High school teachers will need extensive content preparation in these advances, as well as support in reconceptualizing the organization of school knowledge, to achieve the new vision.

In addition, as discussed earlier, instruction at the high school level remains textbook-dominated, with relatively little use of technology and little opportunity for students to engage in scientific inquiry and reasoning (in the NSSME, for example, 61 percent of high school teachers reported asking students to use evidence in developing claims even once a week). That is, while calls for the reform of science teaching are not new in this country, science instruction remains largely didactic, with curriculum coverage taking priority over substantial inquiry-oriented experiences for students. Rising to the challenge of the new vision will require shifting away from traditional instruction and toward instruction that is more student- and practice-centered.

Although block scheduling could give teachers greater opportunity to design a more interactive and inquiry-oriented approach to science learning, the use of this form of scheduling was reported by only about one-third of high schools surveyed for the NSSME. Most teachers, even if inclined toward inquiry-oriented instruction and prepared to employ it, face the constraints of the common 50-minute class period.

While organizational structures may account for some of the failure to reform science education, it is also likely, as discussed earlier, that high school teachers will need to acquire more knowledge of how to meet the needs of diverse learners, including how to adapt instruction in ways that tap into students' funds of knowledge. They will also need opportunities to enhance their pedagogical content knowledge, including how to use new technologies to engage in activities that integrate disciplinary core ideas, crosscutting concepts, and scientific practices. As new curricula emerge that are aligned with the new vision, teachers will need extensive experiences with trying these curricula out and adapting them to their contexts.

The School Context:
Leadership, Support, and Opportunities for Collaboration

Administrative leadership and access to colleagues are important characteristics of the school context that shape teachers' learning opportunities. The significance of administrative leadership and support is a common refrain in the research on policy implementation and school reform (e.g., Bryk et al., 2010; Sykes and Wilson, in press). In the most recent national survey conducted by Horizon Research, the principal's support was the factor in promoting effective science instruction cited most frequently by both middle school (Weis, 2013) and high school (Banilower et al., 2013) teachers, and was the second most important factor (after students' motivation, interest, and effort) cited by elementary teachers (Trygstad, 2013). A state-wide study of science education in California elementary schools found that virtually all school principals attach a high value to science instruction for all students (99 percent), and nearly as many (92%) believe that science instruction should begin as early as kindergarten (Dorph et al., 2011). In the present accountability and funding climate, however, principals and other school-level administrators may struggle to translate their support into material resources and professional opportunities for teachers.

Research dating back decades shows that gains in schools' academic performance and teachers' successful implementation of new curriculum or instructional practices are furthered by a collaborative and improvement-oriented culture (e.g., Bryk et al., 2010; Little, 1982; McLaughlin and Talbert, 2001, 2006; Stein and D'Amico, 2002). Yet science and mathematics teachers generally lack opportunities to observe their colleagues teaching (Smith et al., 2002). Peer observation has never been a frequent and systematic phenomenon in U.S. schools, even though it has been found to spur teacher learning and innovation (Little, 1982; Little et al., 1987). In 1993, only 11 percent of teachers in grades 1-4 and 5-8 reported regularly observing their colleagues teaching classes; by 2000, that percentage had fallen to 4 percent for grades 1-4 and 5 percent for grades 5-8 (Smith et al., 2002). Only one in four teachers had time during the week to collaborate with colleagues in their school, and even these discussions were not devoted to decisions about curriculum. Items related to peer observation and collaborative practices were dropped from the most recent iteration of the NSSME, but one-quarter of teachers surveyed reported that the allocation of their time during the school week actively inhibited their ability to plan for their science classes either individually or with colleagues, and fewer than 60 percent reported that time allocation promoted such planning opportunities during school time (Banilower et al., 2013, p. 120).

The extent to which teachers have administrative support for effective science instruction and opportunities to work with and learn from colleagues influences their learning needs. Teachers in schools that have placed relatively less emphasis on science or where teachers have had little opportunity to work with colleagues with science expertise will likely need more opportunities to develop expertise for science teaching than teachers who work in settings where science has received more emphasis.

Of course, teacher support is not limited to a teacher's specific classroom or school, and there are myriad learning opportunities that teachers both encounter and actively seek out in the larger ecology in which they work. These issues are discussed in greater depth in Chapter 7.

CONCLUSION

This chapter has considered both what teachers need to know and be able to do to teach to high and rigorous standards and their associated learning needs. A number of specific issues will need to be addressed to support teachers in achieving the vision of the Framework and NGSS.

As noted in the previous chapter, many science teachers have not had sufficiently rich experiences with the content relevant to the science courses they currently teach, let alone a substantially redesigned science curriculum. This is especially true in schools that serve high percentages of low-income students, where teachers are often newer and less qualified.

Furthermore, science teachers lack a coherent and well-articulated system of learning opportunities to enable them to continue developing expertise for teaching science while in the classroom. Such opportunities are unevenly distributed across grade bands, schools, districts, and regions, with little attention to sequencing or how to support science teachers' learning systematically. Access to learning experiences related to science is particularly limited for elementary teachers.

Conclusion 4: Science teachers' learning needs are shaped by their preparation, the grades and content areas they teach, and the contexts in which they work. Three important areas in which science teachers need to develop expertise are

- *the knowledge, capacity, and skill required to support a diverse range of students;*
- *content knowledge, including understanding of disciplinary core ideas, crosscutting concepts, and scientific and engineering practices; and*
- *pedagogical content knowledge for teaching science, including a repertoire of teaching practices that support students in rigorous and consequential science learning.*

Teachers have unique learning needs depending on the context in which they teach: who their students are, how well resourced their school is, the average level of experience of teachers in the school, access to supportive cultural institutions, and the like. Teachers will learn more in schools that are organized for their learning (as well as the learning of students). They also will have more human resources available to them in schools in which there are seasoned, veteran teachers who have deep knowledge of the students in the community, the content to be covered, and ways to connect that content to the lives and experiences of the students. Thus, designing the optimal learning opportunities for teachers in a particular school will require careful attention to those details and others, a point to which we return later in this report.

While this tailoring is important, research also has identified some important trends that warrant attention. As previously noted, elementary teachers have spent little time teaching science, and helping them prepare for more intensive science instruction will take time and resources. Middle and high school teachers typically have a greater understanding of science than their elementary school colleagues but may not know how to teach it in ways that help students connect ideas through crosscutting concepts or engage in the scientific practices to bring content alive and make it relevant to students' lives.

REFERENCES

Ball, D.L., and Forzani, F. (2009). The work of teaching and the challenge for teacher education. *Journal of Teacher Education, 60*(5), 497-511.

Ball, D.L., Thames, M.H., and Phelps, G. (2008). Content knowledge for teaching: What makes it special? *Journal of Teacher Education, 59*(5), 389-407.

Banilower, E.R., Smith, P.S., Weiss, I.R., Malzahn, K.A., Campbell, K.M., and Weis, A.M. (2013). *Report of the 2012 National Survey of Science and Mathematics Education.* Chapel Hill, NC: Horizon Research.

Berry, A., Friedrichsen, P., and Loughran, J., (Eds.). (2015). *Re-examining Pedagogical Content Knowledge in Science Education.* New York: Routledge.

Boyer Commission on Educating Undergraduates in the Research University. (1998). *Reinventing Undergraduate Education: A Blueprint for America's Research Universities.* Stony Brook, NY: Boyer Commission on Educating Undergraduates in the Research University.

Brown, M. (2009). The teacher-tool relationship: Theorizing the design and use of curriculum materials. In J.T. Remillard, B. Herbel-Eisenman, and G. Lloyd (Eds.), *Mathematics Teachers at Work: Connecting Curriculum Materials and Classroom Instruction* (pp. 17-36). New York: Routledge.

Bryk, A., Sebring, P., Allensworth, E., Suppescu, S., and Easton, J. (2010). *Organizing Schools for Improvement: Lessons from Chicago.* Chicago, IL: The University of Chicago Press.

Cuevas, P., Lee, O., Hart, J., and Deaktor, R. (2005). Improving science inquiry with elementary students of diverse backgrounds. *Journal of Research in Science Teaching, 42*(3), 337-357.

Davis, E.A., and Boerst, T. (2014). *Designing Elementary Teacher Education to Prepare Well-Started Beginners.* TeachingWorks Working Paper. Ann Arbor: University of Michigan. Available: http://www.teachingworks.org/images/files/TeachingWorks_Davis_Boerst_WorkingPapers_March_2014.pdf [June 2015].

Davis, E.A., Petish, D., and Smithey, J. (2006). Challenges new science teachers face. *Review of Educational Research, 76*(4), 607-651.

diSessa, A.A. (2006). A history of conceptual change research: Threads and fault lines. In K. Sawyer (Ed.), *Cambridge Handbook of the Learning Sciences* (pp. 265-281). Cambridge, UK: Cambridge University Press.

Donnelly, D.F., Linn, M.C., and Ludvigsen, S. (2014). Impacts and characteristics of computer-based science inquiry learning environments for precollege students. *Review of Educational Research, 20*(10), 1-37.

Dorph, R., Goldstien, D., Lee, S., Lepori, K., Schneider, S., and Venkatesan, S. (2007). *The Status of Science Education in the Bay Area: Research Brief.* Berkeley: Lawrence Hall of Science, University of California. Available: http://lawrencehallofscience.org/rea/bayareastudy/pdf/final_to_print_research_brief.pdf [January 2015].

Dorph, R., Shields, P., Tiffany-Morales, J., Hartry, A., and McCaffrey, T. (2011). *High Hopes—Few Opportunities: The Status of Elementary Science Education in California.* Sacramento, CA: The Center for the Future of Teaching and Learning at WestEd.

Ericsson, K.A. (2007). Deliberate practice and the modifiability of body and mind: Toward a science of the structure and acquisition of expert and elite performance. *International Journal of Sport Psychology, 38*, 4-34.

Ericsson, K.A., Nandagopal, K., and Roring, R.W. (2009). Toward a science of exceptional achievement: Attaining superior performance through deliberate practice. *Annals of New York Academy of Science, 1172*, 199-217.

Faulstich Orellana, M. (2009). *Translating Childhoods: Immigrant Youth, Language and Culture.* New Brunswick, NJ: Rutgers University Press.

Feiman-Nemser, S. (2001). From preparation to practice: Designing a continuum to strengthen and sustain teaching. *Teachers College Record, 103*(6), 1013-1055.

Geier, R., Blumenfeld, P.C., Marx, R.W., Krajcik, J.S., Fishman, B., Soloway, E., and Clay-Chambers, J. (2008). Standardized test outcomes for students engaged in inquiry-based science curricula in the context of urban reform. *Journal of Research in Science Teaching, 45*(8), 922-939. Available: http://deepblue.lib.umich.edu/bitstream/handle/2027.42/61206/20248_ftp.pdf?sequence=1 [June 2015].

Gerard, L.F., Varma, K., Corliss, S.C., and Linn, M.C. (2011). Professional development for technology-enhanced inquiry science. *Review of Educational Research, 81*(3), 408-448.

Gerard, L.F., Liu, L., Corliss, S., Varma, K., and Spitulnik, M. (2013). Professional development programs for teaching with visualizations. In C. Mouza and N. Lavigne (Eds.), *Emerging Technologies for the Classrooms: A Learning Sciences Perspective* (Ch. 5, pp. 63-78). New York: Springer.

Gess-Newsome, J., and Lederman, N.G. (Eds). (1999). *Examining Pedagogical Content Knowledge: The Construct and Its Implications for Science Education.* Norwell, MA: Kluwer Academic.

Gonzalez, N., Moll, L., and Amanti, C. (2005). *Funds of Knowledge: Theorizing Practices in Households, Communities, and Classrooms.* Mahwah, NJ: Lawrence Erlbaum Associates.

Grossman, P., Hammerness, K., and McDonald, M. (2009). Redefining teaching, re-imagining teacher education. *Teachers and Teaching: Theory and Practice, 15*(2), 273-289.

Gutiérrez, K.D., and Rogoff, B. (2003). Cultural ways of learning: Individual traits or repertoires of practice. *Educational Researcher, 32*(5), 19-25.

Hartry, A., Dorph, R., Shields, P., Tiffany-Morales, J., and Romero, V. (2012). *The Status of Middle School Science Education in California.* Sacramento, CA: The Center for the Future of Teaching and Learning at WestEd.

Heller, J.I., Daehler, K.R., Wong, N., Shinohara, M., and Miratrix, L.W. (2012). Differential effects of three professional development models on teacher knowledge and student achievement in elementary science. *Journal of Research in Science Teaching, 49*(3), 333-362.

Lederman, N.G. (1992). Students' and teachers' conceptions of the nature of science: A review of the research. *Journal of Research in Science Teaching, 29*(4), 331-359.

Lee, O., Deaktor, R., Enders, C., and Lambert, J. (2008). Impact of a multiyear professional development intervention on science achievement of culturally and linguistically diverse elementary students. *Journal of Research in Science Teaching, 45*(6), 726-747.

Little, J.W. (1982). Norms of collegiality and experimentation: Workplace conditions of school success. *American Education Research Journal, 19*(3), 325-340.

Little, J.W., and Lieberman, A. (1987). Teachers as colleagues. In V. Richardson-Koehler (Ed.), *Educators' Handbook: A Research Perspective* (pp. 491-518). New York: Longman.

Luft, J.A. (2009). Beginning secondary science teachers in different induction programmes: The first year of teaching. *International Journal of Science Education, 31*(17), 2355-2384.

Luft, J.A., Firesont, J.B., Wong, S.S., Ortega, I. Adams, K., and Ban, E.J. (2011). Beginning secondary science teacher induction: A two-year mixed methods study. *Journal of Research in Science Teaching, 48*(10), 1199-1224.

McLaughlin, M.W., and Talbert, J.E. (2001). *Professional Communities and the Work of High School Teaching.* Chicago, IL: University of Chicago Press.

McLaughlin, M.W., and Talbert, J.E. (2006). *Building School-based Teacher Learning Communities: Professional Strategies To Improve Student Achievement.* Chicago, IL: University of Chicago Press.

Moll, L., Amanti, C., Neff, D., and Gonzalez, N. (1992). Funds of knowledge for teaching: Using a qualitative approach to connect homes and classrooms. *Theory into Practice, 31*(2), 132-141.

National Research Council. (1999). *Transforming Undergraduate Education in Science, Mathematics, Engineering and Technology.* Committee on Undergraduate Science Education. Center for Science, Mathematics, and Engineering Education. Washington, DC: National Academy Press.

National Research Council. (2002). *Studying Classroom Teaching as a Medium for Professional Development: Proceedings of a U.S.-Japan Workshop.* H. Bass, Z. Usiskin, and G. Burrill (Eds.). U.S. National Commission on Mathematics Instruction, Board on International Scientific Organizations, Policy and Global Affairs Division. Washington, DC: The National Academies Press.

National Research Council. (2003). *Evaluating and Improving Undergraduate Teaching in Science, Technology, Engineering, and Mathematics.* Committee on Recognizing, Evaluating, Rewarding, and Developing Excellence in Teaching of Undergraduate Science, Mathematics, Engineering, and Technology, Board on Science Education, Division of Behavioral and Social Sciences and Education, Washington, DC: The National Academies Press.

National Research Council. (2007). *Enhancing Professional Development for Teachers: Potential Uses of Information Technology, Report of a Workshop.* Committee on Enhancing Professional Development for Teachers, National Academies Teacher Advisory Council, Center for Education, Division of Behavioral and Social Sciences and Education. Washington, DC: The National Academies Press.

National Research Council. (2010). *Preparing Teachers: Building Evidence for Sound Policy.* Committee on the Study of Teacher Preparation Programs in the United States, Center for Education. Division of Behavioral and Social Sciences and Education. Washington, DC: The National Academies Press.

National Research Council. (2011). *Successful K-12 STEM Education: Identifying Effective Approaches in Science, Technology, Engineering, and Mathematics.* Committee on Highly Successful Science Programs for K-12 Science Education. Board on Science Education and Board on Testing and Assessment, Division of Behavioral and Social Sciences and Education. Washington, DC: The National Academies Press.

National Science Board. (1986). *Undergraduate Science, Mathematics and Engineering Education: Role for the National Science Foundation and Recommendations for Action by Other Sectors to Strengthen Collegiate Education and Pursue Excellence in the Next Generation of U.S. Leadership in Science and Technology.* NSB86-100. Washington, DC: National Science Foundation.

Next Generation Science Standards Lead States. (2013). *Next Generation Science Standards: For States, By States.* Washington, DC: The National Academies Press.

Ochs, E. (1993). Constructing social identity: A language socialization perspective. *Research on Language and Social Interactional, 26*(3), 287-306.

Ochs, E., and Schieffelin, B.B. (2008). Language socialization: An historical overview. In P.A. Duff and N.H. Hornberger (Eds.), *Encyclopedia of Language Education* (vol. 8, 2nd ed., pp. 3-15). New York: Springer.

Ochs, E., and Schieffelin, B.B. (2011). The theory of language socialization. In A. Duranti, E. Ochs, and B. Schieffelin (Eds.), *The Handbook of Language Socialization* (pp. 1-21). Malden, MA: Wiley-Blackwell.

Pardhan, H., and Wheeler, A.E. (1998). Enhancing science teachers' learning through pedagogical content knowledge. *Science Education International, 9*(4), 21-25.

Pardhan, H., and Wheeler, A.E. (2000). Taking "stock" of pedagogical content knowledge in science education. *School Science Review, 82*(299), 80-86.

Project Kaleidoscope. (2006). *Recommendations for Action in Support of Undergraduate Science, Technology, Engineering, and Mathematics.* Washington, DC: Project Kaleidoscope.

Rogoff, B. (2003). *The Cultural Nature of Human Development.* New York: Oxford University Press.

Ryoo, K.L., and Linn, M.C. (2012). Can dynamic visualizations improve middle school students' understanding of energy in photosynthesis? *Journal of Research in Science Teaching, 49*(2), 218-243.

Schieffelin, B.B., and Ochs, E. (1986). Language socialization. *Annual Review of Anthropology,* 163-191.

Shen, J., and Linn, M.C. (2011). Connecting scientific explanations and everyday observations: A technology-enhanced unit of modeling static electricity. *International Journal of Science Education, 33*(12), 1597-1623.

Shulman, L.S. (1986). Paradigms and research programs in the study of teaching. In M.C. Wittrock (Ed.), *Handbook of Research on Teaching* (3rd ed., pp. 3-36). New York: MacMillan.

Shulman, L.S. (February, 1987). Knowledge and teaching: Foundations of the new reform. *Harvard Educational Review.* 1-22.

Smith, P.S., Banilower, E.R., McMahon, K.C., and Weiss, I.R. (2002). *The National Survey of Science and Mathematics Education: Trends from 1977 to 2000.* Chapel Hill, NC: Horizon Research.

Stein, M.K., and D'Amico, L. (2002). Inquiry at the crossroads of policy and learning: A study of a district-wide literacy initiative. *Teachers College Record, 104*(7), 1313-1344.

Sykes, G., and Wilson, S.M. (in press). Instructional policy. In D. Gitomer and C. Bell (Eds.), *Handbook of Research on Teaching* (5th ed.). Washington, DC: American Educational Research Association.

Trygstad, P.J. (2013). *2012 National Survey of Science and Mathematics Education: Status of Elementary School Science.* Chapel Hill, NC: Horizon Research.

van Driel, J.H., Verloop, N., and de Vos, W. (1998). Developing science teachers' pedagogical content knowledge. *Journal of Research in Science Teaching, 35*(6), 673-695.

Watson, K., Steele, F., Vozzo, L., and Aubusson, P. (2007). Changing the subject: Retraining teachers to teach science. *Research in Science Education, 37*(2), 141-154.

Weis, A.M. (2013). *2012 National Survey of Science and Mathematics Education. Status of Middle School Science.* Chapel Hill, NC: Horizon Research.

Windschitl, M., and Calabrese-Barton, A. (forthcoming). Rigor and equity by design: Seeking a core of practices for the science education community. In *AERA Handbook of Research on Teaching* (5th ed.).

Windschitl, M., Thompson, J., Braaten, M., and Stroupe, D. (2012). Proposing a core set of instructional practices and tools for teachers of science. *Science Education, 96*(5), 878-903.

Zhang, Z.H., and Linn, M.C. (2013). Learning from chemical visualizations: Comparing generation and selection. *International Journal of Science Education, 35*(13), 2174-2197.

6

Professional Development Programs

This chapter reviews what is known about formally organized programs of professional development in science, which are the focus of the majority of available research on teacher learning. For purposes of this discussion, formal professional development programs are defined as learning experiences for teachers that (1) are purposefully designed to support particular kinds of teacher change; (2) include a focused, multiday session for teachers that takes place outside of the teacher's classroom or school; (3) may include follow-up opportunities over the school year; and (4) have a finite duration (although they can take place over a period of 2 to 3 years). These kinds of experiences often are provided by organizations or individuals outside of the school system—universities, cultural institutions, publishers, or contracted providers—but may also be provided by states, districts, or schools.

Depending on access, teachers select from various offerings; in one recent study, The New Teacher Project (2015) found that one district had more than 1,000 professional development opportunities listed in its catalog for 1 year. While the professional development landscape sprawls, it is also disjointed and incoherent; school districts rarely have professional development systems that are aligned with the curriculum and/or opportunities that offer teachers increasingly more advanced study over time (e.g., Wilson et al., 2011). Often, teachers must make choices about programs in which to participate with little outside guidance on their relative benefits or on how a set of experiences might fit together to contribute to

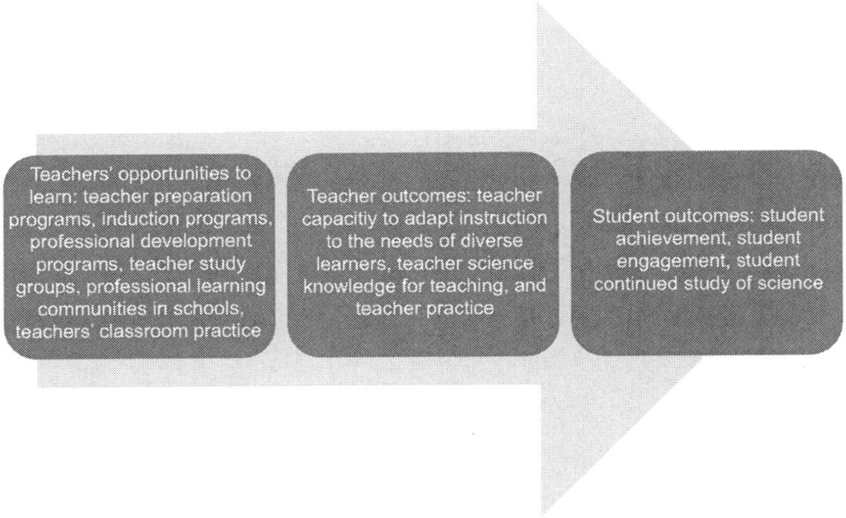

FIGURE 6-1 Connecting the dots: Linking teacher learning opportunities to teacher learning to student learning.

achieving a learning goal. For many teachers, the result is a diffuse and uncoordinated set of learning experiences.

In examining the impact of professional development programs in science, the committee focused on outcomes for teachers and students. Outcomes for teachers include the three domains enumerated in Chapter 5: teachers' capacity to adapt instruction to the needs of diverse learners, their content knowledge, and their pedagogical content knowledge and actual instructional practices. While the assumption often is made that teachers who develop professional knowledge and practices in each of these domains will have students who learn more, we also were interested in the extent to which the research literature demonstrates improvements in student outcomes. Therefore, we examined the literature for insights that would help us understand these linkages (see Figure 6-1).[1]

This chapter begins by describing features of effective professional

_____

[1]Given our conception of teacher learning as both individual and collective and of teachers as participants in larger communities and contexts, the representation in Figure 6-1 is limited. The linearity of the model illustrated in the figure, while helping us emphasize the logic of connecting teacher learning to teacher outcomes to student outcomes, obscures the fact that we view learning as both iterative and dynamic, and as embedded in contexts that fundamentally shape what teachers learn and how they exercise their knowledge and skill. For the purposes of parsing the research literature, however, we use this relatively simple framing of the process.

development programs, drawing on research that is not specific to science. It then examines existing research on professional development programs for science teachers, with a particular focus on the impact of these programs and the nature of the research base. We then consider an emerging field of research on professional development—online learning—which has the potential to expand learning opportunities for science teachers in new and exciting ways.

FEATURES OF EFFECTIVE PROFESSIONAL DEVELOPMENT PROGRAMS

Organized opportunities for teacher development have a long history in the United States, dating to the 19th century and the origins of the current system of schooling (e.g., Clifford, 2014; Warren, 1989). Attention to professional development as a central lever in school reform rose in the last half of the 20th century, linked to curricular innovations following the launch of Sputnik in the late 1950s, to successive large-scale initiatives following passage of the Elementary and Secondary Education Act in 1965, and to efforts at systemic and standards-based reform in the 1980s and 1990s.

In recent decades, syntheses of research across multiple subject areas have yielded what Desimone (2009) characterizes as "an empirical consensus on a set of core features and a conceptual framework for teacher learning" (p. 192). Garet and colleagues (2001) analyzed survey responses of a cross-sectional sample of 1,027 mathematics and science teachers who participated in the Eisenhower Professional Development Program and identified three core features and three structural features of effective professional development. The core features were (1) a focus on content (e.g., science or mathematics), (2) opportunities for active learning, and (3) coherence with other professional learning activities. The structural features identified were (1) the form of the activity (e.g., workshop or study group); (2) collective participation of teachers from the same school, grade, or subject; and (3) the duration of the activity. In a related analysis, Desimone and colleagues (2002) analyzed survey responses from a longitudinal survey of teachers in the Eisenhower program and found that the teachers' participation in professional development that was focused on particular teaching strategies (such as use of technology), specific instructional approaches, or new forms of student assessment predicted their increased use of those practices in the classroom. These effects were independent of teachers' prior use of the practices, as well as the subject area.

Numerous syntheses have offered other ways to characterize and conceptualize features of effective professional development (e.g., Abdal-Haqq, 1995; Ball and Cohen, 1999; Blank et al., 2008; Borko, 2004; Borko et al., 2010; Darling-Hammond et al., 2009; Hawley and Valli, 2006; Little, 1988; Loucks-Horsley et al., 1998, 2003; Putnam and Borko, 1997; Wilson and Berne, 1999; Yoon et al., 2007). Drawing on these findings, as well as those of other studies, Desimone (2009) nominated five core features and suggested that they be used to guide research on professional development. We refer to this as the consensus model of effective professional development:

- content focus—learning opportunities for teachers that focus on subject matter content and how students learn that content;
- active learning—can take a number of forms, including observing expert teachers, followed by interactive feedback and discussion, reviewing student work, or leading discussions;
- coherence—consistency with other learning experiences and with school, district, and state policy;
- sufficient duration—both the total number of hours and the span of time over which the hours take place; and
- collective participation—participation of teachers from the same school, grade, or department.

While this consensus view has shaped the design of many professional development programs, it draws on a research base that consists mainly of correlational studies and teachers' self-reports (Wilson, 2011; Yoon et al., 2007). Few studies have systematically examined each feature to identify variations within and among features and how these variations connect to teacher learning, fewer still have looked at the impact of programs on teaching practice, and even fewer have examined impacts on student learning (Desimone, 2009; National Research Council, 2011). However, recent research has begun to explore these connections (e.g., Heller et al., 2012; Roth et al., 2011). When the elements of the consensus model have been studied using designs that allow for testing of each feature, the results have not consistently supported the model (Garet et al., 2008, 2011; Scher and O'Reilly, 2009), suggesting that these features may capture surface characteristics and not the mechanisms that account for teacher learning.

Consider duration—perhaps the most consistently reported key feature of effective professional development, and perhaps the most difficult element of the consensus model to specify. Studies vary in the number of hours of participation found to be associated with changes in instruction, as well as in the period over which teachers were engaged. Desimone's (2009) review suggests the need for at least 20 hours of professional development time spread out over at least a semester. Kennedy's (1999) review of mathematics and science professional development indicates that 30 hours or more of participation was associated with positive effects on student learning. A review of projects funded by the National Science Foundation's (NSF) Local Systemic Change through Teacher Enhancement Program suggests that changes in teaching practice were evident only after 80 hours of participation, and changes in investigative culture only after 160 hours (Supovitz and Turner, 2000).

Duration may be a proxy for how intensely a teacher engages with a new idea, or it may be related to a teacher's persistence in trying out new practices until they work. It appears likely that the school and district context, a teacher's entering knowledge and skill, the type of knowledge that is emphasized (e.g., using a device, knowing a fact, understanding a concept), and the networks in which a teacher participates all influence how readily a professional development experience leads to changes in a teacher's knowledge and practice.

The contribution of program duration to changes in teachers' knowledge and practice also appears to be interdependent with other key features of the learning opportunity. In their analysis of a survey of California mathematics teachers' participation in professional development and classroom practice, Cohen and Hill (2001) conclude that "time spent had a potent influence on practice" (p. 88), but only if the time was spent on content, curriculum, and student tasks. Similarly, the national survey of teachers conducted for an evaluation of the Eisenhower professional development programs (Garet et al., 2001) revealed that the "duration" of professional development (defined in terms of both total contact hours and span of time over weeks or months) achieved its effect primarily through other program features (in a program of longer duration, for example, the greater likelihood that teachers would experience active forms of professional learning).

The consensus model has informed the design of professional development programs in science. In two recent reviews of science professional development (Capps et al., 2012; van Driel et al., 2012), most of the programs studied reflected the consensus model. Across the studies reviewed by van Driel and colleagues (2012), for example, all of the programs stressed active learning, often including inquiry-based activities, and most entailed some degree of collaborative participation and aimed for extended duration.

IMPACT OF PROFESSIONAL DEVELOPMENT PROGRAMS IN SCIENCE

The committee examined the impact of professional development in science on outcomes that align with the logic model in Figure 6-1: teachers' outcomes, including knowledge and beliefs about adapting instruction to students' backgrounds and needs, content knowledge, pedagogical content knowledge, and instructional practices; and students' learning and engagement. Our review of the research on professional development programs in science was aided by five recent reviews of the related research literature: Capps et al. (2012), Gerard et al. (2011), Luft and Hewson (2014), Scher and O'Reilly (2009), and van Driel et al. (2012). These reviews differ in scope and focus, but together they cover much of the research on professional development in science published in peer-reviewed journals in the last decade. We also examined studies published after these reviews were conducted.

From an initial pool of 145 available evaluations, Scher and O'Reilly (2009) eventually were able to use only 18 studies: 7 in mathematics, 8 in science, and 3 that concerned mathematics and science. The authors focused on experimental or quasi-experimental evaluations of mathematics and science professional development that had been conducted since 1990. None of the evaluated programs involved a one-shot workshop; all of the programs took place over one or several academic years. Only one study was a randomized controlled trial. Capps and colleagues (2012) reviewed 22 studies published during 1997-2008 covering 17 distinct professional development programs (in some cases, multiple studies addressed the same program). The authors focused on professional development emphasizing the use of inquiry in science classrooms. The review by van Driel and colleagues (2012) included 44 studies (excluding informal in-service and preservice education studies) published from 2007 to 2011. Luft and Hewson (2014) reviewed 50 studies published after 2003 in science education and major education research journals. And Gerard and colleagues (2011) reviewed 43 studies of professional development in technology-enhanced, inquiry-oriented science, focusing on how the professional development enhanced teachers' support for students' pursuit of scientific investigations.

Reflecting the trend in the general literature on professional development, few studies included measures of all three outcomes for teachers (their knowledge and beliefs about adapting instruction to students' backgrounds and needs and about pedagogical content knowledge, and their practice), and none systematically examined each feature of the consensus model. Many studies relied on teachers' self-reports through questionnaires and interviews. A small number of studies employed rigorous designs—the use of control or comparison groups, random assignment, or large numbers of teachers across different schools or districts. Fewer studies measured student outcomes, so it is difficult to make a strong argument for effects on student learning and achievement. For example, from the original 145 evaluations that Scher and O'Reilly identified for their meta-analysis, only 18 were left in the pool after the authors reviewed the rigor of the designs and the technical quality of the reported research.

While the committee drew on a wide range of literature concerning science teacher learning, for the analysis reported here we emphasized studies that employed comparative designs or included relatively large numbers of teachers drawn from more than one school or district. We also gave particular attention to studies that examined changes in both instructional practices and student outcomes.

Changes in Teachers' Knowledge and Beliefs

Changes in knowledge and beliefs as a result of participation in a professional development program are widely reported in the literature. Teachers' knowledge for science teaching—content knowledge and pedagogical content knowledge—is measured in a variety of ways, including tests, interviews, and surveys. Teachers' beliefs are measured using surveys or interviews.

Of the 22 studies reviewed by Capps and colleagues (2012), 8 report enhanced teacher knowledge as a result of professional development focused on inquiry; however, only 6 of those include measures of teacher knowledge (content knowledge or knowledge of process skills or inquiry) both before and after the professional development experience (Akerson and Hanuscin, 2007; Akerson et al., 2009; Basista and Matthews, 2002; Jeanpierre et al., 2005; Lotter et al., 2006, 2007; Radford, 1998; Shepardson and Harbor, 2004; Westerlund et al., 2002). Two additional studies report on teachers' knowledge during their first year of participation in professional development, but knowledge before participation was not measured; rather, the results reported are based on teachers' own perceptions of their change in knowledge (Lee et al., 2005, 2008). Four studies reviewed by Capps and colleagues report positive changes in teachers' beliefs as a result of participation in professional development in science (Basista and Matthews, 2002; Johnson, 2007; Lee et al., 2004; Luft, 2001).

Among the 44 studies reviewed by van Driel and colleagues (2012), 4 focused only on teachers' knowledge or beliefs. These studies included relatively small numbers of teachers and used surveys, interviews, and reflective journals to measure outcomes.

Numerous studies reviewed by Luft and Hewson (2014) investigated the effects of professional development on teachers' knowledge and beliefs. For example, several qualitative studies found shifts in teachers' understanding of the nature of science through professional development (e.g., Akerson et al., 2009; Lederman et al., 2002; Posnanski, 2010).

Fewer studies examined the impact of professional development in science on teachers' pedagogical content knowledge. One such study found that professional development could lead to changes in teachers' pedagogical content knowledge for argumentation (McNeill and Knight, 2013). This study examined how three professional development programs impacted 70 elementary, middle, and high school teachers' pedagogical content knowledge related to scientific argumentation. Pre- and post-assessments, video recordings of the professional development workshops, artifacts produced by the teachers during the professional development, and classroom learning tasks related to student work were used to assess two elements of teachers' pedagogical content knowledge: (1) knowledge of students' conceptions for argumentation, and (2) knowledge of instructional strategies for argumentation. The researchers found that the workshops led to teachers' increased pedagogical content knowledge in relation to scientific argumentation with regard to the structural components of students' writing. But teachers struggled to analyze classroom discussions in terms of both structural and dialogic characteristics of argumentation, had difficulty applying the reasoning component of argumentation to classroom practice, and found designing argumentation questions to be challenging.

In another study reporting on the impact of professional development in science on teachers' pedagogical content knowledge outcomes, Roth and colleagues (2011) examined upper-elementary teachers' pedagogical content knowledge related to student thinking and the coherence of science activities and ideas. The researchers used a video analysis task that engaged teachers in watching video clips of science lessons pre-, mid- and postprogram. Teachers then wrote an analysis of anything of educational interest regarding the teaching, content, context, and/or students. Teachers in the treatment lesson analysis program became more analytical and made more comments about the science content and about pedagogical content issues after program participation relative to teachers in a comparison group that focused only on deepening teachers' content knowledge.

Studies on teachers' beliefs have varied over time. Most studies suggest that professional development programs can shape teachers' beliefs (Jones and Leagon, 2014). Lumpe and colleagues (2012), for instance, studied the beliefs of more than 30 elementary teachers in a state-wide professional development program. They reported that elementary teachers who participated in more than 100 contact hours displayed significant gains in their beliefs. Larger studies related to teachers' beliefs and professional development tend to focus on elementary and middle school teachers, which is potentially a result of the widespread use of the Science Teaching Efficacy Belief Instrument (STEBI) (Enochs and Riggs, 1990, Luft and Hewson, 2014).

Looking across these results, there is evidence that professional development programs in science can enhance teachers' knowledge of science content and teachers' beliefs. However, it is difficult to determine what features of the programs are most important in enhancing teachers' knowledge or fostering positive beliefs.

Changes in Instructional Practice

Most professional development programs in science are intended to catalyze changes in teachers' instruction, and researchers may use direct classroom observations, teachers' self-reports, or, less frequently, students' reports to document such changes. Even when instructional changes are observed, it often is difficult to determine what elements of the professional development program were most important in catalyzing the observed changes. Many studies examining instructional changes involved a small number of teachers and did not employ a control or comparison group.

Of the studies reviewed by Scher and O'Reilly (2009), five examined the effects of professional development on teachers' practice. In general, the research found positive effects on teachers' instruction in three studies that examined mathematics and science professional development and one study of science professional development (Lott, 2003). The pooled effect size for the relationship between professional development and teacher instruction was more pronounced than that for professional development and student learning, leading the researchers to conjecture that professional development may have a stronger effect on teacher practice than on student learning. However, the small number of studies that provided sufficiently rigorous evidence on these relationships inhibits the ability to make any causal claims.

Among the studies reviewed by Capps and colleagues (2012), 14 document changes in teachers' instruction as a result of professional development focused on inquiry-based instruction. Eleven of these studies used classroom observation to assess changes, while 2 (Jeanpierre et al., 2005; Lee et al., 2004) used both teachers' self-reports and classroom observation. Lee and colleagues (2004) found that teachers' self-reports of instructional changes conflicted with direct observations, with teachers reporting changes that were not then observed. In contrast, Jeanpierre and colleagues (2005) found that self-reports and observations were consistent and reflected changes in teachers' practice.

Of the studies reviewed by van Driel and colleagues (2012), 25 measured changes both in teachers' knowledge and in their instruction, but did not employ measures of students' learning. Most of these studies involved fewer than 20 teachers and included some form of direct classroom observation. All of the studies showed a positive effect of professional development on teachers' instruction.

Of the studies reviewed pertaining to newly hired teachers of science (Luft and Hewson, 2014), six observational studies found changes in beginning teachers' instruction as result of participating in professional development. Borman and Dowling (2008) investigated the results of a professional development program that supported teachers in using inquiry in the classroom. The study involved 80 schools, with approximately half not participating in the professional development program. New teachers who participated in the program had positive student scores, while more experienced teachers had negative effects.

In a review of programs designed to further teachers' use of technology to support inquiry in science, Gerard and colleagues (2011) found that for programs that lasted 1 year or less, teachers' use of technology in the first year after participating in the program was influenced primarily by technical and instructional challenges related to implementing the technology in the classroom for the first time, rather than by the design of the professional development program. When professional development was sustained beyond 1 year, teachers and researchers were able to overcome these kinds of challenges.

In one of the few large-scale studies that included teachers from multiple schools and districts, Banilower and colleagues (2007) found that participation in professional development programs in science was positively related to teachers' attitudes toward science instruction and their perceptions of their preparedness with respect to pedagogical and science content knowledge (see Box 6-1). In addition, teachers were more likely to implement a set of instructional materials if they had received training in the use of those materials. Professional development around instructional materials also was associated with increases in the amount of instructional time devoted to science and was positively correlated with teachers' use of teaching practices aligned with standards.

Few studies of instructional change in response to professional development in science have used control or comparison groups. Grigg and colleagues (2013) report on a 3-year large-scale randomized trial in the Los Angeles Unified School District focused on studying the effects of a professional development program concerning inquiry science on the instruction of 4th- and 5th-grade teachers in 73 schools. During the study, the school district introduced another district-wide professional development initiative on scientific inquiry. The researchers found that the two interventions increased the frequency of inquiry-based science teaching, and the impact of the professional development was selective: teachers tended to display instructional change in those areas of scientific inquiry that were more emphasized in the professional development. For

---

BOX 6-1
A Large-Scale Study of Professional Development

Banilower and colleagues (2007) drew on a large-scale study from the Local Systemic Change Initiative funded by the National Science Foundation (NSF). NSF began this initiative (through its Teacher Enhancement Program) in 1995. The initiative's primary goal was to improve instruction in science, mathematics, and technology through teacher professional development within schools or school districts. By 2002, NSF had funded 88 projects that targeted science or mathematics (or both) at the elementary or secondary level (or both). The projects were designed for all teachers in a jurisdiction; each teacher was required to participate in a minimum of 130 hours of professional development over the course of the project. The initiative also emphasized preparing teachers to implement district-designated mathematics and science instructional materials in their classes (Banilower et al., 2006).

In addition to providing professional development for teachers, the Local Systemic Change Initiative promoted efforts to build a supportive environment for improving instruction in science, mathematics, and technology. The initiative's projects were expected to align policy and practice within targeted districts and to engage in a range of activities to support reform. Those activities included

- building a comprehensive, shared vision of science, mathematics, and technology education;
- conducting a detailed self-study to assess the system's needs and strengths;
- promoting active partnerships and commitments among an array of stakeholders;
- designing a strategic plan that included mechanisms for engaging teachers in high-quality professional development activities over the course of the project; and
- developing clearly defined, measurable outcomes for teaching and an evaluation plan that would provide formative and summative feedback.

Banilower and colleagues (2007) analyzed the results for 18,657 teachers across 42 different projects involving science teachers in grades K-8 to examine the impact on teachers' attitudes, perceptions of preparedness, and classroom practices of professional development that was content based, situated in classroom practice, and sustained over time. The professional development model used in the projects targeted all teachers in a jurisdiction and emphasized preparing them to implement project-designated materials.

---

example, analysis of classroom observations showed increases in scientific questioning and in students formulating explanations using evidence. There was no increase in students connecting explanations to scientific knowledge, an aspect of scientific inquiry less emphasized in the professional development programs.

A small number of studies have explicitly compared different models of professional development in science. In one such study, Penuel and colleagues (2009) compared three different professional development programs in earth science for teachers from 19 middle schools in a large urban district. Teachers were randomly assigned to one of three program models or a control group. The three professional development programs differed in how teachers were engaged in designing, adopting, or adapting curriculum materials. All of the programs had a positive impact on how teachers planned and carried out their instruction. However, none of the teachers in any of the three programs or the control condition used students' preconceptions in class, and there were no differences in whether they elicited students' prior ideas about the concepts taught that day.

Findings across studies suggest that participation in professional development can lead to changes in teachers' instructional practice, but that those changes often are tightly linked to the aspects of instruction emphasized in the professional development.

Changes in Student Outcomes

As noted above, few studies of professional development for science teachers have measured student outcomes, although this trend is gradually shifting. Nine of the studies reviewed by Capps and colleagues (2012) report enhanced student learning. Two of these studies did not use a control or comparison group, and a third used only a posttest. Only 6 of the 44 studies reviewed by van Driel and colleagues (2012) directly assessed student learning, while 9 asked teachers to report on whether their students had benefited. All 6 of the former studies showed a positive effect on student learning. The review by Gerard and colleagues (2011) indicates that students' science learning experiences were enhanced for more than 60 percent of teachers who participated in professional development programs that (1) helped the teachers elicit students' ideas and support them in using evidence to distinguish among ideas and in reflecting on and integrating ideas; and (2) were sustained for more than 1 year.

Scher and O'Reilly (2009) located 18 studies that provided sufficient evidence for inclusion in their meta-analysis (8 of these were in science, and 3 included mathematics and science teachers). The researchers found a positive effect on student achievement, stronger for mathematics than for science programs. They also report that mathematics professional development taking place over multiple years had a more pronounced effect on student achievement than 1-year programs; they did not find the same result in their analysis of the science professional development evaluations. Among the mathematics professional development programs, the researchers also found a more pronounced effect on student achievement for those programs that focused on content and pedagogy, not pedagogy alone. A similar trend was noted for science, but not as strong statistically. Mathematics professional development programs that included coaching as part of the intervention also had a more pronounced effect. None of the science professional development programs studied included a coaching component.

In general, across all five of the literature reviews the committee consulted, the studies that employed a control or comparison group (thereby allowing for stronger inferences about the effect of the professional development program itself on observed outcomes) report evidence for positive effects on student learning, including among students from economically disadvantaged schools and English language learners. Still, most of the studies employing control or comparison groups included a small number of teachers from a single district.

Lara-Alecio and colleagues (2012) examined how professional development paired with specific science lessons about inquiry-based teaching affected achievement among 5th-grade English language learners. Based on earlier research demonstrating that inquiry-based interventions can improve English language learners' conceptual understanding of science (Amaral et al., 2002; August et al., 2009; Lee et al., 2005), the researchers examined the children's learning in a literacy-embedded science instructional intervention. Twelve teachers in 10 lower middle schools participated in professional development that explored science concepts and curriculum materials developed to aid in teaching those concepts in an inquiry-oriented manner. Students whose teachers participated in the professional development and who used the materials had significantly higher scores on five benchmark tests in science and on reading assessments relative to students in the control group. This result accords with the findings of Penuel and colleagues (2011), who also found that students demonstrated greater gains in their understanding of earth science when their teachers had participated in professional development focused on the development of curriculum units.

The Science Teachers Learning from Lesson Analysis (STeLLA) Program features video-based analysis of instructional practice aimed at upper elementary teachers (Roth et al., 2011). This year-long professional development program is organized around a conceptual framework that focuses teachers' attention on analyzing science teaching and learning through two lenses: the Science Content Storyline Lens and the Student Thinking Lens (see Box 6-2 for further detail). The researchers studied the influence of the professional development program on teachers' science content knowledge (multiple-choice test), teachers' pedagogical content

---

BOX 6-2
The Science Teachers Learning from Lesson Analysis
(STeLLA) Program

The STeLLA Program is an intensive, year-long, videocase-based, analysis-of-practice professional development program in science for upper-elementary teachers. Central to the program is a coherent conceptual framework that encompasses two lenses for looking at science teaching more closely—the Science Content Storyline Lens and the Student Thinking Lens. Drawing on research, this framework identifies eight specific teaching strategies designed to support teachers in making students' thinking more visible and nine strategies designed to support the development of coherent science content storylines that help students make the links between science ideas and classroom activities. This framework provides strong program coherence by focusing teachers' attention on a small set of core teaching strategies and supporting them in analyzing and understanding these strategies and using them well. The program's goals are to deepen teachers' science content knowledge and pedagogical content knowledge about student thinking and about science content storylines in two content areas in the teachers' curriculum.

Teachers meet in small, grade-level study groups (5 to 10 members), led by a STeLLA professional development leader. Teachers first learn about the STeLLA lenses and teaching strategies in a 2-week summer institute, where they analyze STeLLA-prepared videocases from classrooms outside of their own study group. A videocase includes a set of videos from one classroom along with associated materials, including students' written work/pre-posttests, educative curriculum materials that highlight the STeLLA lenses and strategies (e.g., lesson plans, content and pedagogical content knowledge background readings, compendium of common student ideas), and videos of student and teacher interviews. During the

---

knowledge (video analysis task), teachers' practice (lesson videotapes), and students' science knowledge (pre-post science unit tests).

Students whose teachers had participated in the STeLLA Program showed statistically significant learning improvement relative to students of the control teachers in a quasi-experimental study involving 48 teachers (Roth et al., 2011). Similar results were found in a follow-up study of the STeLLA Program using larger numbers of teachers (144 teachers in 77 schools) and over 2,800 students, PD leaders who were not program developers, a new geographical context, and a stronger comparison PD program. In this randomized, controlled study, students of teachers in the STeLLA Program significantly outperformed students of teachers in the comparison content deepening program on a science content knowledge test (Taylor et al., in press).

In a study focused specifically on strategies related to reading and

school year, participating teachers teach STeLLA lesson plans and analyze videos of their own teaching with their colleagues in monthly 3.5-hour study group meetings. During these meetings, teachers regularly generate questions about their own and their students' understandings of the science content, so that science content issues are intertwined with pedagogical issues.

Results from a quasi-experimental study (Roth et al., 2011) of 48 teachers, half of whom participated in the STeLLA Program, showed that, in comparison with teachers who received professional development focused only on deepening science content knowledge, program participants developed deeper science content knowledge and stronger abilities to use pedagogical content knowledge to analyze science-teaching practice. In addition, participants in the STeLLA Program increased their use of teaching strategies that made students' thinking visible and contributed to the coherence of the science lesson. Most important, their students' learning showed significant improvement. Hierarchical linear modeling analyses revealed that predictors of student learning included teachers' science content knowledge; their ability to analyze students' thinking; and their use of four science content storyline teaching strategies: (1) identify one main learning goal, (2) select content representations matched to the learning goal and engage students in their use, (3) make explicit links between science ideas and activities, and (4) link science ideas to other science ideas. Analysis of students' science content learning showed that students of teachers participating in the STeLLA Program outperformed those of teachers in the content deepening only program. Similar results emerged from a scale-up randomized, controlled study where students whose teachers participated in the STeLLA Program showed stronger science content knowledge than students whose teachers participated in a content deepening PD program of equal duration (Taylor et al., in press).

reading comprehension in science, Greenleaf and colleagues (2011) examined the effects of the Reading Apprenticeship Professional Development Program on high school biology teachers and their students. In a group-randomized experimental design, they used multiple measures of teachers' practice and students' learning about both biology and literacy, targeting schools serving many low-achieving students from groups historically unrepresented in the sciences. In total, 105 biology teachers in 83 schools participated (56 in the treatment group, 49 in the control group). Outcome measures for teachers included pre-post survey assessments of teacher knowledge, beliefs, and instructional practices in science and literacy; postintervention interviews; and the National Center for Research on Evaluation, Standards and Student Testing's Teacher Assignment instrument, which incorporates student work samples as a measure of teaching practice (Aschbacher, 1999; Clare, 2000). Student outcomes were measured using student surveys and pre-post assessments of student learning in biology and reading comprehension. Teachers participated in 10 days of professional development in Reading Apprenticeship, an instructional framework that integrates metacognitive inquiry teaching routines (such as think-alouds, text annotation, metacognitive logs, and teacher modeling of reading and reasoning processes) and reading comprehension protocols (such as ReQuest and Reciprocal Teaching) into subject area instruction.

Compared with control teachers, intervention teachers showed increased support for literacy learning in science and increased knowledge of the role of reading in learning and in their repertoire of instructional practices. They also demonstrated increased support for the use of metacognitive inquiry teaching routines, reading comprehension instruction, and collaborative learning structures relative to control teachers. Analysis of their teaching assignments revealed higher ratings for the cognitive challenge in their lessons, both in literacy and in biology, and higher frequencies of reading engagement support compared with control teachers. Students in treatment classrooms performed better than controls on state standardized assessments in English language arts, reading comprehension, and biology.

A program focused on whole-school science professional development developed by Johnson and Fargo (2010) also showed positive effects on students. The researchers employed a randomized controlled research design to study the impact of Transformative Professional Development (TPD) on teacher practice and student learning in a high-needs urban school district. The professional development program spanned 2 years, with a total of 200 hours of professional development. Sixteen teachers participated (8 in the treatment group, 8 in the control group).

Essential to the TPD model is the approach of "critical mass"—that the program includes all science teachers in a building participating together. Careful attention is paid to building relationships between teachers and their colleagues, between teachers and students, and between teachers and university faculty members. In addition, teachers' voices are honored as the program becomes increasingly co-developed by teachers and university partners over the 2-year period.

Over the 2 years, teachers in the treatment school improved in the design and implementation of their lessons, while teachers in the control schools declined. Pre-post tests for students included items taken from state tests. There was no significant difference between the performance of students in the treatment and control conditions after year 1; in year 2, however, students in the treatment group showed twice as much growth as students in the control group.

In one of the few studies employing a randomized design with a control group and a large number of teachers across multiple sites, Heller and colleagues (2012) compared three different models of professional development. The study included 270 elementary teachers and 7,000 students in eight sites across six states who were randomly assigned to one of three experimental models of professional development or to a control condition (see Box 6-3 for details). All three models produced significant

---

BOX 6-3
A Comparison of Three Models of Professional Development for Elementary Teachers

In a large-scale study of 270 elementary teachers and 7,000 students in eight sites across six states, Heller and colleagues (2012) compared three professional development models for elementary teachers. Teachers were randomly assigned to one of the three models or a control group that received no treatment. All three intervention models involved the same science content; however, they differed in the ways in which they supported teachers in developing content teaching knowledge. Each intervention involved 24 hours of contact time divided into eight 3-hour sessions. The interventions were delivered by staff developers trained to lead the teacher courses in their regions. The models were as follows:

- In one intervention model (Teaching Cases), teachers discussed narrative descriptions of extended examples from actual classrooms, which included samples of student work, accounts of classroom discussions, and descriptions of the teachers' thinking and instructional decisions.
- In a second intervention model (Looking at Students' Work), teachers examined and discussed their own students' work in the context of ongoing lessons.
- In the third intervention model (Metacognitive Analysis), teachers engaged in reflection and analysis about their own learning as they participated in science investigations. They considered ideas that could be learned through the investigation, tricky or surprising concepts, and implications for students' learning.
- The control group received no treatment during the initial study year, but participants were offered a delayed opportunity to receive the professional development.

All three intervention models improved both teachers' and students' scores on tests of science content knowledge relative to the scores of teachers and students in the control group. In addition, the effects of the intervention on teachers' students were stronger in the follow-up year than during the intervention year. Achievement also improved for English language learners in both the study and follow-up years. Only the Teaching Cases and Looking at Students' Work models improved the accuracy and completeness of students' written justifications of test answers in the follow-up year. Only the Teaching Cases model had sustained effects on teachers' written justifications.

changes in student scores on selected-response tests of science content, with no significant differences by gender or race/ethnicity. English language learners demonstrated significant gains in content knowledge as well, and students showed significant increases in content test scores a year later. Although all three models generated positive results in terms of student knowledge, the models varied with respect to the quality of students' written explanations. Only students who worked with teachers who participated in the intervention involving looking at student work from their own classrooms showed improved written explanations during the initial study year; in the follow-up year, written explanations improved significantly for students of teachers participating in both models that included an examination of student work samples. English language learners' written justifications did not show significant effects during the study year; a year later, however, those whose teachers participated in the intervention that entailed looking at student work had marginally higher scores relative to the control group of English language learners.

Benefits and Challenges of Professional Development Programs in Science

Professional development programs in science offer a number of benefits. First, they can potentially bring coherence to teacher learning. The fact that professional development programs are planned with a focus on specific goals and experiences with which to meet those goals can help teachers step aside from the activities and multiple goals they are addressing each day in their classrooms and persist with a set of key ideas over enough time to make real progress toward transformative change. The time required to develop such coherent programs often is in short supply within school systems, however.

Programs that incorporate a substantial off-site component also have the potential to enable intense teacher engagement as other obligations and distractions are temporarily removed, and teachers are afforded a time and a place conducive to reflection and study. Teachers for whom reform-oriented practices are entirely new may require such immersion to effect the paradigm shift in teaching attitudes and beliefs needed to achieve the vision of science education set forth in *A Framework for K-12 Science Education* and the *Next Generation Science Standards* (NGSS). Moreover, professional development leaders from outside teachers' workplaces have an advantage in creating a safe space for challenging teachers' thinking because they are not linked in any way to evaluations that would affect the teachers' employment status.

The intensive programs reviewed in this chapter also provide a mechanism for connecting teachers with expertise and experiences in science and science teaching that may not be available in their schools and districts. For example, teachers can interact with scientists who can help them better understand the science they are teaching to their students.

Formal programs can be effectively linked with teachers' work in schools in a variety of ways. Several of the examples discussed in this chapter include sessions during the school year that are based in teachers' schools. These kinds of school-based efforts are discussed in more detail in the next chapter. Finally, the findings of Scher and O'Reilly (2009) reinforce the idea that sustained professional development leads to increased student learning.

The programs discussed in this chapter also have challenges. One major challenge is that programs that include an intensive, multiday, off-site component can be quite expensive and difficult to sustain. Also, such programs typically reach a small percentage of the teachers who could benefit from professional learning experiences in science. In addition, the coherence that is so valuable in professional development programs can be a problem if it is so preplanned that it cannot be responsive to the varying needs of teachers at different stages of their professional development. Online professional learning may provide a mechanism for overcoming problems of scale and being more responsive to individual needs, but more research is needed to understand how online experiences can maintain the coherence that is such a benefit of professional development programs (see the discussion of online programs in the next section).

Another challenge of professional development programs is that even sustained programs have an end point—rarely do such programs continue for more than 2-3 years. Thus, these programmatic experiences are relatively short-lived, often with no mechanism for providing teachers with ongoing support. Because these programs typically are not embedded in schools, it is difficult to ensure that teachers are supported in implementing the ideas and practices they have learned. A program of 90 hours of professional development in science is meaningless if a teacher's principal discourages her from teaching science so as to place more emphasis on English language arts and mathematics. Teachers who participate in science professional development programs outside of their school also may feel isolated as they try to implement new teaching strategies, lacking colleagues at their school who can help them plan, debrief, and problem solve. And this isolation also prevents the development of the collective capacity of the science teachers in a school and district. The learning of that one isolated teacher benefits her and her students but is not disseminated to enhance the learning of all.

Summary

In summary, a solid body of research on professional development programs for science teachers examines impacts on teachers' knowledge, beliefs, and instructional practice. Using a range of methods, researchers have found intriguing evidence that when designed and implemented well, professional development in science can lead to sustainable changes in teachers' knowledge and beliefs and their instruction. There is suggestive evidence that professional development programs in science that incorporate many of the features of the consensus model (science content focus, active learning, coherence, sufficient duration, and collective participation) can lead to changes in teachers' knowledge and beliefs and instructional practice. Many fewer studies have measured student outcomes, making it difficult to offer a strong argument for the effect of these programs on students' learning and achievement. Still, there is suggestive evidence for the potential of certain strategies to support changes in teachers' knowledge and beliefs and their instruction that lead to improved student learning. These promising strategies include analysis of elements of instruction, close attention to students' thinking and analysis of their work, opportunities for teachers to reflect on their own instruction in science, time for teachers to try out instructional approaches in their classrooms, and coherence with school and district policies and practices. Programs typically include a multiday "off-campus" component led by an individual with expertise in science pedagogy and content. Teachers then return to their classrooms to implement some of the instructional approaches they have learned about, during which time they have opportunities to talk with one another and with the professional development providers about their progress.

Findings from those studies that employed a strong design and connected the dots in the teacher learning model depicted in Figure 6-1 by studying the relationships among teachers' opportunities to learn, teacher learning outcomes, and student learning outcomes suggest a preliminary list of program characteristics that lead to improved student learning in science and go beyond the consensus model:

- Teachers' science content learning is intertwined with pedagogical activities such as analysis of practice (Heller et al., 2012; Roth et al., 2011).
- Teachers are engaged in analysis of student learning and science teaching using artifacts of practice such as student work and lesson videos (Greenleaf et al., 2011; Heller et al., 2012; Roth et al., 2011).

- There is a focus on specific, targeted teaching strategies (Greenleaf et al., 2011; Johnson and Fargo, 2010; Penuel et al., 2011; Roth et al., 2011).
- Teachers are given opportunities to reflect on and grapple with challenges to their current practice (Greenleaf et al., 2011; Johnson and Fargo, 2010; Penuel et al., 2011; Roth et al., 2011).
- Learning is scaffolded by knowledgeable professional development leaders (Greenleaf et al., 2011; Heller et al., 2012; Penuel et al., 2011; Roth et al., 2011).
- Analytical tools support collaborative, focused, and deep analysis of science teaching, student learning, and science content (Greenleaf et al., 2011; Roth et al., 2011).

The committee offers this list of characteristics with cautious optimism. On the one hand, it is clear that, as Scher and O'Reilly (2009) argue, "Most reasonable people agree that professional development for math and science teachers is a useful and necessary investment [but that] researchers, practitioners, and policymakers need to be more realistic about what we know" (p. 235). Despite these promising findings, the research base remains uneven, and inconsistencies in results need to be explored. As van Driel and colleagues (2012) point out, most studies focus on one program in one setting with a small number of teachers, and there has been an overreliance on teachers' self-reports. Few studies used strong research designs incorporating pre-post measures of both sets of outcomes shown in Figure 6-1 (teachers' knowledge and instruction and students' learning) and a control or comparison group. The field lacks consistently used, technically powerful measures of science teachers' knowledge and practice, as well as measures that capture the full range of student outcomes.

There are also gaps in the evidence base. As van Driel and colleagues (2012) observe, almost no studies attend to the school organization and context and how they might affect the impact of professional development programs in science. Similarly, no published research examines the role and expertise of science professional development providers and facilitators (Luft and Hewson, 2014), although some research designs allow for that possibility (for one example and preliminary analysis, see Heller et al., 2010, pp. 71-84). Further, given the range of content taught, grade levels, and local and state contexts in which teachers work, even this growing body of research fails to provide definitive answers as to how teachers might best be supported in meeting the challenge of the new vision of science education. Keeping these weaknesses in mind, the committee agrees with Scher and O'Reilly when they remark that "a simple answer that 'the research base of high-quality evaluation is too thin to make informed judgments'. . . discounts the decades' worth of theory and development that have led to many of the current forward-thinking interventions" (p. 237), including those described here. We return to these observations in the chapter's conclusion.

ONLINE PROGRAMS

The explosion of online learning opportunities has led to increased interest in new venues for teacher learning. Professional development designers and leaders have begun exploring the potential of online learning to meet the need for high-quality experiences that are scalable and accessible to large numbers of teachers, flexible enough to meet varying needs and limited schedules, and cost-effective to produce and obtain (Cavanaugh and Dawson, 2010; National Research Council, 2007; Whitehouse et al., 2006). Many also see promise in the online environment as a way to provide professional development experiences that are ongoing, timely, and closely tied to teachers' classroom practices, as a viable alternative to the one-shot workshops in which many teachers now participate (National Research Council, 2007; Sherman et al., 2008; Whitehouse et al., 2006). As technological capabilities have rapidly advanced, a wide array of online professional development programs for teachers across the educational spectrum have emerged, including those for science teachers. This section describes the nature of online teacher professional development, its benefits and challenges, and the available evidence regarding its effectiveness. It should be noted, however, that research on online programs has proceeded largely independently of the research reviewed in the previous section, and remains in its early stages.

The Nature of Online Professional Development

The range of online programs for teacher professional development varies by the intended programs' purpose, objectives, content area, and pedagogy, as well as the ways in which the programs are delivered, assessed, and evaluated (Whitehouse et al., 2006). Dede (2006, pp. 2-3) describes the overarching goals of online teacher professional development as "introducing new curricula, altering teachers' instructional and assessment practices, changing school organization and culture, and enhancing relationships between district and community"—goals that overlap with those face-to-face programs. To achieve these goals, online programs employ a range of methods, including providing materials designed to enhance content knowledge, along with opportunities for reflection and discussion; access to subject matter and pedagogical experts; forums for discussing with other teachers experiences in implementing new practices; ongoing mentorship; and libraries of tools, resources, and video examples. Programs that employ these methods may be delivered online only, but some offer a hybrid model with a combination of both face-to-face and online components.

Dede and colleagues (2005) conducted an extensive review of approximately 400 articles published in the previous 5 years regarding online, face-to-face, and hybrid models of professional development. They identified 40 empirical studies that articulated a clear research question, used rigorous data collection methods, and conducted analyses of and interpreted the data related to the research questions. Nearly half of the 40 studies focused on programs in either mathematics (8) or science (9). The remainder focused on programs in multiple subjects, language arts, special education, foreign languages, or technology integration. Pedagogically, the approaches employed in the online programs studied took a largely social constructivist approach, which included problem-based learning, inquiry-based learning, mentoring, and communities of practice.

Effectiveness of Online Professional Development

A body of research has examined the effectiveness of the online professional development approach in engaging teachers, building community, and improving teacher learning. Much of this research has been based on participant satisfaction surveys, course evaluations, and some pre- and posttesting of participants' learning (Dede et al., 2009).

The majority of the studies reviewed by Dede and colleagues (2009) are qualitative and tend to focus on the nature of participant interactions and the design elements and contexts of the online programs that contributed to teacher learning and community. Some compare these elements in online versus face-to-face programs. Although few studies entailed measuring teacher or student outcomes empirically, results of the reviewed studies suggest some of the key elements that may be necessary to make engagement in online professional development productive. First, multiple studies demonstrate the importance of facilitation for interactions among teachers online, echoing a similar and consistent conclusion regarding the importance of facilitation in face-to-face professional development. Merely creating an online forum for connecting was found to be insufficient for on-topic, productive interactions in which teachers feel safe in discussing their understanding of science concepts and their instructional practices. Similar findings emerged regarding the use of video examples: skilled guidance is required to lead discussions around the examples. Some studies found that facilitators need specifically to elicit contributions focused on teacher practices, to pose pointed questions, and to ask for evidence in support of claims.

Studies comparing online and face-to-face interactions also suggest that teachers may be more reflective about practices online than face-to-face. Dede and colleagues (2005) note the very limited empirical data available on teacher and student learning; however, they did find some support for teachers' ability to learn science content more effectively through online than through face-to-face learning.

Few studies have included measures of teacher practices in the classroom or measures of students' learning (Dede et al., 2009). One recent study by Fishman and colleagues (2013) is an exception. This study consisted of a randomized experiment evaluating two different approaches to professional development designed to prepare high school teachers to implement an environmental science curriculum. One condition consisted of a 6-day, 48-hour face-to-face workshop; the other consisted of an online workshop with a series of self-paced short courses that teachers completed on their own, and included a facilitator who was available to assist teachers and answer questions. Although teachers in the second condition completed the courses online, they also participated in a 2-day face-to-face orientation session designed to prepare them to be successful with the online tools. Thus, the second condition may more appropriately be considered a hybrid approach to professional development.

Researchers measured teachers' beliefs and knowledge, coded videos of their classroom practices with particular lessons from the curriculum, and measured student learning on a multiple-choice test about environmental science. Overall, 25 teachers participated in the online condition and 24 in the face-to-face condition, with 596 and 493 high school students, respectively. Findings indicated that teachers and students in both groups improved in their content knowledge but did not differ significantly in this regard from one another. Teachers in the two groups also did not differ significantly in their beliefs about efficacy and teaching environmental science, or in a range of beliefs about their knowledge and inquiry practices. Nor did the groups differ significantly on measured classroom practices. In their discussion of these findings, Fishman and colleagues suggest that the variability of total contact hours among the online group members, who were able to pace their own learning, indicates the potential effectiveness of this type of flexibility to fit the needs of various participants. However, the authors and others (e.g., Moon et al., 2014) caution that these findings should not be taken as representative of all online professional development, which should be seen more as a delivery vehicle than as a specific approach. Rather, these findings point to conditions that may enable teachers to capitalize on the efficiency, timeliness, and reach of an online environment.

Results of an evaluation of a hybrid model of professional development aimed at helping middle and high school teachers across subjects adopt inquiry-based practices in teaching about energy suggest that online programs may not always lead to positive changes in teachers' beliefs and instruction (Seraphin et al., 2013). The program consisted of a 2-day face-to-face workshop, followed by participation in an online segment that included a peer forum with expert presentations that participants reviewed and discussed. The researchers found that the program was effective at generating interest in teaching about energy. However, teachers' confidence in their ability to teach about energy adequately through inquiry-based methods remained low, as did their knowledge and application of inquiry practices (based on teacher self-reports).

A pilot study of modules created by the National Science Teachers Association to improve the science content knowledge of teachers compared an online-only form with a hybrid form that included a 6-hour in-person workshop in addition to the online segment, which was designed to take a total of 6-10 hours (Sherman et al., 2008). Forty-five middle school teachers across three states participated. Scores in teachers' science knowledge increased from pretest to posttest in the online-only condition, but not among the hybrid group. However, the authors caution that these gains were still quite modest and may not be sufficient for proficiency in the content. Moreover, confidence scores improved a great deal among the hybrid group, "suggesting a disconnect between feeling confident in teaching a particular subject and actually knowing the content well" (p. 30).

Finally, studies have begun to examine the elements and conditions that make online professional development effective, as well as whether there are some teachers for whom this approach works best. In an attempt to better understand why there are high levels of noncompletion of online courses among teachers, for example, Reeves and Pedulla (2011) conducted a pre- and postsurvey of satisfaction among 3,998 elementary and secondary teachers participating in the e-Learning for Educators initiative across nine states. Overall, prior experience with online courses, course organization, helpful feedback from a facilitator, quality of learner interactions, clarity of expectations, user-friendliness of the interface, ease of content transferability, beneficial nature of discussion topics, and effective linking of content and pedagogy were positive predictors of satisfaction. Perhaps somewhat counterintuitively, facilitator expertise, materials that were culturally unbiased, clarity of goals, and the facilitators keeping discussions on topic were negative predictors of satisfaction. Taken together, these positive and negative predictors explained nearly half of the variance in teacher satisfaction. Silverman (2012) notes that when teachers are more active contributors to online discussions, they achieve greater gains in mathematical content knowledge learning.

Russell and colleagues (2009) evaluated the effects of four different levels of support and pacing of online professional development for middle school algebra teachers. They randomly assigned participating teachers to one of four conditions: self-paced online-only, high support with a mathematics instructor, and two different intermediate supports—online facilitator only and facilitated peer support. The purpose of the study was to help determine the relative importance of maximizing flexibility for participants and maximizing interactions with facilitators and peers. Of an initial sample of 235 teachers who agreed to participate, almost half dropped out of the study, with a greater percentage dropping out of the high-support group, although characteristics of those not completing the 8-week course did not differ among groups. Although the researchers had anticipated that the condition with facilitated peer support would yield the greatest gains in teacher beliefs and pedagogical practices (e.g., using worksheets, asking students to explain their thinking), they found that the groups did not differ on either front.

Summary

To summarize, intriguing and emerging research examines the promise and pitfalls associated with online learning as a venue for professional development. In particular, Reiser (2013) suggests that professional development for the NGSS should "structure teachers' sense making around rich images of classroom enactment" (p. 15), noting that the online environment is an important vehicle for making videocases more widely available to teachers.

However, the research base is not yet strong enough to support claims about the relationships between online professional development and changes in teachers' knowledge or practice and their students' learning. Other research on online learning across K-12 and higher-education settings suggests that effective online learning is the product of high-quality program design and implementation, supportive contexts, and understanding of how learner characteristics interact with technology (Means et al., 2014). Thus, future work in this domain will need to be as sensitive to issues of context as the research reviewed here and in the following chapter.

CONCLUSIONS

This chapter has focused on professional development programs that are purposefully designed to improve aspects of teacher knowledge and practice. These programs typically are developed and led by educators from outside schools and districts—university researchers, informal science education leaders, researchers at research and development centers, and so on. These professional development experiences, while linked to teachers' classroom experience, commonly take teachers out of their school setting for a significant block of time (often at summer institutes).

Most professional development programs documented in the research literature have been found to have positive impacts on teachers' learning and practice. A growing body of evidence also traces the effects of professional development programs on teacher knowledge, teacher practice, and student learning. Effective professional development programs provide teachers with opportunities to practice and reflect on new instructional strategies, to analyze student thinking and student work, and to analyze examples of the target instructional practices.

Conclusion 5: *The best available evidence based on science professional development programs suggests that the following features of such programs are most effective:*

- *active participation of teachers who engage in the analysis of examples of effective instruction and the analysis of student work,*
- *a content focus,*
- *alignment with district policies and practices, and*
- *sufficient duration to allow repeated practice and/or reflection on classroom experiences.*

Conclusion 6: *Professional learning in online environments and through social networking holds promise, although evidence on these modes from both research and practice is limited.*

That said, the evidence base on professional development programs in science is not very robust. Many studies focus on one program implemented in a single location with relatively few teachers, typically volunteers. Few studies have employed control or comparison groups, and few have measured multiple outcomes for teachers and students. Still, the available evidence is suggestive of elements that hold promise for supporting changes in teachers' science content knowledge, their content knowledge for teaching, and their instructional practices. These elements include engaging teachers in analysis of student thinking and learning; incorporating specific supports to help teachers use new knowledge to change their teaching practice; providing an expert program facilitator; attending to school context, such as principals' support and curriculum alignment; and considering issues of sustainability in the program design. The available evidence also points to numerous issues for future research and policy to consider.

REFERENCES

Abdal-Haqq, I. (1995). *Professional Development Schools: Weighing the Evidence*. Thousand Oaks, CA: Corwin Press.

Akerson, V.L., and Hanuscin, D.L. (2007). Teaching nature of science through inquiry: Results of a 3-year professional development program. *Journal of Research in Science Teaching, 44*(5), 653-680.

Akerson, V.L., Cullen, T.A., and Hanson, D.L. (2009). Fostering a community of practice through a professional development program to improve elementary teachers' views of nature of science and teaching practice. *Journal of Research in Science Teaching, 46*(10), 1090-1113.

Amaral, O.M., Garrison, L., and Klentschy, M. (2002). Helping English learners increase achievement through inquiry-based science instruction. *Bilingual Research Journal: The Journal of National Association for Bilingual Education, 26*(2), 213-239.

Aschbacher, P.R. (1999). *Developing Indicators of Classroom Practice to Monitor and Support School Reform*. Los Angeles: Center for the Study of Evaluation, National Center for Research on Evaluation, Standards, and Student Testing, Graduate School of Education and Information Studies, University of California.

August, D., Branum-Martin, L., Cardenas-Hagan, E., and Francis, D.J. (2009). The impact of an instructional intervention on the science and language learning of middle grade English language learners. *Journal of Research on Educational Effectiveness, 2*(4), 345-376.

Ball, D.L., and Cohen, D.K. (1999). Developing practice, developing practitioners: Toward a practice-based theory of professional education. In G. Sykes and L. Darling-Hammond (Eds.), *Teaching as the Learning Profession: Handbook of Policy and Practice* (pp. 3-32). San Francisco, CA: Jossey-Bass.

Banilower, E.R., Boyd, S.E., Pasley, J.D., and Weiss, I.R. (2006). *Lessons from a Decade of Mathematics and Science Reform: A Capstone Report for the Local Systemic Change through Teacher Enhancement Initiative*. Chapel Hill, NC: Horizon Research.

Banilower, E.R., Heck, D.J., and Weiss, I.R. (2007). Can professional development make the vision of the standards a reality? The impact of the National Science Foundation's local systemic change through teacher enhancement initiative. *Journal of Research in Science Teaching, 44*(3), 375-395.

Basista, B., and Matthews, S. (2002). Integrated science and mathematics professional development programs. *School Science and Mathematics, 102*(7), 359-370.

Blank, R.K., de las Alas, N., and Smith, C. (2008). *Does Teacher Professional Development Have Effects on Teaching and Learning? Analysis of Evaluation Findings from Programs for Mathematics and Science Teachers in 14 States*. Washington, DC: Council of Chief State School Officers.

Borko, H. (2004). Professional development and teacher learning: Mapping the terrain. *Educational Researcher, 33*(8), 3-15.

Borko, H., Jacobs, J., and Koellner, K. (2010). Contemporary approaches to teacher professional development. In E. Baker, B. McGaw, and P. Peterson (Eds.), *International Encyclopedia of Education* (Part 7, 3rd ed., pp. 548-555). Oxford, UK: Elsevier.

Borman, G.D., and Dowling, N.M. (2008). Teacher attrition and retention: A meta-analytic and narrative review of the research. *Review of Educational Research, 78*(3), 367-409.

Capps, D.K., Crawford, B.A., and Constas, M.A. (2012). A review of empirical literature on inquiry professional development: Alignment with best practices and a critique of the findings. *Journal of Science Teacher Education, 23*(3), 291-318.

Cavanaugh, C., and Dawson, K. (2010). Design of online professional development in science content and pedagogy: A pilot study in Florida. *Journal of Science Education and Technology, 19*(5), 438-446.

Clare, L. (2000). *Using Teachers' Assignments as an Indicator of Classroom Practice.* Los Angeles: Center for the Study of Evaluation, National Center for Research on Evaluation, Standards, and Student Testing, Graduate School of Education and Information Studies, University of California.

Clifford, G.J. (2014). *Those Good Gertrudes: A Social History of Women Teachers in America.* Baltimore, MD: Johns Hopkins University Press.

Cohen, D.K., and Hill, H.C. (2001). *Learning Policy.* New Haven, CT: Yale University Press.

Darling-Hammond, L., Wei, R.C., Andree, A., Richardson, N., and Orphanos, S. (2009). *Professional Learning in the Learning Profession: A Status Report on the Teacher Development in the United States and Abroad.* Washington, DC: National Staff Development Council.

Dede, C. (2006). *Online Professional Development for Teachers-Emerging Models.* Cambridge, MA: Harvard Education Press.

Dede, C., Breit, L., Ketelhut, D.J., McCloskey, E.M., and Whitehouse, P. (2005). *An Overview of Current Findings from Empirical Research on Online Teacher Professional Development.* Cambridge, MA: Harvard Graduate School of Education.

Dede, C., Ketelhut, D.J., Whitehouse, P., Breit, L., and McCloskey, E.M. (2009). A research agenda for online teacher professional development. *Journal of Teacher Education, 60*(1), 8-19.

Desimone, L.M. (2009). Improving impact studies of teachers' professional development: Toward better conceptualizations and measures. *Educational Researcher, 38*(3), 181-199.

Desimone, L., Porter, A.C., Garet, M.S., Yoon, K.S., and Birman, B.F. (2002). Effects of professional development on teachers' instruction: Results from a three-year longitudinal study. *Educational Evaluation and Policy Analysis, 24*(2), 81-112.

Fishman, B., Konstantopoulos, S., Kubitskey, B.W., Vath, R., Park, G., Johnson, H., and Edelson, D.C. (2013). Comparing the impact of online and face-to-face professional development in the context of curriculum implementation. *Journal of Teacher Education, 64*(5), 426-438.

Garet, M.S., Porter, A.C., Desimone, L., Birman, B.F., and Yoon, K.S. (2001). What makes professional development effective? Results from a national sample of teachers. *American Educational Research Journal, 38*(4), 915-945.

Garet, M.S., Cronen, S., Eaton, M., Kurki, A., Ludwig, M., Jones, W., Uekaway, K., Falk, A., Bloom, H., Doolittle, F., Zhu, P., Sztejnber, L., and Silverberg, M. (2008). *The Impact of Two Professional Development Interventions on Early Reading Instruction and Achievement.* Washington, DC: U.S. Department of Education, Institute of Education Sciences.

Garet, M.S., Wayne, A.J., Stancavage, F., Taylor, J., Eaton, M., Walters, K., Song, M., Brown, S., Hurlburt, S., Zhu, P., Sepanik, S., and Doolittle, F. (2011). *Two-Year Findings from the Middle School Mathematics Professional Development Impact Study.* Washington, DC: U.S. Department of Education, Institute of Education Sciences.

Gerard, L.F., Varma, K., Corliss, S.B., and Linn, M.C. (2011). Professional development for technology-enhanced inquiry science. *Review of Educational Research, 81*(3), 408-448.

Greenleaf, C.L., Litman, C., Hanson, T.L., Rosen, R., Boscardin, C.K., Herman, J., and Schneider, S. (2011). Integrating literacy and science in Biology: Teaching and learning impacts of reading apprenticeship professional development. *American Educational Research Journal, 48*(3), 647-717.

Grigg, J., Kelly, K.A., Gamoran, A., and Borman, G.D. (2013). Effects of two scientific inquiry professional development interventions on teaching practice. *Educational Evaluation and Policy Analysis, 3*(1), 38-56.

Hawley, W.D., and Valli, N. (2006). Design principles for learner-centered professional development. In W. Hawley (Ed.), *The Keys to Effective Schools* (2nd ed., pp. 1-23). Thousand Oaks, CA: Corwin Press.

Heller, J.I., Daehler, K.R., Wong, N., Shinohara, M., and Miratrix, L.W. (2012). Differential effects of three professional development models on teacher knowledge and student achievement in elementary science. *Journal of Research in Science Teaching, 49*(3), 333-362.

Jeanpierre, B., Oberhauser, K., and Freeman, C. (2005). Characteristics of professional development that effect change in secondary science teachers' classroom practices. *Journal of Research in Science Teaching, 42*(6), 668-690.

Johnson, C.C. (2007). Whole-school collaborative sustained professional development and science teacher change: Signs of progress. *Journal of Science Teacher Education, 18*(4), 629-661.

Johnson, C.C., and Fargo, J.D. (2010). Urban school reform enabled by transformative professional development: Impact on teacher change and student learning of science. *Urban Education, 45*(1), 4-29.

Kennedy, M. (1999). Form and substance in mathematics and science professional development. *NISE Brief, 3*(2), 1-7.

Lara-Alecio, R., Tong, F., Irby, B.J., Guerrero, C., Huerta, M., and Fan, Y. (2012). The effect of an instructional intervention on middle school English learners' science and English reading achievement. *Journal of Research in Science Teaching, 49*(8), 987-1011.

Lederman, N.G., Abd-El-Khalick, F., Bell, R.L., and Schwartz, R.S. (2002). Views of nature of science questionnaire: Toward valid and meaningful assessment of learners' conceptions of nature of science. *Journal of Research in Science Teaching, 39*(6), 497-521.

Lee, O., Hart, J.E., Cuevas, P., and Enders, C. (2004). Professional development in inquiry-based science for elementary teachers of diverse student groups. *Journal of Research in Science Teaching, 41*(10), 1021-1043.

Lee, O., Deaktor, R.A., Hart, J.E., Cuevas, P., and Enders, C. (2005). An instructional intervention's impact on the science and literacy achievement of culturally and linguistically diverse elementary students. *Journal of Research in Science Teaching, 42*(8), 857-887.

Lee, O., Lewis, S., Adamson, K. Maerten-Rivera, J., and Secada, W.G. (2008). Urban elementary school teachers' knowledge and practices in teaching science to English language learners. *Science Education, 92*(4), 733-758.

Little, J.W. (1988). Teachers' professional development in a climate of educational reform. In R.J. Anson (Ed.), *Systemic Reform: Perspectives on Personalizing Education* (pp. 105-135). Washington, DC: U.S. Department of Education, Office of Educational Research and Improvement.

Lott, K.H. (2003). Evaluation of a statewide science inservice and outreach program: Teacher and student outcomes. *Journal of Science Education and Technology, 12*(1), 65-80.

Lotter, C., Harwood, W.S., and Bonner, J.J. (2006). Overcoming a learning bottleneck: Inquiry professional development for secondary science teachers. *Journal of Science Teacher Education, 17*(3), 185-216.

Lotter, C., Harwood, W.S., and Bonner, J.J. (2007). The influence of core teaching conceptions on teachers' use of inquiry teaching practices. *Journal of Research in Science Teaching, 44*(9), 1318-1347.

Loucks-Horsley, S., Hewson, P.W., Love, N., and Stiles, K.E. (1998). *Designing Professional Development for Teachers of Science and Mathematics.* Thousand Oaks, CA: Corwin Press.

Loucks-Horsley, S., Love, N. Stiles, K.E., Mundry, S., and Hewson, P. (2003). *Designing Professional Development for Teachers of Science and Mathematics* (2nd ed.). Thousand Oaks, CA: Corwin Press.

Luft, J. (2001). Changing inquiry practices and beliefs: The impact of an inquiry-based professional development programme on beginning and experienced secondary science teachers. *International Journal of Science Education, 23*(5), 517-534.

Luft, J., and Hewson, P. (2014). Research on teacher professional development in science. In N.G. Lederman and S.K. Abell (Eds.), *Handbook of Research in Science Education* (vol. II, pp. 889-909). New York: Routledge.

McNeill, K.L., and Knight, A.M. (2013). Teachers' pedagogical content knowledge of scientific argumentation: The impact of professional development on K-12 teachers. *Science Education, 97*(6), 936-972.

Means, B., Bakia, M., and Murphy, R. (2014). *Learning Online: What Research Tells Us About Whether, When, and How.* New York: Routledge.

Moon, J., Passmore, C., Reiser, B.J., and Michaels, S. (2014). Beyond comparisions of online versus face-to-face PD: Commentary in response to Fishman et al., "Comparing the impact of online and face-to-face professional development in the context of curriculum implementation." *Journal of Teacher Education, 65*(2), 172-176.

National Research Council. (2007). *Taking Science to School: Learning and Teaching Science in Grades K-8.* Committee on Science Learning, Kindergarten through Eighth Grade. R.A. Duschl, H.A. Schweingruber, and A.W. Shouse (Eds.). Board on Science Education, Center for Education, Division of Behavioral and Social Sciences and Education. Washington, DC: The National Academies Press.

National Research Council. (2011). *Successful K-12 STEM Education: Identifying Effective Approaches in Science, Technology, Engineering, and Mathematics.* Committee on Highly Successful Science Programs for K-12 Science Education. Board on Science Education and Board on Testing and Assessment, Division of Behavioral and Social Sciences and Education. Washington, DC: The National Academies Press.

The New Teacher Project. (2015). *The Mirage: Confronting the Hard Truth About Our Quest for Teacher Development.* Brooklyn, NY: The New Teacher Project.

Penuel, W.R., McWilliams, H., McAuliffe, C., Benbow, A.E., Mably, C., and Hayden, M.M. (2009). Teaching for understanding in earth science: Comparing impacts on planning and instruction in three professional development designs for middle school science teachers. *Journal of Science Teacher Education, 20*(5), 415-436.

Penuel, W.R., Gallagher, L.P., and Moorthy, S. (2011). Preparing teachers to design sequences of instruction in earth systems science: A comparison of three PD programs. *American Education Research Journal, 48*(4), 996-1025.

Posnanski, T. (2010). Developing understanding of the nature of science within a professional development program for inservice elementary teachers: Project nature of elementary science teaching. *Journal of Science Teacher Education, 21*(5), 589-621.

Putnam, R.T., and Borko, H. (1997). Teacher learning: Implications of new views of cognition. In B.J. Biddle, T.L. Good, and I.F. Goodson (Eds.), *International Handbook of Teachers and Teaching* (vol. II, pp. 1223-1296). Dordrecht, the Netherlands: Kluwer Academic.

Radford, D.L. (1998). Transferring theory into practice: A model for professional development for science education reform. *Journal of Research in Science Teaching, 35*(1), 73-88.

Reeves, T.D., and Pedulla, J.J. (2011). Predictors of teacher satisfaction with online professional development: Evidence from the USA's e-Learning for Educators initiative. *Professional Development in Education, 37*(4), 591-611.

Reiser, B.J. (2013). *What Professional Development Strategies Are Needed for Successful Implementation of the Next Generation Science Standards?* Invitational Research Symposium on Science Assessment. Princeton, NJ: K-12 Center at Educational Testing Service.

Roth, K., Garnier, H., Chen, C., Lemmens, M., Schwille, K., and Wickler, N.I.Z. (2011). Video-based lesson analysis: Effective science PD for teacher and student learning. *Journal of Research in Science Teaching, 48*(2), 117-148.

Russell, M., Kleiman, G., Carey, R., and Douglas, J. (2009). Comparing self-paced and cohort-based online courses for teachers. *Journal of Research on Technology in Education, 41*(4), 443-466.

Scher, L., and O'Reilly, F. (2009). Professional development for K-12 math and science teachers: What do we really know? *Journal of Research on Educational Effectiveness, 2*(3), 209-249.

Seraphin, K.D., Philippoff, J., Parisky, A., Degnan, K., and Warren, D.P. (2013). Teaching energy science as inquiry: Reflections on professional development as a tool to build inquiry teaching skills for middle and high school teachers. *Journal of Science Education and Technology, 22*(3), 235-251.

Shepardson, D.P., and Harbor, J. (2004). ENVISION: The effectiveness of a dual-level professional development model for changing teacher practice. *Environmental Education Research, 10*(4), 471-492.

Sherman, G., Byers, A., and Rapp, S. (2008). Evaluation of online, on-demand science professional development material involving two different implementation models. *Journal of Science Education and Technology, 17*(1), 19-31.

Silverman, J. (2012). Exploring the relatioship between teachers prominence in online collaboration and the development of mathematical content knowledge for teaching. *Journal of Technology and Teacher Education, 20*(1), 47-69.

Supovitz, J.A., and Turner, H.M. (2000). The effects of professional development on science teaching practices and classroom culture. *Journal of Research in Science Teaching, 37*(9), 963-980.

Taylor, J., Roth, K.J., Wilson, C., Stuhlsatz, M., and Tipton, E. (in press). The effect of an analysis-of-practice, videocase-based, teacher professional development program on elementary students' science achievement. *Journal of Research on Educational Effectiveness.*

van Driel, J. H., Meirink, J. A., van Veen, K., and Zwart, R.C. (2012). Current trends and missing links in studies on teacher professional development in science education: A review of design features and quality of research. *Studies in Science Education, 48*(2), 129-160.

Warren, D. (Ed.). (1989). *American Teachers: Histories of a Profession at Work.* New York: Macmillan.

Westerlund, J.R., Garcia, D.M., Koke, J.R., Taylor, T.A., and Mason, D.S. (2002). Summer scientific research for teachers: The experience and its effect. *Journal of Science Teacher Education, 18*(1), 63-89.

Whitehouse, P., Breit, L., McCloskey, E.M., Ketelhut, D.J., and Dede, C. (2006). An overview of current findings from empirical research on online teacher professional development. In C. Dede (Ed.), *Online Professional Development for Teachers: Emerging Models and Methods* (pp. 13-29). Cambridge, MA: Harvard Education Press.

Wilson, S.M. (2011). How can we improve teacher quality? Recruit the right candidates, retain teachers who do well, and ensure strong preparation, good working conditions, and quality professional development. *Phi Delta Kappan, 93*(2), 64.

Wilson, S.M., and Berne, J. (1999). Teacher learning and the acquisition of professional knowledge: An examination of research on contemporary professional development. In A. Iran-Nejad and P.D. Pearson (Eds.), *Review of Research in Education* (vol. 24, pp. 173-209). Washington, DC: American Educational Research Association.

Wilson, S.M., Rozelle, J.J., and Mikeska, J.N. (2011). Cacophony or embarrassment of riches: Building a system of support for teacher quality. *Journal of Teacher Education, 62*(4), 383-394.

Yoon, K.S., Duncan, T., Lee, S.-W.-Y., Scarloss, B., and Shapley, K. (2007). *Reviewing the Evidence on How Teacher PD Affects Student Achievement.* Washington DC: U.S. Department of Education, Institute of Education Sciences, National Center for Education Evaluation and Regional Assistance, Regional Educational Laboratory Southwest.

7

Teacher Learning in Schools and Classrooms

Although most of the research on professional development for science teachers focuses on formally organized programs, teachers of science spend a relatively small number of hours or days in such programs during a typical school year that extends to approximately 180 days (and even accounting for nonteaching time in the summer)—on average, less than 35 hours over a 3-year period (Banilower et al., 2013, p. 50). Rather, most of the time for learning available to teachers occurs when they are in school with their students and colleagues. Some of this learning takes place in the classroom when teachers may least expect it—a student makes an enlightening remark, for example. Some of this learning is more planned, as when members of a grade-level team decide to look closely at samples of their students' work and in so doing develop a new understanding of what and how the students are learning. This chapter focuses on what is known about the broad array of such teacher learning opportunities that arise in classrooms and schools.

In one recent report, The New Teacher Project (2015) found that in three large urban districts, teachers self-reported spending an average of 17 hours a month on a broad range of development activities run by their school or district (150 hours a year); they reported their mandated professional development time as 39-74 hours per year. For the purposes of that survey, development activities were conceptualized broadly as formal and informal professional development, curriculum planning activities, teacher evaluation programs, and the like.

For at least the last 30 years, repeated calls have been made to capitalize on teachers' opportunities to learn in schools. Calls for professional development schools (Darling-Hammond, 1994; Goodlad, 1990; Holmes Group, 1990; Levine, 1992; Levine and Trachtman, 1997), for school improvement teams (e.g., Harris, 2001; Spillane and Diamond, 2007), for professional learning communities (DuFour et al., 2005; Fullan, 2005; Hord, 1997), and for schools as learning organizations (Senge et al., 2000) all are grounded in the idea of supporting teachers' learning in their daily lives, not just on "professional development days" (see also Cohen and Hill, 2001; Darling-Hammond and McLaughlin, 1995; Joyce and Showers, 1996; Neufeld and Roper, 2003; Supovitz and Turner, 2000).

Some researchers have conceptualized this learning as "embedded professional development" (Gallucci et al., 2010) or "embedded coaching" (Stein and D'Amico, 2002), highlighting the fact that it is "situated in the context of practice" (Ball and Cohen, 1999; Gallucci et al., 2010). Other researchers have tried to capture a more holistic sense of a school's "professional environment," a combination of formal and informal learning opportunities and supports. One important feature of school-based approaches to professional development is that they target both the development of individual teacher expertise and the collective capacity of the school (Bryk et al., 2010; Louis and Kruse, 1995). Another important feature is attention to specific contextual demands—teaching these students, in this school, in the company of these colleagues. These in-school learning opportunities also may be more scalable than the kinds of intensive programs reviewed in Chapter 6.

The available research on the school and classroom as a learning environment for teachers of science is both limited and diffuse, particularly in science. For this reason, the discussion in this chapter draws in some cases on research on teachers of other subjects, particularly mathematics. The chapter begins by reviewing the literature on teacher learning through collaboration and professional community. It then considers the roles of coaches and mentors and of induction programs for beginning teachers. It is important to note that while the research base on learning opportunities embedded in teachers' everyday work is thin, many innovative approaches currently being developed and implemented may hold promise for enhancing science teachers' learning and expanding the available research in this area.

COLLABORATION AND PROFESSIONAL COMMUNITY

Research spanning more than 30 years offers testimony to the power of teacher collaboration. Advocates credit systems theorist Peter Senge's (1990) book *The Fifth Discipline* with sparking administrators' and reformers' interest in professional learning communities as drivers of improvement in schools (see, for example, Hamos et al., 2009; Hord, 1997). Senge conceived of a "learning organization" as one comprising individuals with a shared vision, a team approach to problem solving, and a disposition toward continual learning through reflection and discussion. Within education, former school and district administrators have popularized the term "professional learning community," or "PLC," promoting it through workshops and books (see, for example, DuFour et al., 2005).

For purposes of this report, however, we find it useful to trace the origins of the concept of a professional learning community as it has developed specifically in educational research. Within education, the concept first emerged in the context of workplace-based studies conducted in the 1980s and 1990s, referring to teachers whose professional relationships are marked by a consistent orientation toward improvement, a focus on student learning, and practices of collaboration and inquiry. Such relationships represent a departure from the more individualistic norms, practices, and cultures that have typically characterized the school workplace (Lortie, 1975). Little (1982, 1984) conducted a year-long ethnographic study of six elementary, middle, and high schools, finding that the schools with well-established "norms of collegiality and experimentation" were better able to adapt to external change pressures and initiatives and better positioned to take advantage of district-sponsored professional development relative to the schools with more individualistic cultures. Rosenholtz (1989) used a combination of surveys and interviews in a study of 78 elementary schools. She distinguished between "learning enriched" and "learning impoverished" schools, with the former more likely to have established practices of collaboration and a stance of continuous improvement. McLaughlin and Talbert (2001) drew on a multiyear, mixed-methods study of the "contexts of teaching" in 16 high schools to differentiate schools and departments with a "professional learning community" (a relatively small number) from those exhibiting either an individualistic culture or a cohesive culture resistant to questioning—what they term a "traditional professional community."

Newmann (1996) argues that a professional community of teachers can provide a supportive context in which teacher learning can occur. For example, the Center on Organization and Restructuring of Schools at the University of Wisconsin conducted a multimethod study of 24 elementary, middle, and high schools undertaking comprehensive restructuring in 22 districts and 16 states, with special attention to the quality of instruction in mathematics and social studies. They found that aspects of school-wide professional community—shared norms and values, a focus on student learning, a habit of reflective dialogue, deprivatization of practice, and collaboration—were associated with more robust instruction and provided supports for teacher learning (Newmann and Associates, 1996;

Louis et al., 1996). In a related analysis of data from the National Education Longitudinal Study of 1988 (NELS:88), Center researchers found that
high schools that had adopted some of the same reform practices as the
24 restructuring schools showed more impressive gains in science, mathematics, reading, and history from grades 8 to 10 and from grades 10 to
12 (Newmann and Wehlage, 1995).

Bryk and colleagues (2010) identify professional community, together
with an improvement-oriented work culture and access to professional
development, as elements of "professional capacity" that were associated
with measured gains in achievement and attendance in Chicago elementary schools over a 6-year period in the 1990s. In a series of papers developed from analysis of the NELS:88 database, Valerie Lee and colleagues
argue that more "communally organized" schools produced higher levels
of teacher satisfaction, positive student behavior, pedagogy supportive
of student problem solving and sense making, and student learning in
mathematics and science (Lee and Smith, 1995, 1996; Lee et al., 1997). They
write, "our results suggest that when a form of a professional community
of teachers predominates—when teachers take responsibility for the success of all their students—more learning occurs" (Lee et al., 1997, p. 142).
This conclusion accords with results of survey and case study research
reported by Bolam and colleagues (2005), who define professional learning communities as communities "with the capacity to promote and sustain the learning of all professionals in the school community with the
collective purpose of enhancing student learning" (p. 145).

Each of these studies points to the generative conditions established
for teacher learning when schools foster collective responsibility for student learning and well-being. A recent study by Kraft and Papay (2014)
reinforces the point. The researchers used a composite measure of the
professional environment constructed from teachers' responses to the
North Carolina Teacher Working Conditions Survey, combined with state
end-of-grade test results in mathematics and reading in grades 3-8. They
found that teachers working in more supportive professional environments, compared with those working in less supportive environments,
improved their effectiveness more over time.

Relatively few studies, however, have delved deeply into the question
of *how* teacher interaction supports teacher learning in particular subject
domains. Researchers associated with the Cognitively Guided Instruction
(CGI) approach to mathematics professional development (Franke et al.,
2001) found that teachers who sustained high levels of CGI-consistent
practice several years after the professional development ended and who
developed their understanding still further over that time tended to be
those who engaged in robust forms of collaboration with school colleagues. Such teachers also were likely to combine school-level collabora-

tion with established ties to external resources (university experts, district mentors). Although the actual dynamics of teacher interaction were not a focus of study for the CGI researchers, the interview-based accounts suggest that collaboration achieved quite variable levels of depth and supplied quite different resources for teacher learning, even within a single school.

In-depth investigations of teacher interaction are relatively scarce, but those that do exist suggest that self-defined collaborative groups may vary substantially in the resources they are able to marshal to support teacher learning. Horn and Little (2010) analyzed audio and video recordings of collaborative groups formed among high school teachers, finding that groups within the same school differed both with regard to their inclination to question their own practice and to delve deeply into questions of student learning and with regard to the resources they brought to such questioning and inquiry. A highly successful group of mathematics teachers (who had achieved demonstrated gains in student learning and advanced course taking) was distinguished from other collaborative groups by a shared framework for talking about teaching and learning in mathematics (derived from collective professional development); the use of collaborative time to delve in detail into problems of practice; leadership roles and expectations that preserved the group's focus on core values, goals, and principles; and the cultivation of external ties to aid the group's own learning. Such external ties—active participation in university-based professional development, collaboration in university-led research projects, and membership in mathematics teacher networks—were a key factor in the strong professional community forged by the teachers within the school and in the student outcomes they were able to generate.

Vescio and colleagues (2008) reviewed 11 studies of the impact of professional learning communities on instruction and on student learning. Most of the studies relied on interview and survey self-reports of positive impact. In a smaller set of empirical studies that employed observation, however, it appeared that well-developed professional learning communities can have a positive impact on both teaching practice and student achievement.

The concept of professional community among teachers thus originated in studies centered on the organic development of learning-oriented professional relationships initiated by teachers in the context of day-to-day work in schools, teams, or departments. These studies of naturally occurring teacher interaction underscore the potential of close collaboration in schools to support teacher learning, while also revealing the difficulty of building and sustaining such collaboration in a workplace that often is poorly organized to support it and the importance of access to some form of external support.

Educators' interest in scaling up meaningful collaboration among teachers now manifests itself in the increasingly widespread use of the term "PLC" to refer to almost all groups of teachers convened at the school level, many of which have been mandated by state or local policies. Yet simply applying this label may lead the conveners of such groups to overlook the conditions required to make them fruitful venues for teacher learning. In scaling up, for example, the fundamental assumptions underlying the ideal of a professional learning community—that teachers' knowledge is situated in their daily practice and that their active engagement in such a community will improve their knowledge and their students' learning—may be neither understood nor valued. With this caution in mind, the committee sought to understand the prevalence of in-school opportunities for science teachers' learning.

Science-Focused Collaboration and Teacher Learning

In the National Survey of Science and Mathematics Education (Banilower et al., 2013), school representatives (one per school) reported that science-related teacher study groups exist in about one-third of elementary schools (32 percent) and approaching half of middle and high schools (43 percent and 47 percent, respectively). Collective analysis of science assessment results constitutes the most prominent activity (73 percent) of such groups, together with analyzing instructional materials (65 percent) and planning lessons together (67 percent); teachers' own engagement in science investigations are the least common activity (25 percent). Representatives of schools with study groups also tended to report that participation in the groups is required (79 percent), but these schools may set expectations for participation without supplying resources of time and space (only 62 percent reported having organized specific times for teachers to meet). In addition, only 56 percent of schools with science-related study groups have designated leaders for those groups. Fewer than 5 percent of elementary teachers reported having served as leader of a teacher study group focused on science teaching. The figures are somewhat higher at the secondary level, with 19 percent of middle school and 26 percent of high school science teachers having led such a group. Overall, the picture is one in which teachers of science, especially at the elementary level, may not have opportunities to collaborate with colleagues.

Fulton and colleagues (2010) drew implications for research, policy, and practice from a review of the available research on science, technology, engineering, and mathematics (STEM)-related professional learning communities, as well as consideration of other, nonempirical research sources (i.e., advice generated by professional education organizations and the guidance proposed by an expert panel of researchers and practitioners). Although the authors employ the popular term "PLC" to frame their review, the search terms they used encompass many professional development configurations or school-based learning contexts (for example, lesson study, critical friends groups, study groups, grade-level teams, and the like) that differ in important respects from and would not necessarily have been termed PLCs by the researchers whose studies they reviewed.

The authors derived their research-based claims from 25 "Type 1" studies—empirical studies published since 1995 that report adequately on the research methods used—and another 22 papers that are described as "empirical studies" but for which the published reports lack methodological detail. Altogether, the 47 studies are heavily weighted toward qualitative methods (78 percent) and toward mathematics (twice as many as those focused on science), but encompass all levels of schooling. All of the studies involved activity designed specifically for the purpose of professional development in STEM domains. Most (including 15 of the 25 Type 1 studies) focused primarily on teachers' experience of the professional development, although nearly half (11 of the 25) also examined subsequent effects on teachers' instructional practice. Only 3 studies—one of which one was a study of preservice teachers—examined effects on student outcomes.

Much of what these authors report regarding professional learning communities—including the significance of skilled facilitation and the benefit of helping teachers learn to elicit, analyze, and respond to students' thinking—appears broadly in studies of professional development across subject domains. However, the authors argue that STEM-related professional learning communities have distinguishing features that warrant attention. In particular, they conclude that advancement of STEM teachers' professional learning would be better ensured by the organization of discipline-specific rather than cross-subject groups, suggesting that the former afford more sustained and in-depth attention to content understanding and to the development of content-related teaching knowledge and practice. For example, Nelson and Slavit (2007) completed case studies of five cross-subject (mathematics and science) and cross-grade (middle and high school) teacher inquiry groups. They found that teachers appreciated the opportunity to familiarize themselves with teaching in other grades or subject domains. However,

> These cross-disciplinary, cross-grade-level collaborations also posed some challenges, especially in relation to the focus of their inquiries.

> Many struggled to define an inquiry question that would cut across the
> disciplines. . . .This led, in most cases, to a focus on pedagogy or class-
> room processes as opposed to specific disciplinary ideas and student
> understanding. (p. 29)

Fulton and colleagues (2010) also cite findings from other studies
whose focus plausibly fits within the professional learning community
designation (regardless of whether that term is used in the original study),
observing that sustained participation in subject-specific teacher groups
"increased teachers' deliberation about students' mathematics or science thinking" (p. 8). For example, Kazemi and Franke (2004) worked
throughout a school year with a group of teachers in a single elementary
school, examining what teachers learned and what instructional changes
they made as a result of focusing consistently and collectively on students' work and students' reasoning about mathematics in classroom
discussions.

Responding to the potential benefits of professional learning communities, the National Science Foundation's (NSF) Math and Science
Partnership (MSP) projects have increasingly incorporated collaborative
teacher groups into their program designs and professional development
models. Hamos and colleagues (2009) summarize seven MSP projects in
which teacher collaboration figured prominently. These seven projects
illustrate the range of contexts in which professional learning community
arrangements have been introduced to support science teachers' learning,
including one such community for rural teachers created entirely in an
online environment. The projects vary widely in the number of participants, in the specific strategies employed, and in the available research
on project processes and outcomes.

Program evaluations and other research conducted in the MSP projects suggest the benefits of collaborative groups in deepening teachers'
science content knowledge and developing inquiry-oriented teaching
practices, although the measures used across the studies varied. Six of
the seven project summaries generated by Hamos and colleagues (2009)
indicate positive results with respect to teacher knowledge and/or practice, and two of them point to measured gains in student learning (see also
Ellet and Monsaas, 2007; Hessinger, 2009; Monsaas, 2006).

As in other research on effective professional development, skilled
facilitation looms large as a factor. According to organizers of Project
Pathways at Arizona State University,

> In the absence of a PLC facilitator who holds teachers to high standards
> for verbalizing the processes involved in knowing, learning, and teach-
> ing content, Pathways research has revealed that PLC discussions tend

to be superficial and teachers make little progress in shifting their classroom practices. (Hamos et al., 2009, p. 19)

In addition to the importance of skilled facilitation, three of the seven
MSP project sites profiled by Hamos and colleagues (2009) identified
administrative support at the school level as a factor in whether teachers
benefited from their participation. Researchers associated with Project
Pathways cited three specific contributions of a school principal: "(1)
willingness to rearrange schedules to accommodate content-focused,
school-based PLCs for one hour during the work week, (2) support of
inquiry-based and conceptually-oriented teaching, and (3) willingness to
work through logistical obstacles to facilitate participation by all teachers' in the workshop or course and weekly PLC meetings" (Hamos et al.,
2009, p. 20).

As part of their broader research and evaluation agendas, MSP
researchers have investigated certain aspects of professional community
and collaboration, including the extent to which project participants at
a site held a shared vision and how they worked together—specifically,
their engagement in reflective dialogue. Much of the available research
relies on teachers' self-reports of collaborative practice, but two of the
projects profiled by Hamos and colleagues (2009) developed observation
protocols.

In a year-long, video-based investigation of a group of secondary
mathematics and science teachers involved in the Project Pathways site at
Arizona State University, researchers analyzed the teachers' discourse at
three points in time (Clark et al., 2008). They saw a shift from early-stage
interactions, in which participants' explanations "remained computational in nature, often incoherent, and each member remained focused on
her or his own ways of thinking" (p. 308), to later interactions, in which
explanations were more conceptually anchored and in which participants
attended closely to and built on one another's reasoning. Clark and colleagues attribute the emergence of mathematically rich discourse within
this professional learning community to the active role taken by the designated facilitator in modeling such discourse himself and in prompting
and guiding it among the other teachers. In addition, the researchers
report that such skilled facilitation required specific training and coaching
of the facilitator, who became demonstrably more focused and strategic
in his facilitation over the course of the year.

Overall, the research conducted by the profiled MSP sites varied
widely with respect to the rigor of the research design, with many studies
lacking control or comparison groups and (with a few exceptions, such
as the study described above) a heavy reliance on outcomes self-reported
via survey or interview. The research results also appear less commonly

in peer-reviewed journals than in conference proceedings or technical reports. That said, the available research points consistently to the likely benefits of well-organized and facilitated professional development-related collaboration among science teachers.

A small number of studies published after the Hamos and colleagues (2009) MSP project profiles and the Fulton and colleagues (2010) review further advance understanding of the kinds of interactions likely to be associated with teacher learning in the context of content-focused collaborative groups. Unlike studies that relied heavily on self-reports, these studies employed audio and/or video recordings of group interaction to trace changes in teachers' demonstrated conceptual understanding, depth of interaction, attention to student thinking, and classroom practice.

In one example, Richmond and Manokore (2011) report on a qualitative study of two science-focused, professional-learning community groups formed by elementary school teachers from multiple schools in a single urban district. The researchers define a professional learning community as "a group of teachers who meet regularly with a common set of teaching and learning goals, shared responsibilities for work to be undertaken, and collaborative development of pedagogical content knowledge (PCK) as a result of the gatherings" (p. 545). The two grade-level groups, one comprising 1st-grade teachers and the other 4th-grade teachers, participated in a multiyear program of inquiry-oriented activity. Each yearly cycle began with a 7- to 10-day summer institute, followed by 2-hour biweekly collaborative group meetings during the school year. Activity was centered on the development, teaching, and post-teaching assessment of a focal science unit (identifying relevant key concepts, linking concepts to assessment benchmarks, exploring curricula, developing instructional tasks and activities, videotaping and discussing classroom instruction, analyzing samples of student work, and proposing refinements to the unit). Meetings were facilitated by a university faculty member (1st grade) or a district science specialist (4th grade).

Researchers used audiotaped records of the group meetings, supplemented by observational field notes and interviews, to explore the extent to which the groups functioned in a manner that was consistent with the definition of a professional learning community and was likely to strengthen teachers' science knowledge and instructional practice. Analysis of teachers' transcribed talk revealed some evidence of participants' increased confidence in science teaching, together with comfort in asking for help or receiving feedback. However, the analysis also underscored the marginal place of science instruction in elementary schools and the pressure experienced by teachers to focus primarily on literacy and mathematics. Participants in the two professional learning communities tended to be the only individuals from their schools to be involved, leaving them with limited support for implementing new practices or having a broader influence on science teaching and learning. Interviews with participating teachers raised additional issues regarding the sustainability of such groups in the absence of a designated facilitator and other supports. As in other studies, skilled facilitation emerged as a key factor in the teachers' ability to make productive use of the time spent in these groups.

Collaborative teacher groups formed one component of a 3-year program of science professional development for elementary and middle school teachers investigated by Lakshmanan and colleagues (2011). The program (also funded by an MSP grant) combined three content courses, taught over three summers by university faculty, with participation in monthly professional learning community groups during the school year that were supported by local coaches. Researchers investigated the impact of participation on 5th- to 8th-grade mathematics and science teachers' reported self-efficacy in teaching, their outcome expectations, and their observed use of inquiry-based practices in the classroom. The researchers report gains in teacher knowledge, self-efficacy, and instructional practices resulting from their participation in professional learning communities ("Educator Inquiry Groups"), but do not describe the nature of the groups' activities.

In a contribution to the emerging research on online professional development (discussed in Chapter 6), McConnell and colleagues (2013) conducted a qualitative study of the effectiveness of videoconferencing in supporting collaborative teacher groups involved in the Problem-Based Learning Project for Teachers, a professional development program for K-12 teachers in Michigan that focused on inquiry-based science lessons. The online group meetings complemented a 7-day training conference and a 3-day "Focus on Practice" meeting in which all teachers met face to face. In the following months, 10 of the 54 participating teachers met via videoconferencing (5 in each of two virtual professional learning community groups), while the remaining teachers were organized in nine face-to-face professional learning communities. This program design afforded the possibility of studying teachers' experience of the virtual community as well as the opportunity to compare virtual with face-to-face groups.

The published paper cited here relies primarily on focus group interviews with participants and written reflections from participants and facilitators, although the project data include recorded videoconference sessions. The core activities and discussion topics were found to be comparable in the virtual and face-to-face settings, as were the benefits cited by teachers in interviews and reflections. Participants agreed that benefits of participation included sharing information, gaining new perspectives, hearing practical solutions, being accountable to the group, keeping discourse professional, and developing friendships. The authors indicate

BOX 7-1
Lesson Study

The promise of teacher study groups focused on analysis of teaching and learning in science can be seen in lesson study in Japan. Lesson study has served as a model for the organization of teacher study groups in some schools in the United States.

Lesson study, a widespread practice in Japanese schools, involves "collaborative inquiry cycles that revolve around planning, observation, and analysis of live instruction" (Lewis, 2011). It is built around "research lessons," which are meant to embody teachers' ideas about "optimal teaching of a particular subject matter to a particular group of students" (Lewis, 2013). The goal usually is not refinement of a single lesson but the use of instructional examples as catalysts to provoke study of the presenters' hypotheses related to teaching and learning.

Lesson study occurs at multiple levels in the Japanese education system, including individual schools, districts, national schools, and subject matter-oriented associations. Nearly all schools in Japan participate in some form of lesson study. According to a recent survey, research lessons occur in 99 percent of Japanese elementary schools, 98 percent of junior high schools, and 95 percent of public high schools (National Education Policy Research Institute, 2011).

At the elementary level, teachers of a given grade often plan collaboratively and conduct three to four research lessons per year focused on a school-wide theme and examined by all educators and administrators in the school (Fernandez and Yoshida, 2004). Themes are chosen collaboratively by the entire faculty, with emphasis on joint thinking about the impact of daily instruction on agreed-upon long-term goals for students. As in many U.S. schools, elementary teachers in

that fostering community during the initial training conferences, before the groups were implemented, was important. Although teachers in the virtual professional learning communities expressed a preference for meeting face-to-face, they judged videoconferences to be a good practical alternative that addressed problems of geographic distance and enabled groupings by grade level and science domain.

As with the research reviewed in Chapter 6, this research is limited to small programs and is heavily reliant on teacher self-reports. There remains relatively little research on the effects of professional learning communities on science teachers' or students' learning. However, the available research is suggestive, illuminating the potential of well-run and -organized teacher study groups to lead to change among participating teachers (see Box 7-1 for discussion of lesson study as an approach to teacher study groups). Among the characteristics that may matter in

Japan are generalists who teach all subjects to their charges. Lesson study programs at the district level offer an opportunity for teachers to cultivate expertise in a specific subject of special interest. Reflection on research lessons at the district level takes place during salaried time after school.

A culture of experimentation has arisen around the lesson study model, a culture that allows both rapid adoption of new curricula and continual refinement of existing content and teaching methods (Hart et al., 2011; Lewis and Tsuchida, 1997; Lewis et al., 2002, 2006; Watanabe and Wang-Iverson, 2005). This culture is enabled both by substantial teacher buy-in and by institutional considerations that give priority to teachers' contributions to their continued development. The Japanese school day includes dedicated time for collaborative planning of instruction and management of noninstructional tasks. Additionally, education is seen as a communal task, and a high premium is placed on cross-pollination of ideas among educators. Those whose contributions are viewed as especially insightful are sought after as commentators on research lessons across Japan. Teachers are recognized as producers of sophisticated, valuable knowledge on teaching and learning and are highly involved in all aspects of their continued professional learning.

Although lesson study is based in another educational system, its potential to serve as a structure around which to design teacher learning opportunities in U.S. schools has enjoyed considerable uptake in the field of mathematics education (e.g., Perry and Lewis, 2011). In a review of effective mathematics professional development conducted by the What Works Clearinghouse (WWC) (Gersten et al., 2011), a study of lesson study (Perry and Lewis, 2011)—one of two studies on mathematics professional development that met the criteria for inclusion in a WWC review—found positive effects on students' mathematics learning.

achieving these effects are those highlighted by Newman (1996) and confirmed in a large-scale, multisite study of workplace-based professional communities in England (Bolam et al., 2005):

- shared values and vision about pupil learning and leadership (Newman, 1996);
- collective responsibility for pupil learning (Newman et al., 1996);
- collaboration focused on learning (Newman, 1996);
- professional learning—individual and collective (Newman, 1996);
- reflective professional enquiry (Newman, 1996);
- openness, networks, and partnerships (Bolam et al., 2005);
- inclusive membership (Bolam et al., 2005); and
- mutual trust, respect, and support (Bolam et al., 2005).

In research on teacher groups organized specifically for professional development purposes, skilled facilitation remains a prominent factor in the groups' reported effectiveness.

Networks

Opportunities for collaboration and for building professional community can extend beyond an individual school. A network of teachers that spans multiple schools or districts, working together to understand and implement changes in their instruction, can be a powerful means of supporting teacher learning (Coburn et al., 2010, 2012; Penuel and Riel, 2007). Such networks provide a mechanism for teachers to share ideas about teaching, learning, and assessment; stories about students' successes and difficulties; strategies for managing learning groups; and tips for using technology (Penuel and Riel, 2007).

There is an expansive literature here, especially in the field of literacy teacher development. For example, in a randomized controlled trial of the National Writing Project's partnership program, researchers documented that interactions with colleagues who changed their own practice as a consequence of their participation in professional development augmented the effects of professional development on their own teaching practice (Penuel et al., 2012; Sun et al., 2013). This same finding of "spillover" effects of interactions with colleagues has been found in observational studies as well (e.g., Jackson and Bruegmann, 2009; Sun et al., 2014). This research builds on a whole tradition of research on teacher networks and instructional change conducted in the early 2000s (e.g., Bidwell and Yasumoto, 1997; Frank and Zhao, 2005; Frank et al., 2004; Yasumoto et al., 2001).

Efforts to build similar networks among science educators are growing. The Knowles Science Teaching Foundation (2015), for example, is building a national network of science teacher leaders who are committed classroom teachers involved in a range of leadership roles intended to improve the quality of the national science teaching workforce. The San Francisco Exploratorium's Teacher Institute is another example. Since 1984, it has been offering summer professional development for practicing middle and high school science teachers. In the Teacher Institute, teachers learn to integrate the hands-on, inquiry-based experiences of the Exploratorium into their classrooms. A Beginning Teacher Program was developed to support new teachers in the first 2 years of their development, while a Teacher Leadership Program trains the most experienced science teachers to serve as mentors and coaches for novice teachers. In addition to summer programs, the museum offers ongoing weekend workshops, digital resources, and online support. Thousands of alumni are connected through an online community, and teachers exchange ideas, offer just-in-time help for colleagues, and comment on new developments in science education.

Other networks have been created through professional organizations and state-wide networks of science and STEM partnerships and teachers. Examples are found in California (Penuel and Riel, 2007), Texas (http://www.thetrc.org [November 2015]), Oklahoma, and Nebraska. The Robert Noyce Teaching Fellowship Program (http://nsfnoyce.org [November 2015]), offered through NSF, provides scholarships, stipends, and programmatic support to recruit and prepare STEM majors and professionals to become K-12 teachers and master teachers to support them.

The proliferation of networks and network initiatives has outpaced the research. Although there are many networks, few research studies document their effects. In addition, existing studies have done more to map the structure of network ties than to delve into the nature, depth, and quality of network interaction (for an exception, see Coburn et al., 2012). This may change as interest in research on teacher networks increases (e.g., Coburn et al., 2012; Daly, 2010; Frank et al., 2004; Penuel et al., 2012) and research methodologies evolve (Avila de Lima, 2010). Nonetheless, some key features of networks have been shown to be more effective than others in supporting sustained change in instruction. Effective networks include strong ties (frequent interaction and social closeness), access to expertise, and deep interactions (focused on underlying pedagogical principles, the nature of the discipline, or how students learn) (Coburn et al., 2012). District policy can shape how teachers engage in networks and whether their participation supports changes in their instruction (Coburn et al., 2013). Policies can support more frequent and deeper interactions and help teachers identify local experts, but they also can disrupt ties, interrupt the flow of resources, and eliminate supports that encourage interaction (Coburn et al., 2013; see Chapter 6 for a more detailed discussion of this study).

A study of 21 California schools engaged in school-wide reforms suggests several additional characteristics of effective teacher networks (Penuel and Riel, 2007). First, receiving help from outside of one's immediate circle (characterized by Granovetter [1973] as "weak ties") is valuable for obtaining new information and expertise. Second, making it clear who has the expertise to assist with a specific challenge is helpful. To this end, it is important to provide venues where teachers can talk about their teaching, as well as to recognize success and achievement publicly in ways that encourage teachers to seek out their colleagues for help and resources. Third, meeting and committee structures in which teachers can participate in multiple meetings that cut across different functions in the school allow teachers to gain different perspectives on the instructional changes they are striving to make.

These insights suggest that networks may be more valuable to teachers when information flows in multiple directions, tapping into the distributed experiences of the members. It also appears that networks are more helpful when participating experts are given time to help others. Such experts may already be in formal roles that allow them to share their expertise, but they also may be informal leaders who have little time outside of their teaching responsibilities to serve as resources to their peers. Recognizing these informal leaders and giving them time to work with peers can be helpful in building effective teacher networks.

COACHING AND MENTORING RESOURCES IN SCHOOLS

Schools and districts have increasingly embraced instructional coaching as a form of workplace-embedded professional development support. The idea of instructional coaching has been around for at least the last 30 years, first stimulated by Bruce and Showers (1981) argument for creating venues for classroom-based assistance for teachers implementing new practices. Recruited from the ranks of experienced teachers, coaches provide a range of professional development activities in schools (Gallucci et al., 2010; Taylor, 2008; Woulfin, 2014). Like teacher study groups and professional learning communities, coaching can take qualitatively different forms, ranging from one-on-one encounters to coaches working with groups or teams of teachers. One-on-one classroom-based coaching remains relatively rare for science teachers—reported by just 17 percent of elementary and middle schools and 22 percent of high schools (Banilower et al., 2013). Coaching resources are less likely in science than in literacy and mathematics and are especially uncommon in rural schools (Banilower et al., 2013).

In addition to variation in coach-to-teacher ratios, coaching can focus on different issues and have varied ends—peer coaching, cognitive coaching, and instructional coaching being three examples. Coaching relationships also can be established through mentoring, which is used as a support strategy for prospective teachers, for teachers in the early stages of their careers, and for teachers who face specific challenges for which they need tailored support. Instructional coaching can be either content based or generic; it can be intended to support all teachers in meeting the demands of new school or district reform mandates, or it can be focused on early-career support or on teachers who are struggling with evaluations (Mangin and Stoelinga, 2008). Knight (2005) defines the instructional coach as an "on-site professional developer who teaches educators how to use proven teaching methods . . . and collaborates with teachers, identifies practices that will effectively address teachers' needs, and helps teachers implement those practices" (p. 17). Among the activities in which coaches engage are (1) assisting teachers in implementing new curricula or assessments; (2) consulting with and mentoring teachers; (3) supporting teachers who are working to apply knowledge and develop new skills or to deepen their understanding; (4) planning for, proposing, and conducting research and evaluation; (5) providing resources; and (6) leading study, inquiry, or book groups (Deussen et al., 2007).

Coaching has been adopted by states, large urban districts, and federally funded reforms (e.g., Deussen et al., 2007), and has been considered a core feature of comprehensive school reform (Sykes and Wilson, 2015) and the scaling up of reforms in mathematics education (Coburn and Russell, 2008). Coaching and mentoring also is seen as a significant means of sharing leadership within schools (Taylor, 2008), and coaches often are viewed as teacher leaders. Given the variations in its settings and in the ways it is conceptualized and implemented, it is difficult to draw conclusions about the potential effects of this form of teacher learning. Compounding the issue is the fact that there is very little research on this practice beyond descriptive case studies (Cornett and Knight, 2008) and a few small-scale studies that cannot easily be generalized (Darling-Hammond et al., 2009; Deussen et al., 2007).

Typical of the existing research is a study by Nam and colleagues (2013), who studied the effects of a 1-year collaborative mentoring program in South Korea consisting of five one-on-one mentoring meetings, weekly science education seminars, weekly mentoring group discussions, and self-evaluation activities. The researchers conducted a field study of three beginning science teachers and their three mentors, and found that the program encouraged the beginning teachers to reflect on their own perceptions and teaching practice in terms of inquiry-based science teaching, which the authors argue led to changes in their teaching practice.

In general, the committee was unable to locate sufficient research on different models of coaching and mentoring, their implementation, and their effects on teacher knowledge and practice and student learning, especially with regard to science teachers (recall that not one of the professional development evaluations included in the Scher and O'Reilly [2009] meta-analysis included the use of coaches for science teachers). In light of the growing interest in professional development that includes coaching as a component, it will be important to examine the potential effects of coaching/mentoring rigorously, especially given the current use of education evaluation systems, some of which include coaching as part of their model.

INDUCTION PROGRAMS

In the last 20 years, it has become clear that retaining new teachers early in their careers is crucial to building a strong workforce. Induction programs for beginning teachers vary considerably in their content and character, and they often involve the use of teacher learning opportunities, such as mentoring, coaching, and networking. Like professional learning communities and coaching, "induction" can have very different meanings in different contexts. Some induction programs are quite thin, involving orientation meetings focused on how to work within the district or school bureaucracy. Others involve working with mentors or coaches; in some programs, these more experienced teachers are trained in how to support new teachers, while in others they are not. Some programs entail structured opportunities with mentors who are matched with new teachers on grade level and/or subject matter expertise. In still other programs, strapped for human and material resources, mentoring is more catch-as-catch-can.

Induction programs also vary in duration. Goldrick and colleagues (2012) report that 13 states require induction programs for 1 year, while 11 require induction programs for 2 or more years. Some school districts have provided formal induction programs (e.g., Flowing Wells Unified School District, School District of Philadelphia), which often involve an overview of school district policies and general guidance on management. Support for new teachers also is offered by organizations that transcend school boundaries (e.g., Exploratorium, The New Teacher Center). These programs can be focused on teaching science or on teaching in general. Other programs consist of small groups of teachers who collaborate (e.g., Forbes, 2004), are university based (e.g., Luft and Patterson, 2002), exist online (e.g., Simonsen et al., 2009), or involve study of one's own instruction (e.g., Mitchener and Jackson, 2012).

Within the support offered to newly hired teachers of science, the terrain is different for secondary and elementary teachers. As noted earlier, beginning secondary teachers typically have stronger content knowledge than elementary teachers and are focused on science as their main teaching assignment. Elementary teachers often have weak science knowledge, and support for them in science competes with that in the other subject areas. Induction programs will need to be organized differently at the elementary and secondary levels to be responsive to teachers' needs.

Most teachers have little opportunity to engage in authentic scientific experiences during their preservice training but instead are offered courses defined by didactic lectures and "cookbook-style" labs (Gess-Newsome and Lederman, 1993). Even those few teachers fortunate enough to experience student-centered instruction in their preservice courses tend to revert to traditional practices once in the classroom (Simmons et al., 1999). Induction programs ideally serve as bridges from the student-centered theory characteristic of many teacher education programs to the realities of the classroom.

Teachers' preservice experiences influence how they respond to induction programs. Roehrig and Luft (2006) found this to be the case within a cohort of secondary science teachers. They tracked the induction-elicited change in teaching beliefs and attitudes of 24 teachers with a range of preservice experiences who participated in an induction program known as ASIST (Alternative Support for the Induction of Science Teachers). This program incorporated ongoing support to participants through classroom visits, trips to teacher conferences, technology-mediated dialogue, and monthly meetings. Changes in the teachers' beliefs were measured through semistructured interviews. Additionally, classroom observations allowed researchers to note changes in the teachers' instructional practice. Finally, program evaluations were completed by each participant at the conclusion of the induction program.

The various facets of ASIST were found to aid the development of productive knowledge, skills, and dispositions differentially, depending on teachers' preservice background. For example, those individuals from alternative or elementary certification pathways derived great benefit from workshops that immersed them in inquiry-based teaching methods. More traditionally certified secondary science teachers were already familiar with the themes of these induction workshops and so found them less beneficial. Researchers further noted the potential of open discussion on teaching philosophy, structured to build participants' awareness of best practices in inquiry-based instruction, to effect changes in teachers' beliefs and subsequent adjustments to classroom practice. Results from Roehrig and Luft's (2006) work indicate that designers of induction programs need to be mindful of the heterogeneous backgrounds of educators when developing these programs and, to the extent possible, build in activities intended to address different levels of expertise.

Regardless of program design, one of the primary goals of many induction programs is reducing teacher turnover. Ingersoll and Strong (2011) reviewed 15 empirical studies of the effects of induction programs on beginning teachers. Most of the studies revealed that the programs led to higher teacher retention and that students of teachers who participated in the programs showed higher gains on achievement tests. The researchers also found that induction programs generally had positive effects on teachers' classroom practices.

Smith and Ingersoll (2004) analyzed data from the nationally representative 1999-2000 Schools and Staffing Survey to identify the most effective aspects of induction programs. The 1999-2000 sample included

52,000 educators, 3,235 of whom were in their first year of teaching. Approximately 80 percent of the first-year teachers in public school settings had participated in some kind of induction program, compared with 60 percent of private school teachers. Common forms of induction included mentorship (66 percent of surveyed beginning teachers), collaborative planning time (68 percent), and "supportive communication" (81 percent). Reduced workload was a far less common aid provided to first-year teachers (11 percent). As measures to reduce the rate of teacher turnover, the most successful induction programs included mentorship by a teacher in one's field (a reduction of approximately 30 percent in the risk of departure) and common planning time with other educators in one's field (around a 43 percent reduction).

Induction supports for new teachers often were deployed in combination, so it may be difficult to isolate the effect of individual features. To gain some sense of the synergistic effects of multiple induction supports, Ingersoll and Kralik (2004) calculated the additive effect of three support "packages" incorporating progressively more components. More comprehensive support packages were associated with decreased turnover.

Among the different program configurations, certain components appear to be important to the success of newly hired science teachers: support, knowledge, and examination of classroom practice. Newly hired teachers need someone who can provide support during their initial years, whether it be a designated mentor, an influential teacher, or a group of teachers. When support is provided to newly hired science teachers, it can be instructional and/or psychological. Specifically, these teachers need help in all three of the domains on which the committee focused: tailoring of instruction for all students, disciplinary knowledge and scientific practices, and pedagogical content knowledge and instructional practices. Here, too, however, we found the research to be of uneven quality. Moreover, little of the existing research focuses specifically on science teachers, and thus it is difficult to draw any definitive conclusions about the power of induction programs to support the development of early-career science teachers.

CONCLUSIONS

Teachers spend the majority of their professional time in classrooms and schools, and it is imperative that those settings support their professional learning, both individually and collectively. For students to have opportunities to develop the skills, knowledge, and practices envisioned in *A Framework for K-12 Science Education* and the *Next Generation Science Standards*, teachers will need to have similarly rich learning experiences that are ongoing and embedded in their daily work, involve the practices of science, and account for the specific demands of their context (e.g., students' prior learning and experience, the availability of materials, teacher colleagues). A growing body of research documents the generative conditions established for teacher learning when schools foster collective responsibility for student learning and well-being. However, the evidence base related to learning opportunities for teachers that are embedded in schools and classrooms is weak, especially with regard to science. Despite the relative lack of research, innovative approaches to individual and collective teacher growth and development are appearing regularly in the education marketplace. It is important to understand these innovations better so their potential to support teachers as they work to improve their science instruction can be harnessed.

Conclusion 7: Science teachers' professional learning occurs in a range of settings both within and outside of schools through a variety of structures (professional development programs, professional learning communities, coaching, and the like). There is limited evidence about the relative effectiveness of this broad array of learning opportunities and how they are best designed to support teacher learning.

Conclusion 8: Schools need to be structured to encourage and support ongoing learning for science teachers, especially given the number of new teachers entering the profession.

Two themes arise from the varied body of research on embedded opportunities for teacher learning that accord with findings from research on professional development programs reviewed in Chapter 6. First is the importance of opportunities for teachers to analyze student thinking and student work, as well as examples of the target instructional practices, and to reflect on and attempt to change their own classroom instruction. Second, the involvement of individuals with expertise in science content and pedagogy who can act as facilitators is critical as context that supports and promotes continuous instructional improvement.

REFERENCES

Avila de Lima, J. (2010). Studies of networks in education: Methods for collecting and managing high-quality data. In A. J. Daly (Ed.), *Social Network Theory and Educational Change* (pp. 243-258). Cambridge, MA: Harvard Education Press.

Ball, D.L., and Cohen, D.K. (1999). Developing practice, developing practitioners: Toward a practice-based theory of professional education. In G. Sykes and L. Darling-Hammond (Eds.), *Teaching as the Learning Profession: Handbook of Policy and Practice* (pp. 3-32). San Francisco, CA: Jossey-Bass.

Banilower, E.R., Smith, P.S., Weiss, I.R., Malzahn, K.A., Campbell, K.M., and Weis, A.M. (2013). *Report of the 2012 National Survey of Science and Mathematics Education.* Chapel Hill, NC: Horizon Research.

Bidwell, C.E., and Yasumoto, J.Y. (1997). The collegial focus: Teaching fields, colleague relationships, and instructional practice in American high schools. *Sociology of Education, 72*(4), 234-256.

Bolam, R., McMahon, A., Stoll, L., Thomas, S., Wallace, M., Greenwood, A., Hawkey, K., Ingram, M., Atkinson, A., and Smith, M. (2005). *Creating and Sustaining Effective Professional Learning Communities* (Research Report 637). London, UK: DfES and University of Bristol.

Bruce, R.J., and Showers, B. (1981). Transfer of training: The contribution of "coaching." *The Journal of Education, 163*(2), 163-172.

Bryk, A., Sebring, P., Allensworth, E., Suppescu, S., and Easton, J. (2010). *Organizing Schools for Improvement: Lessons from Chicago.* Chicago, IL: University of Chicago Press.

Clark, P.G., Moore, K.C., and Carlson, M.P. (2008). Documenting the emergence of "speaking with meaning" as a sociomathematical norm in professional learning community discourse. *The Journal of Mathematical Behavior, 27*(4), 297-310.

Coburn, C.E., and Russell, J.L. (2008). District policy and teachers' social networks. *Educational Evaluation and Policy Analysis, 30*(3), 203-235.

Coburn, C.E., Choi, L., and Mata, W. (2010). "I would go to her because her mind is math": Network formation in the context of a district-based mathematics reform. In A.J. Daly (Ed.), *Social Network Theory and Educational Change* (pp. 33-50). Cambridge, MA: Harvard Education Press.

Coburn, C.E., Russell, J.L., Kaufman, J., and Stein, M.K. (2012). Supporting sustainability: Teachers' advice networks and ambitious instructional reform. *American Journal of Education, 119*(1), 137-182.

Coburn, C.E., Mata, W., and Choi, L. (2013). The embeddedness of teachers' social networks: Evidence from mathematics reform. *Sociology of Education, 86*(4), 311-342.

Cohen, D.K., and Hill, H.C. (2001). *Learning Policy.* New Haven, CT: Yale University Press.

Cornett, J., and Knight, J. (2008). Research on coaching. In J. Knight (Ed.), *Coaching: Approaches and Perspectives* (pp. 192-216). Thousand Oaks, CA: Corwin Press.

Daly, A.J. (Ed.). (2010). *Social Network Theory and Educational Change.* Cambridge, MA: Harvard Education Press.

Darling-Hammond, L. (1994). *Professional Development Schools: Schools for a Developing Profession.* New York: Teachers College Press.

Darling-Hammond, L., and McLaughlin, M.W. (1995). Policies that support professional development in an era of reform. *Phi Delta Kappan, 76*(8), 597-604.

Darling-Hammond, L., Wei, R.C., Andree, A., Richardson, N., and Orphanos, S. (2009). *Professional Learning in the Learning Profession: A Status Report on Teacher Development in the United States and Abroad.* Dallas, TX: National Staff Development Council.

Deussen, T., Coskie, T., Robinson, L., and Autio, E. (2007, June). *"Coach" Can Mean Many Things: Five Categories of Literacy Coaches in Reading First.* Issues & Answers Report, REL 2007-No. 005. Washington, DC: U.S. Department of Education, Institute of Education Sciences, National Center for Education Evaluation and Regional Assistance, Regional Educational Laboratory Northwest.

DuFour, R., Eaker, R., and DuFour, R. (Eds.). (2005). *On Common Ground: The Power of Professional Learning Communities.* Bloomington, IN: National Educational Service.

Ellett, C.D., and Monsaas, J.A. (2007). *Summary of the Development and Use of the Inventory for Teaching and Learning (ITAL) in the External Evaluation of the Georgia Partnership for Reform in Science and Mathematics (PRISM).* Available: http://hub.mspnet.org/index.cfm/14284 [June 2015].

Fernandez, C., and Yoshida, M. (2004). *Lesson Study: A Case of a Japanese Approach to Improving Instruction through School-Based Teacher Development*. Mahwah, NJ: Lawrence Erlbaum Associates.

Forbes, C.J. (2004). Peer mentoring in the development of beginning secondary science teachers: Three case studies. *Mentoring and Tutoring, 12*(2), 219-239.

Frank, K.A., and Zhao, Y. (2005). Subgroups as a meso-level entity in the social organization of schools. In L.V. Hedges and B. Schneider (Eds.), *The Social Organization of Schooling* (pp. 200-224). New York: SAGE.

Frank, K.A., Zhao, Y., and Borman, K. (2004). Social capital and the diffusion of innovations within organizations: Application to the implementation of computer technology in schools. *Sociology of Education, 77*(2), 148-171.

Franke, M., Carpenter, T., Levi, L., and Fennema, E. (2001). Capturing teachers' generative change: A follow-up study of professional development in mathematics. *American Educational Research Journal, 38*(3), 653-689.

Fullan, M. (2005). Professional learning communities writ large. In R. DuFour, R. Eaker, and R. DuFour (Eds.), *On Common Ground: The Power of Professional Learning Communities* (pp. 209-223). Bloomington, IN: National Educational Service.

Fulton, K., Doerr, H., and Britton, T. (2010). *STEM Teachers in Professional Learning Communities: A Knowledge Synthesis*. Washington, DC: National Commission on Teaching and America's Future and WestEd.

Gallucci, C., Van Lare, M., Yoon, I., and Boatright, B. (2010). Instructional coaching: Building theory about the role and organizational support for professional learning. *American Educational Research Journal, 47*, 919-963.

Gersten, R., Taylor, M.J., Keys, T.D., Rolfus, E., and Newman-Gonchar, R. (2011). *Summary of Research on the Effectiveness of Math Professional Development Approaches*. Available: http://ies.ed.gov/ncee/edlabs/regions/southeast/pdf/REL_2014010.pdf [August 2015].

Gess-Newsome, J., and Lederman, N.G. (1993). Preservice biology teachers' knowledge structures as a function of professional teacher education: A year-long assessment. *Science Education, 77*(1), 25-45.

Goldrick, L., Osta, D., Barlin, D., and Burn, J. (2012). *Review of State Policies on Teacher Induction*. Santa Cruz, CA: New Teacher Center.

Goodlad, J. (1990). *Teachers for Our Nation's Schools*. San Francisco, CA: Jossey-Bass.

Granovetter , M.S. (1973). The strength of weak ties. *American Journal of Sociology, 78*(6), 1360-1380.

Hamos, J.E., Bergin, K.B., Maki, D.P., Perez, L.C., Prival, J.T., Rainey, D.Y., Rowell, G.H., and VanderPutten, E. (2009). Opening the classroom door: Professional learning communities in the Math and Science Partnership Program. *Science Educator, 18*(2), 14-24.

Harris, A. (2001). Building the capacity for school improvement. *School Leadership & Management, 21*(3), 261-270.

Hart, L.C., Alston, A., and Murata, A. (2011). *Lesson Study Research and Practice in Mathematics Education*. New York: Springer.

Hessinger, S. (2009). Professional learning communities. In J.S. Kettlewell and R.J. Henry (Eds.), *Increasing the Competitive Edge in Math and Science* (pp. 101-120). Lanham, MD: Rowan and Littlefield.

Holmes Group. (1990). *Tomorrow's Schools: Principles for the Design of PDSs. A Report of the Holmes Group*. East Lansing, MI: Holmes Group.

Horn, I.S., and Little, J.W. (2010). Attending to problems of practice: Routines and resources for professional learning in teachers' workplace interactions. *American Educational Research Journal, 47*(1), 181-217.

Hord, S.M. (1997). *Professional Learning Communities: Communities of Continuous Inquiry and Improvement.* Austin, TX: Southwest Educational Development Laboratory.

Ingersoll, R.M., and Kralik, J.M. (2004). *The Impact of Mentoring on Teacher Retention: What the Research Says.* Education Commission of the States Research Review. Available: http://www.gse.upenn.edu/pdf/rmi/ECS-RMI-2004.pdf [April 2015].

Ingersoll, R.M., and Strong, M. (2011). The impact of induction and mentoring programs for beginning teachers: A critical review of the research. *Review of Educational Research, 81*(2), 201-233.

Jackson, C.K., and Bruegmann, E. (2009). Teaching students and teaching each other: The importance of peer learning for teachers. *American Economic Journal: Applied Economics, 1*(4), 85-108.

Joyce, B., and Showers, B. (1996). The evolution of peer coaching. *Educational Leadership, 53*(6), 12-16.

Kazemi, E., and Franke, M.F. (2004). Teacher learning in mathematics: Using student work to promote collective inquiry. *Journal of Mathematics Teacher Education, 7*(3), 203-235.

Knight, J. (2005). A primer on instructional coaches. *Principal Leadership, 5*(9), 16-21.

Knowles Science Teaching Foundation. (2015). *Knowles Science Teaching Foundation Announces 2015 Cohort of Teaching Fellows.* Available: http://globenewswire.com/news-release/2015/06/10/743662/10138068/en/Knowles-Science-Teaching-Foundation-Announces-2015-Cohort-of-Teaching-Fellows.html [June 2015].

Kraft, M.A. and Papay, J.P. (2014). Can professional environments in schools promote teacher development? Explaining heterogeneity in returns to teaching experience. *Educational Evaluation and Policy Analysis, 36*(4), 476-500.

Lakshmanan, A., Heath, B.P., Perlmutter, A., and Elder, M. (2011). The impact of science content and professional learning communities on science teaching efficacy and standards-based instruction. *Journal of Research in Science Teaching, 48*(5), 534-551.

Lee, V., Smith, J., and Croninger, R. (1997). How high school organization influences the equitable distribution of learning in mathematics and science. *Sociology of Education, 70*(2), 128-150.

Lee, V.E., and Smith, J.B. (1995). Effects of high school restructuring and size on early gains in achievement and engagement. *Sociology of Education, 68*(4), 241-270.

Lee, V.E., and Smith, J.B. (1996). Collective responsibility for learning and its effects on gains in achievement for early secondary school students. *American Journal of Education, 104*(2), 103-147.

Levine, M. (Ed.). (1992). *Professional Practice Schools: Linking Teacher Education and School Reform.* New York: Teachers College Press.

Levine, M., and Trachtman, R. (Eds.). (1997). *Making Professional Development Schools Work: Politics, Practice and Policy.* New York: Teachers College Press.

Lewis, C. (2011). Teachers and teaching in Japan: Professional mecca or pressure cooker? In Y. Zhao (Ed.), *Handbook of Asian Education* (pp. 231-246). New York: Routledge.

Lewis, C. (2013). *How Do Japanese Teachers Improve their Instruction? Synergies of Lesson Study at the School, District, and National Levels.* Paper commissioned by the Committee on Strengthening Science Education through a Teacher Learning Continuum, Washington, DC.

Lewis, C., and Tsuchida, I. (1997). Planned educational change in Japan: The case of elementary science instruction. *Journal of Educational Policy, 12*(5), 313-331.

Lewis, C., Tsuchida, I., and Coleman, S. (2002). The creation of Japanese and U.S. elementary science textbooks: Different processes, different outcomes. In G. DeCoker (Ed.), *National Standards and School Reform in Japan and the United States* (pp. 44-66). New York: Teachers College Press.

Lewis, C., Perry, R., and Murata, A. (2006). How should research contribute to instructional improvement? The case of lesson study. *Educational Researcher 35*(3), 3-14.

Little, J.W. (1982). Norms of collegiality and experimentation: Workplace conditions of school success. *American Education Research Journal, 19*(3), 325-340.

Little, J.W. (1984). *Professional Development Roles and Relationships: Principles and Skills of "Advising."* San Francisco, CA: Far West Laboratory for Educational Research and Development.

Lortie, D.C. (1975). Schoolteacher: A sociological inquiry. *Teachers College Record, 77*(4), 642-645.

Louis, K.S., and Kruse, S.D. (1995). *Professionalism and Community: Perspectives on Reforming Urban Schools.* Thousand Oaks, CA: Corwin Press.

Louis, K.S., Marks, H.M., and Kruse, S. (1996). Teachers' professional community in restructuring schools. *American Educational Research Journal, 33*(4), 757-798.

Luft, J.A., and Patterson, N.C. (2002). Bridging the gap: Supporting beginning science teachers. *Journal of Science Teacher Education, 13*(4), 267-282.

Mangin, M.M., and Stoelinga, S.R. (Eds.). (2008). *Effective Teacher Leadership.* New York: Teachers College Press.

McConnell, T.J., Parker, J.M., Eberhardt, J., Koehler, M.J., and Lundeberg, M.A. (2013). Virtual professional learning communities: Teachers' perceptions of virtual versus face-to-face professional development. *Journal of Science Education and Technology, 22*(3), 267-277.

McLaughlin, M.W., and Talbert, J.E. (2001). *Professional Communities and the Work of High School Teaching.* Chicago, IL: University of Chicago Press.

Mitchener, C.P., and Jackson, W.M. (2012). Learning from action research about science teacher preparation. *Journal of Science Teacher Education, 23*(1), 45-64.

Monsaas, J.A. (2006). *Engaging Higher Education Faculty in K-16 Learning Communities to Improve Teaching and Learning Science and Mathematics in the K-12 Schools.* Paper presented at the MSP Evaluation Summit II, Minneapolis, MN.

Nam, J., Seung, E., and Go, M. (2013). The effect of a collaborative mentoring program on beginning science teachers' inquiry-based teaching practice. *International Journal of Science Education, 35*(5), 815-836.

National Education Policy Research Institute. (2011). *Report of Survey Research on Improvement of Teacher Quality [Kyouin no Shitsu no Koujou ni Kansuru Chosa Kenkyuu].* Tokyo, Japan: National Education Policy Research Institute.

Nelson, T., and Slavit, D. (2007). Collaborative inquiry amongst science and mathematics teachers in the U.S.A.: Professional learning experiences through cross-grade, cross-discipline dialogue. *Journal of Inservice Education, 33*(1), 23-39.

Neufeld, B., and Roper, D. (2003). *Coaching: A Strategy for Developing Instructional Capacity—Promises & Practicalities.* Washington, DC: Aspen Institute Program on Education and the Annenberg Institute for School Reform.

The New Teacher Project. (2015). *The Mirage: Confronting the Hard Truth About Our Quest for Teacher Development.* Brooklyn, NY: The New Teacher Project.

Newmann, F.M. (1996). *Authentic Achievement: Restructuring Schools for Intellectual Quality.* San Francisco, CA: Jossey-Bass.

Newmann, F.M., and Wehlage, G.G. (1995). *Successful School Restructuring: A Report to the Public and Educators.* Madison: Center on Organization and Restructuring of Schools, University of Wisconsin.

Penuel, W.R., and Riel, M. (2007). The "new" science of networks and the challenge of school change. *Phi Delta Kappan, 88*(8), 611.

Penuel, W.R., Sun, M., Frank, K.A., and Gallagher, H.A. (2012). Using social network analysis to study how collegial interactions can augment teacher learning from external professional development. *American Journal of Education, 119*(1), 103-136.

Perry, R.R., and Lewis, C.C. (2011). *Improving the Mathematical Content Base of Lesson Study: Summary of Results.* Available: http://www.lessonresearch.net/IESAbstract10.pdf [July 2014].

Richmond, G., and Manokore, V. (2011). Identifying elements critical for functional and sustainable professional learning communities. *Science Teacher Education, 95,* 543-570.

Roehrig, G.H., and Luft, J.A. (2006). Does one size fit all? The induction experience of beginning science teachers from different teacher-preparation programs. *Journal of Research in Science Teaching, 43*(9), 963-985.

Rosenholtz, S.J. (1989). *Teachers' Workplace: The Social Organization of Schools.* New York: Longman.

Scher, L., and O'Reilly, F. (2009). Professional development for K-12 math and science teachers: What do we really know? *Journal of Research on Educational Effectiveness, 2*(3), 209-249.

Senge, P.M. (1990). *The Fifth Discipline: The Art and Practice of the Learning Organization.* New York: Doubleday/Currency.

Senge, P.M., Kleiner, A., Roberts, C., Ross, R.D., and Smith, B.J. (2000). *Schools that Learn: The Fifth Discipline Fieldbook for Educators, Parents, and Everyone Who Cares About Education.* New York: Doubleday.

Simmons, P.E., Emory, A., Carter, T., Coker, T., Finnegan, B., Crockett, D., Richardson, L., Yager, R., Crave, J., Tillotson, J., Brunkhorst, H., Twiest, M., Hossain, K., Gallagher, J., Duggan-Haas, D., Parker, J., Cajas, F., Alshannag, Q., McGlamery, S., Krockover, J., Adams, P., Spector, B., LaPorta, T., James, B., Rearden, K., and Labuda, K. (1999). Beginning teachers: Beliefs and classroom actions. *Journal of Research in Science Teaching, 36*(8), 930-954.

Simonsen, L., Luebeck, J., and Bice, L. (2009). The effectiveness of online paired mentoring for beginning science and mathematics teachers. *International Journal of E-Learning and Distance Education, 23*(2), 51-68.

Smith, T., and Ingersoll, R. (2004). What are the effects of induction and mentoring on beginning teacher turnover? *American Educational Research Journal, 41*(3), 681-714.

Spillane, J.P., and Diamond, J.B. (2007). *Distributed Leadership in Practice.* New York: Teachers College Press.

Stein, M.K., and D'Amico, L. (2002). Inquiry at the crossroads of policy and learning: A study of a district-wide literacy initiative. *Teachers College Record, 104*(7), 1313-1344.

Sun, M., Penuel, W.R., Frank, K.A., Gallagher, H.A., and Youngs, P. (2013). Shaping professional development to promote the diffusion of instructional expertise among teachers. *Educational Evaluation and Policy Analysis, 35*(3), 344-369.

Sun, M., Wilhelm, A.G., Larson, C.J., and Frank, K.A. (2014). Exploring colleagues' professional influences on mathematics teachers' learning. *Teachers College Record, 116*(6).

Supovitz, J.A., and Turner, H.M. (2000). The effects of professional development on science teaching practices and classroom culture. *Journal of Research in Science Teaching, 37*(9), 963-980.

Sykes, G., and Wilson, S.M. (2015). Instructional policy. In D. Gitomer, and C. Bell (Eds.), *Handbook of Research on Teaching* (5th ed.). Washington, DC: American Educational Research Association.

Taylor, J.E. (2008). Instructional coaching: The state of the art. In M.M. Mangin, and S.R. Stoelinga (Eds.), *Effective Teacher Leadership: Using Research to Inform and Reform* (pp. 10-35). New York: Teachers College Press.

Vescio, V., Ross, D., and Adams, A. (2008). A review of research on the impact of professional learning communities on teaching practice and student learning. *Teaching and Teacher Education, 24*(1), 80-91.

Watanabe, T., and Wang-Iverson, P. (2005). The role of knowledgeable others. In P. Wang-Iverson and M. Yoshida (Eds.), *Building our Understanding of Lesson Study* (pp. 85-92). Philadelphia, PA: Research for Better Schools.

Woulfin, S.L. (2014). Charting the research on the policies and politics of coaching. *Education Policy Analysis Archives, 22*(50).

Yasumoto, J.Y., Uekawa, K., and Bidwell, C. (2001). The collegial focus and student achievement: Consequences of high school faculty social organization for students on achievement in mathematics and science. *Sociology of Education, 74,* 181-209.

8

Creating a Supportive Context
for Teacher Learning

Teachers work within contexts, and those contexts matter. The committee's view of teacher learning is one of a dynamic process contingent on its context—including the policies, practices, and norms of the groups with which teachers interact—as well as teachers' own individual characteristics. Science teachers work in classrooms, departments, schools, districts, and professional organizations. They work within a larger, ever-expanding and shifting educational system, characterized by ongoing state and federal reform efforts and changing student and teacher populations (Cuban, 2010; Cusick, 2014). These shifts and others are important to both acknowledge and take into account as one considers the resources necessary to nurture and sustain teachers in the reform of science education. For example, state standards are significant drivers of curriculum, instruction, assessments, and the allocation of various resources for teachers. In general, the last 20 years have seen an increase in expectations for children's scientific literacy (National Research Council, 2010; President's Council of Advisors on Science and Technology, 2010). The *Next Generation Science Standards* (hereafter referred to as NGSS) represent an important step in that evolution, articulating a vision for science education that is profoundly different from the status quo, and that will require science teachers to have a new set of skills.

School, district, and state contexts can feed or starve teachers' efforts to grow. Many teachers want to develop new approaches to improve their teaching, but they encounter policy and organizational constraints that place obstacles in their way. Previous chapters of this report have established a vision for science teaching and learning, characterized the science teaching workforce, identified teachers' learning needs to achieve the vision, and analyzed what is known about meeting those needs. Understandably, the focus of those chapters is largely on teachers, and the driving goal—whether implicitly or explicitly stated—is to promote changes in teachers' practice that will improve student outcomes. Here, we shift from a focus on teachers to a broader look at the conditions, structures, and resources that could support science teachers' individual and collective learning in ways that might lead to improved outcomes for students.

Schools and districts are complex organizations. Identifying a single factor that will drive improvements is difficult. Research on comprehensive school reforms has shown that widespread gains in student achievement often are associated with reforms that address simultaneously several aspects of the education system—from curriculum, to assessment, to school organization and leadership, to the development of human capital (e.g., Bryk et al., 2010; Desimone, 2002; Sykes and Wilson, in press). Notably, a longitudinal study of more than 100 low-income, low-performing elementary schools in Chicago identified five supports that must be in place at the school level to improve student learning: professional capacity, coherent instructional guidance, leadership, parent-community ties, and a student-centered learning environment (Bryk et al., 2010). Schools that were strong in three or more of these supports were 10 times more likely than other schools to demonstrate significant learning gains in mathematics and reading. While this research did not assess the effects of these supports on science learning, there is no reason to believe that its findings would not hold for science as well.

In a similar vein, in an analysis of three comprehensive school reform models, Rowan and colleagues (2009) found comparable results: the most effective networks of schools provide systematic support for coherent curricula, aligned and substantively rich teacher professional development, and reliably effective classroom instruction that is guided by a well-articulated vision of good teaching. The work of Cohen and his colleagues reinforces this finding (Cohen et al., 2013).

These and other similar analyses provide an important backdrop for the present discussion of the school, district, and state contexts for supporting teachers' learning (see Figure 8-1). One important lesson from research on instructional improvement is that improving students' outcomes requires working on multiple fronts, and a sustained weakness in any one support undermines attempts to improve students' learning. In thinking about supporting teachers' individual learning and promoting collective capacity in schools, then, it is important to consider how a variety of factors work together to support teachers, instead of focusing on only one factor (e.g., time for collective planning). As Cohen and Hill

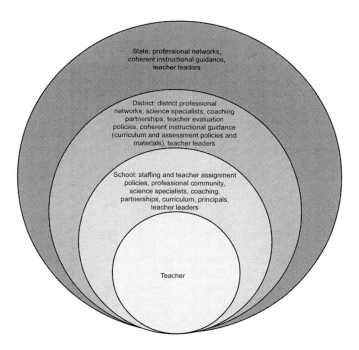

FIGURE 8-1 Contexts for teachers' learning.

(2000, p. 110) observe in their study of mathematics education reforms in California,

> When teachers attended the student curriculum workshops, their classroom practices changed to reflect reformers' ideas, and when those same teachers also attended to California Learning Assessment System (CLAS) as a learning opportunity, their teaching methods changed even more. This result suggests the importance of using a variety of policy instruments in coordinated efforts to enable changes in practice, rather than placing all policy eggs in a single basket.

The committee found little research that investigated the effects of school, district, and state contexts on science teachers and their instruction or on students' learning of science. That said, a wide-ranging and gradually accumulating research literature examines various aspects of teacher development in different contexts. The contexts and cultures that nurture or constrain teacher learning are myriad and overlapping (see Figure 8-1). Here we examine research related to three of the five supports identified by Bryk and colleagues (2010): professional capacity (e.g., professional networks, coaching, partnerships), coherent instructional guidance (e.g., state and district curriculum and assessment/accountability policies), and leadership (e.g., principals and teacher leaders). We also discuss conventional resources (Cohen et al., 2001) such as time and funding, and consider the implications for science teacher development that can advance achievement of the new vision for science education in *A Framework for K-12 Science Education* (hereafter referred to as the Framework) and the NGSS. We note that contexts have permeable boundaries—a district can have staffing policies that shape and are shaped by a school's staffing policies—and the summary provided here is intended to capture the interactive, dynamic, iterative ways in which contexts influence one another.

PROFESSIONAL CAPACITY

The challenge of developing the expertise teachers need to implement the NGSS is daunting. Even so, it presents an opportunity to rethink professional learning for science teachers—specifically, to shift the focus from individual to collective learning for teachers at the department, school, district, and school network levels. Thinking about professional learning within a system in this way means that not all of the needed expertise must reside in one teacher, one coach, or one school. It potentially also means that resources can be used more cost-effectively to support that student and teacher learning. In addition, teachers' learning becomes more public—as do the learning opportunities available to them—and easier to monitor. Here we consider four domains in which educators have attempted to influence school and district contexts for building professional capacity: professional community and collaboration, staffing policies, teacher evaluation, and school/district partnerships.

Professional Community and Collaboration

Professional community is one component of professional capacity that is repeatedly cited as important, and this observation resonates with the literature on professional learning communities described in Chapter 7. The idea here is that teachers "relinquish some of the privacy of their individual classrooms to engage in critical dialogue with one another as they identify common problems and consider possible solutions to these concerns" (Bryk et al., 2010, p. 55). This kind of community involves creating opportunities for faculty to discuss classroom work with their colleagues, establishing processes for allowing constructive dialogue about classroom practice, and providing mechanisms for sustained collaboration that focuses on strengthening instruction.

One way to support collective learning is by developing policies that provide teachers with time to work together and that value collaboration, such as by offering incentives for engaging in collaboration. Providing such support for collaborative learning would lend needed structure to efforts now emerging along these lines in many schools and districts.

Also critical is for teachers to have access to others with greater expertise, such as science specialists, lead teachers, or outside consultants. Meeting this need requires identifying the expertise among colleagues in a building, across the district, in those associations and organizations that surround school communities, and in online environments and then providing mechanisms for teachers to access that expertise. Teachers also may require help in connecting with national groups such as the National Science Teachers Association (NSTA), particularly through the NSTA Learning Center which connects teachers through discussion forums and e-mail lists, and links teachers to thousands of free resources—webinars readings, a portfolio system, and an index of professional development opportunities. There are also teacher-mentors who answer teachers' questions and connect them with resources. Other networks include Scitable, a collaborative learning space for teachers and scientists with resources on genetics and cell biology connected with the journal *Nature*.

District policies can influence teachers' social networks in formal and informal ways. This point is illustrated by a study of a district mathematics reform effort over a 3-year period (Coburn et al., 2013). The district initiated reform of elementary mathematics over 2 years, then pulled back on the initiative in year 3. In year 1, the district created the role of mathematics coach. Each school was required to have at least one half-time mathematics coach who worked with teachers. A district-level team supported the coaches, providing them with regular professional development and observing them once a month. The district instituted weekly grade-level teacher meetings to facilitate joint planning and offered biweekly school-based professional development. Finally, the district provided professional development for selected teachers during the summer and during intersessions.

In year 2, the district offered additional professional development to teachers in cross-district settings. The school-based professional development shifted to cross-grade groupings of teachers. The focus of the professional development deepened to examine how students learn mathematics, the nature of mathematics, and how to solve mathematics problems. In year 3, as a result of a new superintendent and changes in policy, the district abandoned and dismantled the mathematics reform initiative.

Teachers' social networks changed in response to these district policies. In years 1 and 2 of the initiative, teachers' networks expanded in number and diversity, but they then contracted in year 3. In year 1, teachers' networks were small and tended to be grade level-specific, but they expanded in year 2 to include more individuals and more teachers interacting across grade levels. The initiative also allowed teachers to identify those with expertise related to mathematics instruction, and this enabled them to make strategic decisions about whom to ask for advice.

District policy influenced the resources teachers accessed through their social networks by providing information and materials and deepening expertise through professional development. The district also influenced the nature of teachers' interactions by providing professional development for coaches on how to engage with teachers around mathematics, focused in such areas as task analysis, investigation of students' problem-solving strategies, structured reflection on practice, and routines for reviewing student data. These kinds of interactions began between coaches and teachers, but then appeared in teacher-to-teacher interactions even in year 3, when the initiative was abandoned. These kinds of interactions fostered an in-depth discussion of mathematics and mathematics pedagogy.

In summary, a growing body of research suggests that teacher capacity is enhanced in environments that nurture collegiality. Teacher collaborations do not naturally arise in the busy world of schooling. Instead, policies that encourage the joint work of teachers, provide them with time to collaborate, and task them with significant work to accomplish in those groups can play an important role.

Staffing Policies and Science Expertise

Expertise in science teaching and learning is important for supporting teacher collaboration and enhancing professional capacity in science. This expertise entails both general knowledge of science pedagogy and a specific understanding of state standards and assessments. It also entails deep knowledge of students so that instruction is designed, from the beginning, in ways that respond to students' backgrounds, interests, and differences. Yet, staffing schools with sufficient expertise is challenging across all grade levels.

For elementary schools, ensuring teachers have access to expertise in science may be more challenging than is the case for other subjects. In response to policy pressures associated with the No Child Left Behind Act, many school districts created new roles for teachers, including literacy and mathematics specialists. The responsibilities and titles of these specialists often differ across the contexts in which they work, and may include teaching, coaching, and leading school reading and mathematics programs. These specialists also may serve as a resource in reading, writing, and mathematics for educational support personnel, administrators, teachers, and the community; provide professional development based on historical and current literature and research; work collaboratively with other professionals to build and implement instructional programs for individuals and groups of students; and serve as advocates for struggling students.

There are a limited number of science specialists at the state and district levels (Trygstad et al., 2013). However, new specialists can be identified through multiple programs, including Einstein Fellows, National Board Certified Teachers, Knowles Science Foundation Teaching Fellows, the National Science Teachers Association Leadership Institute, and the U.S. Department of Education Teaching Ambassador Fellowships, to name just a few. The state of Virginia has invested considerable resources in the development of mathematics and reading specialists, and has initiated similar efforts in science. Building on an earlier definition of the mathematics specialist (Reys and Fennell, 2003), the Virginia Mathematics and Science Coalition's Science Specialist Task Force defines a science specialist as "a teacher whose interest and distinctive preparation in content and pedagogy are coordinated with particular teacher leadership assignments to support teaching and learning in the context of science instruction" (Reys and Fennell, 2003; Sterling et al., 2007, p. 8). However, such specialists, who could bring targeted and informed support at time of heightened demand, have been cut and not restored.

Fewer than 40 percent of districts have staff dedicated to support for science instruction, although larger districts are more likely to employ science specialists. The use of science specialists in schools, either in place of or in addition to regular classroom teachers, is uncommon (10-16 percent of schools) (Banilower et al., 2013). Weiss and colleagues (2001, p. 4) report similar results: "In the United States, approximately 15 percent of elementary students receive science instruction from a science specialist in addition to their regular teachers, and another 12 percent receive science instruction from a science specialist instead of their regular classroom teachers." Pull-out instruction, whether for remediation or enrichment, also is quite rare (7-10 percent of schools). The picture is quite different in elementary mathematics instruction. Students are pulled out for remediation in almost 60 percent of schools, and for enrichment in roughly one-third of schools. The prevalence of these practices may be due in part to the fact that testing for accountability purposes is more common in mathematics than in science. In addition, Title 1 funds are more likely to be targeted for remediation in mathematics and reading than in science (Banilower et al., 2013, p. 109).

Although 61 percent of district officials report having policies or suggested guidelines regarding the number of minutes per week science should be taught in elementary classrooms, district support for elementary science is limited. More than 60 percent of districts have no district staff dedicated to elementary science, and another 13 percent report having less than 0.5 full-time equivalent district staff in this role. A closer look at district support by district size shows that large districts are more likely to have such staff than smaller districts, but it is striking that there are none in more than a third of large districts (Dorph et al., 2011, p. 37).

When resources allow, offering one-on-one coaching to help teachers improve their practice also can be a powerful tool. Yet at both the elementary and middle school levels, schools are significantly more likely to provide coaching in mathematics than in science; there is no significant difference at the high school level (Banilower et al., 2013, p. 47). As standardized testing in science begins to take hold in public education, however, it is likely that districts and school networks will begin to use coaching and mentoring for science teachers more often.

Schools with differing proportions of students eligible for free/reduced-price lunches are about equally likely to provide assistance to science teachers in need. In contrast, the largest schools are significantly more likely than the smallest ones to offer science-focused teacher study groups. The greatest variation is in the percentage of schools providing one-on-one coaching, which is more likely to be offered in schools in the highest quartile of proportion of students eligible for free/reduced-price lunches than in those in the lowest quartile (Banilower et al., 2013, p. 49).

At the high school level, challenges around school staffing have concerned teachers' misassignment. Ingersoll (2002) notes that out-of-field teaching "typically involves the assignment of otherwise well qualified individuals to teach subjects that do not match their qualifications" (p. 2). Further, his analyses demonstrate that out-of-field teaching often takes place in schools that do not have teacher shortages in general. In science, teacher certification policies muddy the waters, as states vary in how they license teachers in the sciences. Ingersoll (2002) explains:

> For example, a broad definition of the field of science might include anyone who teaches any science course and define as in-field those instructors with a major or minor in any of the sciences, including chemistry, physics, geology, space science, or biology. This definition assumes that simply having a major or minor in one science qualifies a teacher to teach any of the sciences...the obvious shortcoming of this broad definition is that it overlooks the problem of within-department, out-of-discipline, teaching; a teacher with a degree in biology may not be qualified to teach physics. (p. 25)

Analyses reported both in *Rising Above the Gathering Storm* (National Academy of Sciences et al., 2010) and by Ingersoll (2003) indicate that about 28-30 percent of middle and high school teachers who taught one or more science classes did not have a minor in the relevant science or in science education, and 41 percent did not have a major or regular certification in one or more of the science courses they were teaching. For example, Ingersoll (2003) found that 60 percent of those teaching physical science classes (chemistry, physics, earth or space science) lacked a major or minor in any of the physical sciences.

In sum, staffing policies have clear implications for the qualifications of teachers assigned to teach the sciences. Little to no research exists on policies that can address the issues discussed here. A school system committed to the improvement of its science teacher workforce would want to attend to staffing policies as well as to recruitment, retention, and professional development.

Teacher Evaluation

Although not always aligned with instructional policies, teacher evaluation is becoming increasingly salient as a lever for teacher development. Notably, the federal Race to the Top initiative provided incentives for states to seek ways of tying teacher evaluations more closely to student learning (Institute of Education Sciences, 2014). The initiative promoted teacher evaluation policies that call for multiple measures and multiple rating categories, which could help provide more valid and reliable measures of teacher quality. Many states responded to the initiative, instituting new teacher evaluation systems that include teachers and school leaders making plans for teacher learning over the course of the year, repeated observations of teachers' practice, and the gathering of evidence of student learning through standardized tests.

Two genres of teacher evaluation have emerged out of the renewed interest in this area: value-added measurement and standards-based observations (Milanowski, 2004; Papay, 2012). The former calculates a teacher's effectiveness based on student standardized achievement scores. However, the American Statistical Association (2014) has concluded that value-added measurement is inappropriate for the purpose of teacher evaluation, and it was beyond the scope of this study to explore the challenges associated with using this approach to determine teacher quality. We note, however, the importance of the linkages between teacher evaluation policies and teacher hiring, retention, and assignment policies, as well as student accountability policies.

Standards-based teacher evaluation entails a school district developing instructional standards, a rubric and evaluation process for comparing teachers' practice with those standards, and feedback to teachers about how their practice aligns with the norms established in the standards

(Danielson and McGreal, 2000). It also entails the collection of considerable information, including multiple observations and student work
samples. It is this second form of teacher evaluation that holds the most
promise for helping teachers improve, as value-added assessments do not
provide information on practice (Hill and Grossman, 2013).

Teacher evaluation policies can be positive. For example, some
schools are using systems that encourage teachers to embrace teacher
evaluation as a way to shape their own learning opportunities. In other
contexts, however, punitive consequences are emphasized, and teachers
must undergo mandatory experiences that may or may not improve their
practice. In some schools, curricular and assessment reforms are aligned
with teacher evaluation, with the evaluations using metrics that align with
curricular guidance concerning what science instruction should focus
on and look like. When schools are organized in ways that support all
teachers in continually working to improve their practice, teacher evaluations can be used to highlight teachers' learning needs in a positive way,
thus supporting a generative learning environment for teachers. Yet this,
unfortunately, is not the mainstream experience of most U.S. teachers.

Partnerships

Partnerships between outside organizations and schools and districts
can be mechanisms for enhancing professional capacity in science. Such
partnerships can take many forms: universities can partner with schools,
school districts can partner with each other, scientific and cultural/infor-
mal institutions can partner with schools and districts, scientific societies
and professional organizations can partner with educators.

One kind of partnership entails opportunities for teachers to collaborate with practicing scientists in industry or in cultural institutions,
whether through summer research experiences working with scientists
or professional development programs designed to support the development of science teachers' content knowledge and pedagogical content
knowledge. Research laboratories and cultural institutions across the
United States offer such programs. For example, the Teacher Research
Academy at the Lawrence Livermore National Laboratory offers middle
school, high school, and community college faculty five levels of professional development, including learning about research design from practicing scientists, participating in research projects, and receiving extensive
exposure to content knowledge and instructional activities designed to
engage middle and high school students in active learning. Science teachers in Seattle can spend 9 weeks in the summer conducting research at the
Fred Hutchinson Cancer Research Center. Since 1990, the National Oce-
anic and Atmospheric Administration's (NOAA) has offered its Teacher

at Sea Program through which teachers have real-world research experience working at sea with NOAA scientists and crews.[1] Collaboration and networks outside of a school may be especially important at the elementary level, where, as noted throughout this report, individuals with deep science expertise may be lacking. Many of these programs include program evaluations. However, while the evaluations offer rich detail about the programs, they tend to focus on participant satisfaction and do not include the use of rigorous methods for assessing teacher learning. Thus, little is known about how these experiences shape individual and collective teacher knowledge and practice, or student learning.

Urban Advantage (UA) is a partnership between the New York City Public Schools and informal science education institutions located across New York City. Currently in its eleventh year, UA works with one in three middle schools in the city. In the 2014-2015 school year, the program served 222 schools, 643 middle school science teachers, and 62,504 public school students across the five boroughs. This program was initially developed to address a school district requirement that every 8th-grade student complete a long-term science investigation before moving on to high school but has grown to include 6th- and 7th-grade science teachers as well. UA's core mission is to build teachers', students', administrators', and parents' understanding of scientific inquiry and investigation by providing teachers with professional development, parents and teachers with access to cultural institutions, and principals with insight into the program's content and character. An evaluation of the program indicates that attending a UA school increases student performance on the New York State 8th-grade science assessment (Weinstein et al., 2014).

UA is unusual in that the focus of the partnership was determined by the school district's identifying a curricular need that the informal science community in New York City then built a program with resources and support to address. Often, formal/informal partnerships are initiated by the informal community, which develops resources and professional development opportunities for schools and districts that may not be designed specifically to meet specific curricular needs. While such resources can play important roles for schools and districts, UA represents a new kind of collaborative partnership between formal and informal institutions in which cultural institutions and schools create materials together.

Another partnership of note is the Merck Institute for Science Education (MISE). Launched in 1992, MISE worked with four partner school districts (three in New Jersey, one in Pennsylvania). It helped school

---

[1]See https://www.science.gov/internships/k-12.html [November 2015] for a listing of some of these opportunities.

districts select curricular materials and collaborated in the development and implementation of professional development, which included teacher leader development and peer teacher workshops. Over the course of the partnership, the partner districts drafted science curriculum frameworks that aligned with state and national standards and sought out assessments that were aligned with the new frameworks, and teachers were supported as they took on new roles as advocates, coaches, and lead teachers. The partners co-planned and offered conferences designed to address the felt needs of the schools and to build the capacity of principals, teachers, and central administrators to offer high-quality science instruction to all students. Annual evaluations suggested that the investment paid off in improved teacher knowledge and practice (Corcoran et al., 2003). Classroom observations and interviews with teachers also indicated that student performance changed in positive directions. In addition to these results, the partnership led to some insights relevant to the present study. These include the crucial role of a shared vision of instruction, a deep respect for teachers and knowledge of teaching, a conception of professional development as a continuous process, the ongoing support of principals, and high-quality curriculum materials and aligned assessment (Corcoran et al., 2003).

COHERENT INSTRUCTIONAL GUIDANCE

Teachers are eager to pick up new practices from their professional learning experiences. However, they often lack the guidance and opportunities they need to adapt those new practices to different conditions. As a result, they may patch new practices onto old ones or adopt the most superficial aspects of a practice (Cohen, 1990). Bryk and colleagues (2010) identify instructional guidance as one of the core supports needed for successful school reform, as do Rowan and colleagues (2009) and Cohen and colleagues (2013). At least three elements of instructional guidance are relevant:

- the curriculum organization, that is, the arrangement of subject matter content and pacing over time and grades;
- the intellectual depth expected of students when they engage in the subject matter, as reflected in their learning tasks; and
- the pedagogical strategies, tools, and materials made available to teachers to support students and the expectations for teachers' role in the classroom.

Beyond these aspects of instructional guidance are other relevant and linked policies, including student accountability and teacher evaluation.

The science standards adopted by the state provide some guidance on curriculum organization. However, those standards become operational as teachers and instructional leaders learn about them and use them to guide discussion about the adequacy of their current approach to science instruction, as well as to organize efforts to improve instruction (Bryk et al., 2010). The new vision for science education calls for an approach to instruction that engages students in scientific and engineering practices and requires a more sophisticated engagement with science content relative to previous standards. Making this shift will require most teachers to change their approaches to instruction substantially, and they will need to see examples of these new approaches in action, receive guidance on the new expectations, have opportunities to reflect on their own pedagogy, and collaborate with curriculum developers and others in realizing the new vision in concrete ways for classrooms (see Box 8-1 for an example of a program designed to support teachers in this way).

The committee considered available research concerning two aspects of instructional guidance: curriculum materials and their potential to support teacher learning and assessment and accountability policies and practices.

Curriculum Materials

Curriculum materials—the resources that teachers use with their students—also can provide opportunities for teacher learning, and there has been increasing interest in designing these materials in ways that support the learning of both students and their teachers. Schools and districts play an important role in providing curriculum materials in science.

Teachers' use of and learning from text-based curriculum materials depend not only on the characteristics of the materials but also on the type of teaching activity in which a teacher is engaged, the teacher's persistence or lack thereof in reading the materials over time, what the teacher chooses to read or ignore, the teacher's own knowledge and beliefs (e.g., about content, learners, learning, teaching, and curriculum materials), how those beliefs are aligned with the goals of the curriculum, and the teacher's disposition toward reflective practice (Collopy, 2003; Remillard, 2005; Schneider and Krajcik, 2002). These factors interact in a complex and dynamic way (Lloyd, 1999) as teachers interpret the materials and shape the enacted curriculum (Clandinin and Connelly, 1991; see also Brown, 2009).

Researchers have suggested a variety of features that can make curriculum materials more supportive of teachers' learning (see Box 8-2 for an example). Some argue that it is important to provide teachers with rationales for the instructional approaches included in a curriculum, as

---

BOX 8-1
Next Generation Science Exemplar
Professional Learning System (NGSX)

The Next Generation Science Exemplar Professional Learning System (NGSX) is a program aimed at supporting teachers as they work to implement the NGSS. NGSX offers a blended model for science educators, including K-12 teachers, informal science institutions, and teacher education faculty.

As a blended model, NGSX has a high-functioning online platform that provides a curriculum or "pathway" of resources, video images, and tasks for study group participants. The other half of this blended model is a face-to-face component whereby science educators work as adult learners as part of an 18- to 22-member study group using all the functionality and resources provided by the NGSX web platform. In this process, NGSX study group participants work with the help of a skilled facilitator in moving through the curricular units that constitute a particular progression for students, watching and analyzing video-based classroom cases that show students and teachers working together to develop, apply, and refine their understanding of core practices. Likewise, challenges are posed in this pathway for study group participants, who are asked to work with a science phenomenon and engage in modeling as they build a "case" or an argument for their understanding of that phenomenon.

NGSX is designed around five research-based principles for professional development:

- organized around teaching sense making of classroom cases;
- focuses on high-leverage teaching practices;
- organizes teacher study groups that work to apply reforms to their own practice;
- combines a focus on science, student thinking, and pedagogy; and
- develops capacity for teacher leaders.

---

this allows them to transfer what they learn when teaching one unit to subsequent units (Ball and Cohen, 1996; Beyer and Davis, 2012a, 2012b; Davis and Krajcik, 2005). In particular, narratives describing how other teachers have taught lessons and why they made certain adaptations appear to help motivate teachers to read educative curriculum materials and envision lessons (Beyer and Davis, 2012b). Teachers draw in similar ways on other educative features of curriculum materials that also provide representations of the work of teaching (e.g., rubrics with examples of student work and sample teacher comments) (Arias et al., in press), and of students' work (Bismack et al., 2015). For instance, when teachers used educative rubrics that highlighted important characteristics of a scientific practice, such as making and recording observations of a natural phenomenon, the written and drawn observations of the teachers' elementary students tended to reflect those characteristics. This finding suggests that educative curriculum materials intended to support teachers in learning to engage students meaningfully in scientific practice integrated with science content can help them begin to do so.

Some evidence shows that teachers learn from curriculum materials. Schneider and Krajcik (2002) found that teachers read, understood, and adopted ideas from the subject matter supports in the curriculum materials they were using, in addition to learning subject matter from the descriptions of students' alternative ideas. Wyner (2013) found that teachers who enacted a high school curriculum program emphasizing data analysis and media on science research developed more positive orientations toward using those approaches in their teaching. Beyer and Davis (2012a, 2012b) found that when preservice elementary teachers used science curriculum materials in conjunction with teacher education instructional experiences intended to support them, they were able to develop both pedagogical content knowledge and pedagogical design capacity. For example, they came to develop more robust and sophisticated repertoires of criteria they could use in considering changes they should make to curriculum materials for their classrooms.

Some evidence also suggests that teachers' instructional practices in science can be shaped by their use of curriculum materials. For example, Cervetti and colleagues (2015) compared two groups of teachers. One group had access to a version of science curriculum materials with educative features intended to support them in using instructional strategies effective with English language learners. The other group used the same curriculum materials without the educative features. These authors found that teachers who had access to the educative curriculum materials used more strategies to support English language learners and used a wider range of strategies. Similarly, Enfield and colleagues (2008) found that curriculum materials could support changes in teachers' engagement of elementary students in epistemic practices. Furthermore, teachers' uptake of ideas embedded in curriculum materials concerning ambitious science teaching can be associated with stronger student learning outcomes relative to those achieved by teachers whose enactments align less well with ideas in reform-oriented curriculum materials (McNeill, 2009). Other work, however, suggests how challenging it can be for such change to happen (e.g., Alozie et al., 2010; Zangori et al., 2013), reinforcing the need for multiple levers working toward change.

The majority of elementary teachers have access to curriculum materials that are unlikely to be educative for them (Banilower et al., 2013). Furthermore, typical science textbooks for high school tend not to be highly supportive of teachers' learning (Beyer et al., 2009), although there are a few exceptions. Even curriculum materials that are not particularly

---

BOX 8-2
Developing Educative Curriculum

Davis and Krajcik (2005) provide guidance for developing educative curriculum materials that are informed by research on teacher learning in science. According to their guidelines, which built on the existing literature (e.g., Ball and Cohen, 1996; Heaton, 2000; Remillard, 2000; Schneider and Krajcik, 2002), educative curriculum materials could

- help teachers learn how to anticipate and interpret what learners may think about or do in response to instructional activities;
- support teachers' learning of subject matter;
- help teachers consider ways to relate units during the year;
- make the developers' pedagogical judgment visible; and
- promote a teacher's pedagogical design capacity (Brown, 2009)—that is, his or her ability to use personal resources and the supports embedded in curriculum materials (i.e., the curricular resources) to adapt curriculum to achieve productive instructional ends.

Working from these guidelines, Davis and Krajcik (2005) articulate a set of heuristics for designing educative science curriculum materials, with examples. Educative curriculum materials should support teachers in

- engaging students with topic-specific scientific phenomena;
- using scientific instructional representations;
- anticipating, understanding, and working with students' ideas about science;
- engaging students in questions;

---

educative for teachers, though, play important roles in shaping students' opportunities to learn.

Curriculum materials, particularly those designed to be educative for teachers, can provide a direct point of leverage for moving toward alignment of students' opportunities to learn with the Framework and NGSS (see Chapter 5 for additional discussion). To serve this function, the curriculum materials also need to be aligned with the Framework and NGSS so as to provide grade level-appropriate opportunities to learn that accord with specific standards. They need to be coherent and driven by learning goals, provide opportunities for students' investigations and support discourse and elicitation of students' ideas.

Experienced teachers are also central collaborators in the design of new curricula (e.g., Connelly and Ben-Peretz, 1997; Gunckel and Moore, 2005; Remillard, 2005). Ben-Chaim and colleagues (1994) argued that successful implementation of new curricula requires "full active participation

- engaging students in collecting and analyzing data;
- engaging students in designing investigations;
- engaging students in making explanations based on evidence;
- promoting scientific communication; and
- developing subject matter knowledge.

For example, Davis and Krajcik (2005) make the following recommendation for supporting teachers in engaging students in making explanations based on evidence:

> Curriculum materials should provide clear recommendations for how teachers can support students in making sense of data and generating explanations based on evidence that the students have collected and justified by scientific principles that they have learned. The supports should include rationales for why engaging students in explanation is important in scientific inquiry and why these particular approaches for doing so are scientifically and pedagogically appropriate. (p. 11)

Davis and colleagues (2014) updated and built on these design heuristics by proposing a theoretically and empirically informed design process for educative curriculum materials. They recommend a process that entails analyzing existing curriculum materials, describing teachers' enactment through pilot observations to characterize students' opportunities to learn, and assessing students' learning outcomes, and then combining this empirical work with the field's theoretical understandings of teaching and learning and with the recommendations in the design heuristics. Through this process, teachers can be better supported in meeting reform expectations such as the three-dimensional learning associated with the NGSS vision for science education.

of the teachers involved in the decision-making process associated with the curriculum reform" (p. 365). Parke and Coble (1997) studied the effects of collaborations between teachers and curriculum specialists charged with creating new middle-grade science curriculum in North Carolina. Teachers in six schools who participated in the collaboration reported that they wanted students to develop hypotheses, design experiments, and collect, analyze, and report data. Their goals included having students make connections between concepts, achieve content mastery, and engage productively in laboratory and cooperative work. Teachers in six additional schools who were part of a control group reported using more traditional science teaching methods, including the memorization of facts and terminology and a focus on "the scientific method." While there were significant differences in how teachers conceptualized effective science instruction, there were no statistical differences in the performance of students in the experimental and control schools on the state science tests, which were aligned with state standards that had been developed in 1960.

As the major resource teachers use in their practice, curricula play an important role in teachers' lives. The effects of schools and districts plan programs for building teacher capacity will be enhanced by considering the varied roles that creating and learning from curricula could play.

Assessment and Accountability

Accountability policies are another important part of the instructional guidance system. In every state and district, science standards, science curriculum frameworks, and science requirements (including testing requirements) exist alongside those for other subjects. Since 2002, the No Child Left Behind Act has mandated that students in grades 3-8 be tested annually and that states demonstrate adequate yearly progress in raising test scores. The law gives priority to mathematics and English language arts, subjects that make up the bulk of states' accountability formulas. As a result, especially in elementary schools, testing pressures in mathematics and English language arts have largely squeezed science out of the curriculum (Banilower et al., 2013). Nationally, elementary students have had fewer opportunities to experience sound science instruction relative to students at other levels, and their teachers report feeling inadequately prepared for and supported in teaching science (Banilower et al., 2013; Dorph et al., 2007, 2011; Smith et al., 2002; see further discussion in Chapter 2). Even at the high school level, where science enjoys a relatively secure position, federal and state accountability metrics generally weigh performance in mathematics and English language arts more heavily than performance in science. In California, for example, the state's Academic Performance Index accords nearly 86 percent of the weight to mathematics and English language arts and only about 7 percent to science (Hatry et al., 2012).

Assessment can play important formative roles, as well as summative, accountability roles. The learning and assessment tasks in which students engage are a key part of the instructional guidance system (Bryk et al., 2010). Classroom assessments include formative tasks that can inform future instruction and summative tasks that are designed to assign students grades or scores. Assessment tasks designed for the NGSS will need to combine all three dimensions (scientific practices, disciplinary core ideas, and crosscutting concepts) into performances that require students to use their knowledge as they engage in practices (National Research Council, 2014). A recent report from the National Research Council (2014) recommends that tasks designed to assess the performance expectations in the NGSS:

- include multiple components that reflect the connected use of different scientific practices in the context of interconnected disciplinary core ideas and crosscutting concepts;
- address the progressive nature of learning by providing information about where students fall on a continuum between expected beginning and ending points in a given unit or grade; and
- include an interpretive system for evaluating a range of student products that are specific enough to be useful for helping teachers understand the range of student responses and provide tools for helping teachers decide on next steps in instruction.

These recommendations accord with current research on formative assessment more generally (e.g., Stiggins, 2005; Stiggins and Conklin, 1992; Wiliam, 2011). Teachers design and develop their own assessments to help them better understand what students are learning so they can adjust instruction. Teachers also use assessments to enable learning, encouraging students to synthesize and extend their learning. During the course of instruction, for example, students need opportunities to use multiple practices in developing a particular core idea and to apply each practice in the context of multiple core ideas. Effective use of the practices often requires that they be used in concert with one another. Many of the tasks designed for supporting students' learning will also provide assessment information, but teachers will need support to learn how to gather information from these tasks.

Formative and summative assessments produce information about student performance that requires interpretation and professional judgment (e.g., Popham, 2003, 2007). Teachers understand the difference between measuring something and interpreting the evidence, and the role of professional judgment in all formative and summative assessments. Notably, teachers increasingly need to analyze data produced by district- and state-wide testing programs, a task that calls for "data literacy" (Mandinach and Gummer, 2013; Mandinach and Honey, 2008). Teachers not only need to make sense of data on student performance but also need to evaluate the technical quality and relevance of the information collected (e.g., American Federation of Teachers et al., 1990; National Research Council, 2001). For summative assessments, teachers need to apply basic statistical concepts including variability, correlation, percentiles, norming, and combining scores for grading, to engage in the systematic analysis of evidence in technically sound and professionally responsible ways (Sykes and Wilson, 2015). District and school policies and practices associated with assessment and accountability can enable or restrain the ongoing development of teachers' data literacy.

LEADERSHIP

Over the last 20-30 years of education research, the role of leadership, particularly the role of the principal in effecting school-level change, has emerged as particularly important to education reform efforts (e.g., Hallinger and Heck, 1998; Ladd, 2009; Leithwood et al., 2004; Louis et al., 2010; Roehrig et al., 2007; Spillane and Diamond, 2007; Wahlstrom, 2008). They key role of the principal in supporting teachers' learning in science is clear in the literature reviewed in the previous two chapters. Teacher leaders have important roles to play as well.

Principals

In a study of reform in Chicago public schools by Bryk and colleagues (2010), leadership is identified as one of the core supports necessary for changes in students' achievement. In their analysis, the authors focus on principals as the key leaders in schools and describe three dimensions of a principal's leadership. The most basic of these is the managerial dimension, which includes a well-run school office, a regular schedule, good communication with parents and staff, attention to ensuring that supplies are always available, and administrative support for new programs. Weaknesses in this dimension undermine teachers' classroom work by eroding the amount of effective instructional time and can also create a negative perception of the school. With regard to science, principals' managerial responsibilities include the scheduling of science classes and the availability of lab space and materials and supplies needed to teach the classes.

The instructional dimension of school leadership is crucial to reform. This dimension includes deliberate actions by the principal to enhance instructional time and the effectiveness of instructional programs. Principals can advance student learning through initiatives aimed at building the school's professional capacity and the quality of its instructional guidance capacity. Effective instructional leadership makes broad demands on a principal's knowledge and skills with regard to both student and teacher learning. Principals must be knowledgeable about the tenets of learning theory and curriculum, and able to analyze instruction and provide effective, formative feedback to teachers. Successful leadership also entails the deliberate orchestration of people, programs, and available resources. A strategic orientation must guide these efforts so that resources (time and money) are allocated effectively to support the continuous improvement of classroom practice. With regard to science, principals' instructional responsibilities include assessing the capacity of teachers to be effective instructors in science, particularly given the demands of the NGSS, and identifying, allocating, and supporting resources for teachers' professional learning.

Finally, the inclusive-facilitative dimension refers to how principals nurture individuals and build the school's collective capacity. A key factor is the principal's ability to inspire teachers, parents, school community leaders, and students around a common vision. This role often includes ensuring that teachers have a sense of being able to influence decisions affecting their work. It may also include supporting other individuals in the school in assuming leadership roles. This latter function can be especially important in science because relatively few principals have science backgrounds, and they may need to rely on others to provide instructional leadership for science teachers. Principals' inclusive-facilitative role with respect to science also includes having and promoting a vision for science instruction and ensuring access to the expertise needed to increase the capacity of science teachers.

Teacher Leaders

Teacher leaders are central to all genuine school improvement. There is a growing sense of the urgency of developing science, technology, engineering, and mathematics (STEM) teacher leaders, as reflected in the Presidential Awards for Excellence in Mathematics and Science Teaching program and the National Science Foundation's STEM Teacher Leader Initiative. A project currently under way is analyzing existing programs that support and develop STEM master teachers.[2] The National Research Council held a convocation in 2013 to draw attention to the issue (National Research Council, 2014).

At the elementary and middle school levels, the role of teacher leaders in science may be especially important because many teachers at these levels have had insufficient preparation in the science subjects they teach (Ingersoll and Perda, 2010, see also Chapter 4). Teacher leaders may support science teachers by providing professional development, classroom support, mentoring, just-in-time help, and other means of strengthening instruction and curriculum.

Although teacher leaders play many different roles, their contribution is distinct from the work of school administrators (Neumerski, 2012; Wynne, 2001). Some teacher leaders help colleagues improve instruction (Neumerski, 2012), while others focus on more visible roles in school and system improvement (Curtis, 2013). Teacher leaders can be leaders of professional development, mentors, union representatives, academic

---

[2]See http://www.sri.com/work/projects/stem-master-teacher-leader-program-analysis-and-support [November 2015].

department chairs, coaches, or curriculum specialists, or work more infor-
mally with colleagues. They may work in multiple schools or only one,
and they may specialize in one subject or grade level or work across many
(Neumerski, 2012; York-Barr and Duke, 2004). They may conduct action
research, or collaborate with educational researchers or teacher preparation programs.

The research base on teacher leadership is not robust (Goodwin, 2013;
Neumerski, 2012; York-Barr and Duke, 2004). The majority of published
work is descriptive. The possibilities for large-scale studies have been limited by the difficulty of identifying variables that could capture as diverse
and complex a phenomenon as teacher leadership, and the committee
could find no quantitative studies focused on science teacher leadership.
Moreover, very little qualitative research has focused specifically on science teacher leaders. Indeed, reviews of research on mathematics and science teacher leadership, reveal that the majority of the published research
in this area focuses on mathematics teacher leadership or on programs
with mathematics and science teacher leaders, with reporting of results
not distinguishing between the two (see, e.g., http://www.mspkmd.net/
blasts/tl.php [November 2015]).

The few science-specific studies (e.g., Gigante and Firestone, 2008;
Larkin et al., 2009) are small scale. A number of qualitative studies also
have suggested that teacher leaders are most respected and trusted by
their colleagues when they are recognized for their subject matter and
pedagogical knowledge, and when their leadership roles are focused on
teaching and learning rather than on administrative issues (e.g., Center
for Comprehensive School Reform and Improvement, 2005).

The literature has done more to identify the characteristics of teacher
leaders than to describe how such teachers lead or to explore the results
of efforts to foster teacher leadership. However, a few themes, discussed
below, are evident in the research.

Roles of Teacher Leaders

Because the formal roles played by teacher leaders vary, the ways
they support other teachers also vary. When teachers function as mentors,
they may influence both their colleagues and school and district policies
(York-Barr and Duke, 2004). When they play a role in school or district
governance, they influence decisions that affect the work of other teachers. Scholars have documented numerous specific functions performed
by teacher leaders, which fall into several broad categories (Harrison and

Killion, 2007; Institute for Educational Leadership, 2008; York-Barr and Duke, 2004):[3]

- administrative tasks (e.g., coordinating schedules, providing resources);
- academic leadership (e.g., serving as curriculum specialist, mentor, instructional coach, or department leader; providing classroom support; serving as workshop leader, functioning as data specialist);
- school leadership (e.g., participating in school-wide improvement efforts or budget or other decision making; participating in hiring, teacher evaluation, or the development of professional development opportunities; participating in research; building networks inside and outside of the school); and
- contributing to the development or selection of curricula, standards, or other activities that take place beyond the school.

Teacher leaders also play less formal roles, which are even less well studied than the formal roles discussed above. York-Barr and Duke (2004) report that case studies have supported the idea that teachers may be highly influential without having assigned roles that impose hierarchical relationships, and even that all teachers may think of their professional responsibilities as including collaboration with other teachers in examining their instructional practices and their effectiveness. A study of "extraordinary" teachers, for example, suggests that many exert influence through their actions and attitudes; a number of studies identify collaboration and the establishment of professional networks as principal modes of influence (Fairman and Mackenzie, 2014; York-Barr and Duke, 2004). However, the authors caution that other studies suggest there are discrepancies between what teacher leaders report doing and what their colleagues perceive they have done.

While the literature does not provide a detailed understanding of how teacher leaders interact with their colleagues or which leadership activities are most effective (and under what conditions), it does clearly suggest that the objectives for teacher leadership are "not about 'teacher power,'" but about using collaborative and collegial relationships to harness experienced teachers' skills and attributes (Institute for Educational Leadership, 2008). A consortium of educators, teacher leaders, state education agencies, education organizations, and scholars developed a set of

---

[3]See http://www.mspkmd.net/blasts/tl.php [April 2014] for a series of brief synopses of research on some of the practices of teacher leadership collected by the Math and Science Partnership, a project of the National Science Foundation.

recommendations to guide teacher leaders (Teacher Leader Exploratory Consortium, 2010). Based on research and practice, these recommendations reflect both the consortium's findings with respect to what teacher leaders do and its goals for the future. The consortium identified seven key contributions teacher leaders can make (p. 9):

- fostering a collaborative culture,
- assessing and using research,
- promoting professional learning,
- facilitating improvements in instruction and student learning,
- promoting the use of assessments and data for school and district improvement,
- improving outreach and collaboration with families and community, and
- advocating for student learning and the profession.

The Importance of Context

The roles played by teacher leaders are influenced by the contexts in which they work. District and school policies and the ways they are implemented may foster or undermine the development of the professional learning communities that have been identified as most likely to benefit from teacher leaders, but the research literature focuses on the school and the actions and attitudes of principals (Coburn and Lin, 2008).

Qualitative studies of the factors that promote teacher leadership suggest that school culture is important, and that schools in which openness and collaboration are the norm are more hospitable to the development of teacher leaders and the success of leadership programs relative to other schools (Birky et al., 2006; Institute for Educational Leadership, 2008; Muijs and Harris, 2007; Wynne, 2001; York-Barr and Duke, 2004). This literature suggests that leaders may thrive and be most effective in schools in which collective learning and continuous improvement are paramount. Observations from practice also emphasize the importance of encouragement from administrators and an atmosphere in which risk taking is encouraged (Danielson, 2007). However, researchers also note that U.S. teachers have tended to adopt an independent and egalitarian approach to their work, and that both of these tendencies can be obstacles to teacher leadership (Natale et al., 2013; Wynne, 2001).

More recent work has focused on the concept of "distributed leadership," a way of taking into account the roles of the multiple individuals who contribute to leadership within a school (Spillane and Diamond, 2007; Supovitz and Riggan, 2012). A survey of the literature on principal, teacher, and instructional coach leadership, for example, points out that although these three types of leaders have been addressed separately by researchers, they work together in practice and influence one another (Goodwin, 2008; Neumerski, 2012). A related idea is that all teachers can benefit from the opportunity to specialize according to their interests and expertise, and to share their expertise in particular areas with others (Natale et al., 2013).

Relationships with colleagues and principals also are cited as important in case studies of teacher leadership programs (York-Barr and Duke, 2004). Factors identified as likely to contribute to the effectiveness of teacher leader arrangements include support and encouragement from principals, and colleagues who respect teacher leaders for their expertise in the subject they teach and in pedagogy. Case studies suggest that, in addition to promoting a favorable school culture, principals can encourage teacher leadership by, for example, creating opportunities for leadership, trusting teachers to make decisions, and relinquishing authority (Center for Comprehensive School Reform and Improvement, 2005; Neumerski, 2012). However, survey results suggest that principals may not always have the knowledge and experience to encourage teacher leaders in these ways, despite having the intention to do so. Theoretical analysis of school governance and leadership relationships reinforces this point, as several authors note that traditional hierarchical organizational structures hamper effective teacher leadership (Neumerski, 2012; York-Barr and Duke, 2004).

Cultivating Teacher Leaders

The literature provides some insights into policies and approaches that can promote the development of school leaders on a broader scale. The limited evidence on the role of school and district policies that specifically promote teacher leadership appears to suggest that school-level policies have a greater impact than district ones (e.g., Coburn and Lin, 2008). At the same time, qualitative studies indicate that formal preservice and professional development for teachers and principals is important (Parise and Spillane, 2010; York-Barr and Duke, 2004). Specifically, studies suggest that the development of leadership may be supported by programs that encourage all educators to view principals as leaders whose job is to develop a community of leaders and that encourage teachers to view continuous learning and leadership as integral aspects of their careers. Qualitative research points to positive results from school-based seminar sequences, master's programs for experienced teachers, and preservice programs with teacher leadership as a theme, for example. Most important, the literature suggests, is for the training to occur in the context of a learning community of either other aspiring teachers or school colleagues.

A survey of teachers recognized as leaders (Dozier, 2007) found that they engage in multiple leadership activities, such as providing professional development, serving as department or grade-level chairs, mentoring new teachers, and participating in curriculum development. These teachers report that they are eager to take on leadership activities but that they have not been trained adequately for most of these roles.

Well-documented stresses and frustrations experienced by teachers, including low pay and status compared with other careers, have led states to experiment with various ways to provide tiered licenses and compensation and other structures designed to reward teachers who want to assume responsibilities beyond their classrooms (Natale et al., 2013). Research on these programs has not clearly identified the most effective means of addressing these persistent problems, and many such programs have been discontinued, but states continue to pursue a variety of approaches.

Summary

Context shapes teaching and learning. The cultures of schools and districts, the roles assigned to teachers, and the opportunities teachers have to continue growing vary across districts, states, and school networks. In the last 20 years, opportunities for teachers to take on new responsibilities—including helping to induct new teachers into the workforce, participating in school reform, and assisting directly in supporting school-wide instructional improvement—have grown. These opportunities are themselves dependent on policies and practices related to school staffing, teacher development, how teachers are organized to work on instruction, and how decisions are made about curriculum and instruction. Research on how and under what conditions principals and leaders affect the quality of science learning in their schools has yet to be conducted. Also lacking in the research literature are studies of how teachers learn to become leaders. Formal degree programs in teacher leadership are growing in popularity; an informal review of schools of education identified more than 60 such programs (Editorial Projects in Education, 2012). The author of that review notes that the nature of these programs appears to vary, and that the degree may not be widely recognized by districts. There is, moreover, little research on these relatively new programs, and even less on how teachers learn to lead over the course of their careers outside of official programs.

TIME AND FUNDING

Regardless of the policy priorities of a state or district, the successful implementation of those priorities depends on the availability of resources—human (e.g., knowledgeable personnel), social (e.g., teacher networks), and physical (e.g., time, money, materials) (Cohen et al., 1999, 2003). In recent years, state departments of education, district or county offices of education, and intermediary units have been decimated, significantly reducing the curricular and instructional expertise available to teachers in all subjects. As one example, funding for the state-wide California Science Project declined from more than $9 million in 2002 to $1.2 million in 2011 (Hatry et al., 2012). Although funding from the Department of Education's Race to the Top initiative has ameliorated this problem in some states and districts that have been awarded these competitive funds, only a few of those efforts have focused on science, and this funding initiative is not permanent.

Most science teachers have access to certain basic materials and equipment, but more sophisticated science learning technologies are more likely to be present in high schools than in elementary schools (Banilower et al., 2013). At the same time, these resources are not always distributed equitably. Classes composed of mostly high-achieving students are more likely than those composed of mixed or low-achieving students to have access to microscopes and graphing calculators. The amount of money schools report spending per pupil for science instruction is quite small, especially in the elementary grades, where median per-pupil spending is half that in middle schools and less than one-third that in high schools. Elementary science teachers are less likely than their middle and high school counterparts to view their resources as adequate.

This lack of funding and other resources limits effective science teaching (or any science teaching at all) and confounds attempts to improve practice over time in myriad ways. For example, teachers need time to revise their curricula, adopt new materials, plan lessons using those new materials, and collaborate on learning from their experience as they try the new materials out. Yet time is precious, and many schools are not organized to support and enable this kind of ongoing professional work. Despite a range of examples from international comparisons that provide models for how teaching and schools might be organized differently so as to support the ongoing learning of teachers, U.S. schools tend to adhere to a set of basic instructional values, routines, and roles for educators that have typified schooling for the past century (Cuban, 1984, 1994, 1998; Spillane et al., 2002; Tyack and Tobin, 1994). Of particular importance to successful reform is creating the expectation that teachers will work collectively on the improvement of instruction, as well as adding personnel trained in supporting teachers' learning and in materials development. Research on the reform of instruction in mathematics and language arts has demonstrated that coaches, mentors, and school leaders are needed to work alongside teachers while they experiment and adapt to the new standards and assessments (e.g., Desimone, 2002; Gamoran et al., 2003).

The new vision of science teaching also requires new material resources, including equipment and materials for engaging in science practices and new organizational arrangements for teaching, including collaborative arrangements with museums and businesses. These materials need not be expensive, as teachers can use ordinary materials in many ways to do extraordinary things in their classrooms.

The lack of adequate resources has especially affected elementary science education. According to a state-wide survey of elementary science in California (Dorph et al., 2011), the average elementary teacher in that state is unlikely to enjoy any meaningful support from science specialists employed at the district level. At the time of that study, fewer than 40 percent of school districts employed any staff dedicated to elementary science. Other resource-related factors that affect the amount and quality of science teaching at the elementary level include the elimination of lead science teachers; frequent reassignment of teachers to new grade levels; and inadequate access to instructional materials, including a lack of science textbooks or other supporting materials (Dorph et al., 2011, p. 12).

A similar lack of resources, combined with structural issues, poses challenges at the middle school level. Students with no prior experience in science, growing class sizes, and 55-minute class periods limit the feasibility of engaging students in science investigations.

Offering the wide array of mechanisms needed to support teacher learning—study groups, professional cultures of learning, coaches and mentors, partnerships with museums or industry—requires time and funding. Making these resources available will in turn require revising school schedules and staffing patterns to free up time for collaboration and ensure that teachers with expertise in science and science pedagogy can serve as resources for science teachers. In conjunction with providing time and rethinking scheduling, some targeted funding will be necessary. Districts often have difficulty tracking all of the funds spent on professional development for teachers in general and find it even more challenging to break out the funding targeted at a specific discipline. Across the country, the lack of resources has eroded the infrastructure for helping science teachers meet the curricular and instructional challenges of teaching science well. As a possible indication of this erosion, fewer than half of the science teachers responding to the 2012 National Survey of Science and Mathematics Education (NSSME) (44 percent) had attended any form of national, regional, or state conference or meeting, and few had attended more than 35 hours of any form of professional development over the 3 years prior to the survey (Banilower et al., 2013). Thus, teachers currently do not have extensive opportunities to participate in professional development that is science specific.

Education Resource Strategies (2013) worked with three districts to analyze spending on professional growth and support for teachers across all subject areas, identifying six areas of financial cost:

- direct professional growth (training, conferences, coaching, expert support, and substitute coverage);
- the percentage of salary teachers spend on professional growth, as stipulated in the teacher union contract or calendar or otherwise mandated for use for staff development;
- salary for education credits, which includes the increase in teacher salary that comes with participation in programs for professional growth;
- curriculum development and support, which includes staff, stipends, and contracts aimed at developing and writing curriculum, as well as ongoing payments for instructional management or guidance systems;
- teacher evaluation, which includes staff and contractors who administer an evaluation system, as well as quantification of the cost of staff time or positions for those who observe teachers and document and rate teacher performance; and
- student assessment, which includes spending on both end-of-year testing and ongoing or formative assessments administered by the school system.

Based on this analysis, Education Resource Strategies identified six steps to a more powerful school system strategy for professional growth:

- Quantify current spending on the universe of teacher professional growth and support.
- Capitalize on mandates and growing investments in standards (e.g., the NGSS and the Framework), student assessment systems, and teacher evaluation to create integrated systems for teacher growth.
- Leverage expert support to guide teacher teams that share instructional content.
- Support growth throughout a teacher's career by restructuring compensation and career paths.
- Add and optimize time to address organizational priorities as well as individual needs.
- Overhaul legacy policies, and make strategic tradeoffs.

CONCLUSIONS

While discussing all possible strategies that researchers have used to improve the cultures and contexts of instruction is beyond the scope of this study, the committee's hope is that the discussion in this chapter makes clear how context indeed matters. If science teachers are to embrace the challenging new vision of science learning described in this report, they will need to be part of larger communities of learning that respect their needs and provide necessary supports; they will need to understand the vision, both as it is laid out in such documents as the Framework and the NGSS and as it is embodied in new curricula and assessments. They will need to be supported by their principals and by colleagues who have learned to lead.

Other factors may matter as well. For example, policies concerning teacher evaluation likely will need to be aligned with the new vision of science learning (Hill and Grossman, 2013)—terrain yet to be researched. Other frequently proposed policy initiatives include differentiated pay for science teachers (as they are in a high-demand area) and incentives in performance pay systems that reward teachers for their classroom practice and often for their participation in official learning opportunities offered by their school systems. Given the impassioned interest in raising teacher quality in this country, there is no lack of intriguing initiatives. But research conducted to date has not produced definitive results on many of these singular ideas, suggesting that the observations of Bryk and colleagues (2010), Rowan and colleagues (2009) and others—that successful reform needs to address simultaneously several aspects of the education system—are worth heeding.

> *Conclusion 9:* Science teachers' development is best understood as long term and contextualized. The schools and classrooms in which teachers work shape what and how they learn. These contexts include, but are not limited to school, district, and state policies and practices concerning professional capacity (e.g., professional networks, coaching, partnerships), coherent instructional guidance (e.g., state and district curriculum and assessment/accountability policies), and leadership (e.g., principals and teacher leaders).

> *Conclusion 10:* School and district administrators are central to building the capacity of the science teacher workforce.

Conditions in schools can create contexts that allow teachers to take better advantage of professional learning opportunities both within the workday and outside of the school. Administrators can direct resources toward science and teachers' learning in science (location of teachers, scheduling of classes, materials budget). They also can send messages about the importance of science in schools. As instructional leaders, they need to understand the vision for science education in the Framework and NGSS and align policies and practices in the school to support this vision.

Conclusion 11: *Teacher leaders may be an important resource for building a system that can support ambitious science instruction. There is increasing attention to creating opportunities for teachers to take on leadership roles to both improve science instruction and strengthen the science teacher workforce. These include roles as instructional coaches, mentors, and teacher leaders.*

Expertise in both science and pedagogy in science is an important component of building capacity in schools and districts. The development of science teacher leaders can be an important mechanism for supporting science learning for all teachers. Such leaders can guide school- or district-based professional learning communities, identify useful resources, and provide feedback to teachers as they modify their instructional practice.

REFERENCES

Alozie, N., Moje, E., and Krajcik, J. (2010). An analysis of the supports and constraints for scientific discussion in high school project-based science. *Science Education, 94*(3), 395-427.

American Federation of Teachers, National Council on Measurements in Education, and National Education Association. (1990). Standards for teacher competence in educational assessment of students. *Educational Measurement: Issues and Practice, 9*(4), 30-32.

Arias, A., Bismack, A., Davis, E.A., and Palincsar, A.S. (in press). Interacting with a suite of educative features: Elementary science teachers' use of educative curriculum materials. *Journal of Research in Science Teaching.*

Ball, D.L., and Cohen, D.K. (1996). Reform by the book: What is—or might be—The role of curriculum materials in teacher learning and instructional reform? *Educational Researcher, 25*(9), 6-8, 14.

Banilower, E.R., Smith, P.S., Weiss, I.R., Malzahn, K.A., Campbell, K.M., and Weis, A.M. (2013). *Report of the 2012 National Survey of Science and Mathematics Education.* Chapel Hill, NC: Horizon Research.

Ben-Chaim, D., Joffe, N., and Zoller, U. (1994). Empowerment of elementary schools teachers to implement science curriculum reforms. *School Science and Mathematics, 94*(7), 355-366.

Beyer, C.J., and Davis, E.A. (2012a). Developing preservice elementary teachers' pedagogical design capacity for reform-based curriculum design. *Curriculum Inquiry, 42*(3), 386-413.

Beyer, C.J., and Davis, E.A. (2012b). Learning to critique and adapt science curriculum materials: Examining the development of preservice elementary teachers' pedagogical content knowledge. *Science Education, 96*(1), 130-157.

Beyer, C.J., Delgado, D., Davis, E.A., and Krajcik, J. (2009). Investigating teacher learning supports in high school biology curricular programs to inform the design of educative curriculum materials. *Journal of Research in Science Teaching, 46*(9), 977-998.

Birky, V.D., Shelton, M., and Headley, S. (2006). An administrator's challenge: Encouraging teachers to be leaders. *NASSP Bulletin, 90*(2), 87-101.

Bismack, A.S., Arias, A., Davis, E.A., and Palincsar, A.S. (2015). Examining student work for evidence of teacher uptake of educative curriculum materials. *Journal of Research in Science Teaching*.

Brown, M. (2009). The teacher-tool relationship: Theorizing the design and use of curriculum materials. In J.T. Remillard, B. Herbel-Eisenman, and G. Lloyd (Eds.), *Mathematics Teachers at Work: Connecting Curriculum Materials and Classroom Instruction* (pp. 17-36). New York: Routledge.

Bryk, A., Sebring, P., Allensworth, E., Suppescu, S., and Easton, J. (2010). *Organizing Schools for Improvement: Lessons from Chicago*. Chicago, IL: The University of Chicago Press.

Center for Comprehensive School Reform and Improvement. (2005). *Research Brief: What Does the Research Tell Us About Teacher Leadership?* Available: http://www.centerforcsri.org/files/Center_RB_sept05.pdf [June 2015].

Cervetti, G., Kulikowich, J., and Bravo, M. (2015). The effects of educative curriculum materials on teachers' use of instructional strategies for English language learners in science and on student learning. *Contemporary Educational Psychology, 40*, 86-98.

Clandinin, D.J., and Connelly, F.M. (1991). Personal knowledge. *The International Encyclopaedia of Curriculum* (pp. 128-131). Oxford, UK: Pergamon.

Coburn, C.E., and Russel, J.L. (2008). District policy and teachers' social networks. *Educational Evaluation and Policy Analysis, 30*(3), 203-235.

Coburn, C.E., Mata, W. and Choi, L. (2013). The embeddedness of teachers' social networks: Evidence from mathematics reform. *Sociology of Education, 86*(4), 311-342.

Cohen, D. (1990). A revolution in one classroom: The case of Mrs. Oublier. *Educational Evaluation and Policy Analysis, 12*(3), 311-329.

Cohen, D.K., and Ball, D.L. (1999). *Instruction, Capacity, and Improvement.* Philadelphia: University of Pennsylvania, Consortium for Policy Research in Education.

Cohen, D.K. and Hill, H.C. (2000). Instructional policy and classroom performance: The mathematics reform in California. *Teachers College Record, 102*(2), 294-343.

Cohen, D.K., and Hill, H.C. (2001). *Learning Policy.* New Haven, CT: Yale University Press.

Cohen, D.K., Raudenbush, S.W., and Ball, D.L. (2003). Resources, instruction and research. *Educational Evaluation and Policy Analysis, 25*(2), 1-24.

Cohen, D.K., Peurach, D.J., Glazer, J.L., Gates, K.E., and Goldin, S. (2013). *Improvement by Design: The Promise of Better Schools.* Chicago, IL: University of Chicago Press.

Collopy, R. (2003). Curriculum materials as a professional development tool: How a mathematics textbook affected two teachers' learning. *The Elementary School Journal, 103*(3), 227-311.

Connelly, F.M., and Ben-Peretz, M. (1997). Teachers, research, and curriculum development. In D.J. Flinders and S.J. Thornton (Eds.), *The Curriculum Studies Reader* (pp. 178-197). New York: Routledge.

Corcoran, T., McVay, S., and Riordan, K. (2003). *Getting It Right: The MISE Approach to Professional Development.* Philadelphia, PA: Consortium for Policy Research in Education.

Cuban, L. (1984). *How Teachers Taught: Constancy and Change in American Classrooms, 1890-1980.* Research on Teaching Monograph Series. New York: Longman. Available: http://files.eric.ed.gov/fulltext/ED383498.pdf [January 2015].

Cuban, L. (1994). The great school scam. *Education Week, 15*, 44-46.

Cuban, L. (1998). How schools change reforms: Redefining reform success and failure. *Teachers College Record, 99*(3), 453-477.

Cuban, L. (2010). *As Good As It Gets: What School Reform Brought to Austin.* Cambridge, MA: Harvard University Press.

Curtis, R. (2013). *Finding a New Way: Leveraging Teacher Leadership to Meet Unprecedented Demands.* Washington, DC: The Aspen Institute.

Cusick, P.A. (2014). The logic of the U.S. educational system and teaching. *Theory into Practice, 53*(3), 176-182.

Danielson, C. (2007). The many faces of leadership. *Educational Leadership, 65*(1), 14-19.

Danielson, C., and McGreal, T.L. (2000). *Teacher Evaluation to Enhance Professional Practice.* Princeton, NJ: Educational Testing Service, Association for Supervision and Curriculum Development.

Davis, E.A., and Krajcik, J. (2005). Designing educative curriculum materials to promote teacher learning. *Educational Researcher, 34*(3), 3-14.

Davis, E.A., Palincsar, A.S., Arias, A., Bismack, A., Marulis, L., and Iwashyna, S. (2014). Designing educative curriculum materials: A theoretically and empirically driven process. *Harvard Educational Review, 84*(1), 24-52.

Desimone, L. (2002). How can comprehensive school reform models be successfully implemented? *Review of Educational Research, 72*(3), 433-479. Available: http://rer.sagepub.com/content/72/3/433.full.pdf [January 2015].

Dorph, R., Goldstein, D., Lee, S., Lepori, K., Schneider, S., and Venkatesan, S. (2007).*The Status of Science Education in the Bay Area: Research Brief.* Berkeley: Lawrence Hall of Science, University of California. Available: http://lawrencehallofscience.org/rea/bayareastudy/pdf/final_to_print_research_brief.pdf [June 2015].

Dorph, R., Shields, P.M., Tiffany-Morales, J., Hartry, A., and McCaffrey, T. (2011). *High Hopes—Few Opportunities: The Status of Elementary Science Education in California.* Sacramento, CA: The Center for the Future of Teaching and Learning at WestEd.

Dozier, T. (2007). Turning good teachers into great leaders. *Educational Leadership, 65*(1), 54-59.

Editorial Projects in Education. (2012). *Teacher-Leadership Degree Programs Aim to Fill Career Gaps, by Anthony Rebora.* Available: http://www.edweek.org/tm/articles/2012/10/17/tl_degree_program.html [April 2014].

Education Resource Strategies. (2013). *A New Vision for Teacher Professional Growth and Support: Six Steps to a More Powerful School System Strategy.* Available: http://www.erstrategies.org/cms/files/1800-gates-pgs-white-paper.pdf [September 2014].

Enfield, M., Smith, E., and Grueber, D. (2008). "A sketch is like a sentence": Curriculum structures that support teaching epistemic practices of science. *Science Education, 92*, 608-630.

Fairman, J.C., and Mackenzie, S.V. (2014). How teacher leaders influence others and understand their leadership. *International Journal of Leadership in Education: Theory and Practice, 18*(1), 61-87.

Gamoran, A., Anderson, C.W., Quiroz, P.A., Secada, W.G., Williams, T., and Ashmann, S. (2003). *Transforming Teaching in Math and Science: How Schools and Districts Can Support Change.* New York: Teachers College Press.

Gigante, N.A., and Firestone, W.A. (2008). Administrative support and teacher leadership in schools implementing reform. *Journal of Educational Administration, 46*(3), 302-331.

Goodwin, A.L. (2008). Defining teacher quality: Is consensus possible? In M. Cochran-Smith, S. Feiman-Nemser, and D.J. McIntyre (Eds.), *Handbook of Research on Teacher Education: Enduring Questions in Changing Contexts* (3rd ed., pp. 399-403). New York: Routledge.

Goodwin, B. (2013). Research says teacher leadership: No guarantee of success. *Leveraging Teacher Leadership, 71*(2), 78-80.

Gunckel, K.L., and Moore, F.M. (2005). *Including Students and Teachers in the Co-Design of the Enacted Curriculum.* Paper Presented at the NARST 2005 Annual Meeting, Dallas, TX.

Hallinger, P., and Heck, R.H. (1998). Exploring the principal's contribution to school effectiveness: 1980-1995. *School Effectiveness and School Improvement, 9*(2), 157-191.

Harrison, C., and Killion, J. (2007). *Ten Roles for Teacher Leaders*. Available: http://www.
    ascd.org/publications/educational-leadership/sept07/vol65/num01/Ten-Roles-for-
    Teacher-Leaders.aspx [April 2014].
Hartry, A., Dorph, R., Shields, P., Tiffany-Morales, J., and Romero, V. (2012). *The Status of
    Middle School Science Education in California*. Sacramento, CA: The Center for the Future
    of Teaching and Learning at WestEd.
Heaton, R.M. (2000). *Teaching Mathematics to the New Standards: Relearning the Dance*. New
    York: Teachers College Press.
Hill, H.C., and Grossman, P. (2013). Learning from teacher evaluations: Challenges and op-
    portunities. *Harvard Education Review, 83*(2), 371-384.
Ingersoll, R.M. (2002). *Measuring Out-of-Field Teaching*. Unpublished manuscript. Graduate
    School of Education, University of Pennsylvania, Philadelphia, PA.
Ingersoll, R.M. (2003). *Out-of-Field Teaching and the Limits of Teacher Policy*. Available: https://
    depts.washington.edu/ctpmail/PDFs/LimitsPolicy-RI-09-2003.pdf [January 2015].
Ingersoll, R.M., and Perda, D. (2010). Is the supply of mathematics and science teachers suf-
    ficient? *American Educational Research Journal, 47*(3), 563-594.
Institute for Educational Leadership. (2008). *Teacher Leadership in High Schools: How Princi-
    pals Encourage It, How Teachers Practice It*. Washington, DC: Institute for Educational
    Leadership.
Institute of Education Sciences. (2014). *State Requirements for Teacher Evaluation Policies Pro-
    moted by Race to the Top*. Washington, DC: Institute of Education Sciences. Available:
    http://ies.ed.gov/ncee/pubs/20144016/pdf/20144016.pdf [January 2015].
Ladd, H. (2009). *Teachers' Perceptions of Their Working Conditions: How Predictive of Policy-
    Relevant Outcomes?* National Center for Analysis of Longitudinal Data in Education
    Research, Working Paper 33. Available: http://files.eric.ed.gov/fulltext/ED509680.
    pdf [June 2015].
Larkin, D., Seyforth, S., and Lasky, H. (2009). Implementing and sustaining science cur-
    riculum reform: A study of leadership practices among teachers within a high school
    science department. *Journal of Research in Science Teaching, 46*(7), 813-835.
Leithwood, K., Louis, K.S., Anderson, S., and Wahlstrom, K. (2004). *How Leadership Influences
    Student Learning: A Review of the Research for the Learning from Leadership Project*. New
    York: The Wallace Foundation. Available: http://www.wallacefoundation.org/knowl-
    edge-center/school-leadership/key-research/documents/how-leadership-influences-
    student-learning.pdf [June 2015].
Lloyd, G.M. (1999). Two teachers' conceptions of a reform-oriented curriculum: Implica-
    tions for mathematics teacher development. *Journal of Mathematics Teacher Education,
    2*(3), 227-252.
Louis, K.S., Leithwood, K., Wahlstrom, K.L., and Anderson, S.E. (2010). *Learning from Leader-
    ship: Investigating the Links to Improved Student Learning. Final Report of Research to the
    Wallace Foundation*. Minneapolis: University of Minnesota. Available: http://www.
    wallacefoundation.org/knowledge-center/school-leadership/key-research/
    Documents/Investigating-the-Links-to-Improved-Student-Learning.pdf [June 2015].
Mandinach, E., and Gummer, E. (2013). A systematic view of implementing data literacy in
    educator preparation. *Educational Researcher, 42*(1), 30-37.
Mandinach, E., and Honey, M. (Eds.). (2008). *Data-Driven School Improvement: Linking Data
    and Learning*. New York: Teachers College Press.
McNeill, K. (2009). Teachers' use of curriculum to support students in writing scientific
    arguments to explain phenomena. *Science Education, 93*(2), 233-268.
Milanowski, A. (2004). The relationship between teacher performance evaluation scores and
    student achievement: Evidence from Cincinnati. *Peabody Journal of Education, 79*(4),
    33-53.

Muijs, D., and Harris, A. (2007). Teacher leadership in (in)action: Three case studies of contrasting schools. *Educational Management Administration Leadership, 35*(1), 111-134.

Natale, C.F., Bassett, K., Gaddis, L. and McKnight, K. (2013). *Creating Sustainable Teacher Career Pathways: A 21st Century Imperative. A Joint Publication of Pearson and National Network of State Teachers of the Year.* Available: http://www.nnstoy.org/download/career_pathways/Final%20updated%20Research%20Report.pdf [June 2014].

National Academy of Sciences, National Academy of Engineering, and Institute of Medicine. (2010). *Rising above the Gathering Storm Revisited: Rapidly Approaching Category 5.* Washington, DC: The National Academies Press. Available: http://www.nap.edu/catalog/12999/rising-above-the-gathering-storm-revisited-rapidly-approaching-category-5 [January 2015].

National Research Council. (2001). *Knowing What Students Know: The Science and Design of Educational Assessment.* Committee on the Foundations of Assessment. J. Pelligrino, N. Chudowsky, and R. Glaser (Eds.). Board on Testing and Assessment, Center for Education. Division of Behavioral and Social Sciences Education. Washington, DC: National Academy Press.

National Research Council. (2014). *Exploring Opportunities for STEM Teacher Leadership: Summary of a Convocation.* S. Olson and J. Labov, Rapporteurs. Planning Committee on Exploring Opportunities for STEM Teacher Leadership: Summary of a Convocation, Teacher Advisory Council, Division of Behavioral and Social Sciences and Education. Washington, DC: The National Academies Press.

Neumerski, C.M. (2012). Rethinking instructional leadership: What do we know about principal, teacher, and coach instructional leadership, and where should we go from here? *Educational Administration Quarterly, 49*(2), 310-347.

Papay, J.P. (2012). Refocusing the debate: Assessing the purposes and tools of teacher evaluation. *Harvard Educational Review, 82*(1), 123-141.

Parise, L.M., and Spillane, J.P. (2010). Teacher learning and instructional change: How formal and on-the-job learning opportunities predict change in elementary school teachers' practice. *The Elementary School Journal, 100*(3), 323-346.

Parke, H.M., and Coble, C.R. (1997). Teachers designing curriculum as professional development: A model for transformational science teaching. *Journal of Research in Science Teaching, 34*(8), 773-789.

Popham, W.J. (2003). *Test Better, Teach Better: The Instructional Role of Assessment.* Alexandria, VA: ASCD.

Popham, W.J. (2007). *Classroom Assessment: What Teachers Need to Know.* Santa Monica, CA: Pearson/Allyn Bacon.

President's Council of Advisors on Science and Technology. (2010). *Prepare and Inspire: K-12 Education in Science, Technology, Engineering and Mathematics (STEM) for America's Future.* Washington, DC: White House Office of Science and Technology Policy. Available: https://www.insidehighered.com/news/2015/01/13/goucher-and-bennington-both-report-success-highly-nontraditional-admissions-options [January 2015].

Remillard, J.T. (2000). Can curriculum materials support teachers' learning? Two fourth-grade teachers' use of a new mathematics text. *The Elementary School Journal, 100*(4), 331-350.

Remillard, J.T. (2005). Examining key concepts in research on teachers' use of mathematics curricula. *Review of Educational Research, 75*(2), 211-246.

Reys, B.J., and Fennell, S. (2003) Who should lead mathematics instruction at the elementary school level? A case for mathematics specialist. *Teaching Children Mathematics, 8*, 277- 282.

Roehrig, G., Kruse, R., and Kern, A. (2007). Teacher and school characteristics and their influence on curriculum implementation. *Journal of Research in Science Teaching, 44*(7), 883-907.

Rowan, B., Corenti, R., Miller, R., and Camburn, E. (2009). School improvement by design: Lessons from a study of comprehensive school reform programs. In G. Sykes, B. Schneider, and D. Plan (Eds.), *Handbook of Education Policy Research,* Washington, DC: American Educational Research Association. Available: http://www.cpre.org/school-improvement-design-lessons-study-comprehensive-school-reform-programs [June 2015].

Schneider, R., and Krajcik, J. (2002). Supporting science teacher learning: The role of educative curriculum materials. *Journal of Science Teacher Education, 13*(3), 221-245.

Smith, P.S., Banilower, E.R., McMahon, K.C., and Weiss, I.R. (2002). *The National Survey of Science and Mathematics Education: Trends from 1977 to 2000.* Available: http://2000survey.horizon-research.com/reports/trends.php [June 2015].

Spillane, J., and Diamond, J. (2007). *Distributed Leadership in Practice.* New York: Teachers College Press.

Spillane, J.P., Reiser, B.J., and Reimer, T. (2002). Policy implementation and cognition: Reframing and refocusing implementation research. *Review of Educational Research, 72*(3), 387-431. Available: http://rer.sagepub.com/content/72/3/387.full.pdf [June 2015].

Sterling, D.R., Dexter, P., Dunn, D.D., Frazier, W., Hepner, J., Klonowski, P., Matkins, J.J., McCauley, E., McDonnough, J.T., Nelson, L.J., Rhoades, E.M., and Smith-Jones, Y. (2007). *Virginia Mathematics and Science Coalition Science Specialist Task Force Report.* Available: http://www.vamsc.org/vms/science_news/science_specialist_task_force_report_full_report_feb_07.pdf [June 2015].

Stiggins, R.J. (2005). Assessment literacy for the 21st century. *Phi Delta Kappan, 77*(3), 238-245.

Stiggins, R.J., and Conklin, N.F. (1992). *In Teachers' Hands: Investigating the Practices of Classroom Assessment.* Albany: State University of New York Press.

Supovitz, J., and Riggan, M. (2012). *Building a Foundation for School Leadership: An Evaluation of the Annenberg Distributed Leadership Project, 2006-2010.* CPRE Research Report #RR-73. Philadelphia, PA: Consortium for Policy Research in Education. Available: http://www.cpre.org/building-foundation-school-leadership-evaluation-annenberg-distributed-leadership-project-2006-2010 [June 2015].

Sykes, G.W., and Wilson, S.M. (2015). *How Teachers Teach: Mapping the Terrain of Practice.* Princeton, NJ: Educational Testing Service.

Sykes, G.W., and Wilson, S.M. (in press). Instructional policy. In D. Gitomer and C. Bell (Eds.), *Handbook of Research on Teaching* (5th ed.). Washington, DC: American Educational Research Association.

Teacher Leader Exploratory Consortium. (2010). *Teacher Leader Model Standards.* Available: https://www.ets.org/s/education_topics/teaching_quality/pdf/teacher_leader_model_standards.pdf [June 2015].

Trygstad, P.J., Smith, S.P., Banilower, E.R., Nelson, M.M. (2013). *The Status of Elementary Science Education: Are We Ready for the Next Generation Science Standards?* Chapel Hill, NC: Horizon Research.

Tyack, D., and Tobin, W. (1994). The "grammar" of schooling: Why has it been so hard to change? *American Education Research Journal, 31*(3), 453-479. Available: http://aer.sagepub.com/content/31/3/453.short [June 2015].

Wahlstrom, K.L. (2008). Leadership and learning: What these articles tell us. *Educational Administration Quarterly, 44*(4), 593-597.

Weinstein, M., Whitesell, E.R., and Schwartz, A.E. (2014). Museums, zoos, and gardens: How formal-informal partnerships can impact urban students' performance in science. *Evaluation Review, 38*(6), 514-545.

Weiss, I.R., Banilower, E.R., McMahon, K.C., and Smith, P.S. (2001). *Report of the 2000 National Survey of Science and Mathematics Education*. Chapel Hill, NC: Horizon Research. Available: http://www.horizon-research.com/horizonresearchwp/wp-content/uploads/2013/04/complete.pdf [June 2015].

Wiliam, D. (2011). *Embedded Formative Assessment*. Bloomington, IN: Solution Tree.

Wyner, Y. (2013). The impact of a novel curriculum on secondary biology teachers' dispositions toward using authentic data and media in their human impact and ecology lessons. *Journal of Science Teacher Education, 24*(5), 833-857.

Wynne, J. (2001). *Teachers as Leaders in Education Reform*. ERIC Digest ED462376. Available: http://files.eric.ed.gov/fulltext/ED462376.pdf [June 2015].

York-Barr, J., and Duke, K. (2004). What do we know about teacher leadership? Findings from two decades of scholarship. *Review of Educational Research, 74*(3), 255-316.

Zangori, L., Forbes, C., and Biggers, M. (2013). Fostering student sense making in elementary science learning environments: Elementary teachers' use of science curriculum materials to promote explanation construction. *Journal of Research in Science Teaching, 50*(8), 989-1017.

9

Conclusions, Recommendations, and Directions for Research

In many ways, the message of this report is a simple one: all students deserve to understand and enjoy science, and helping teachers offer rich instruction will require building similarly rich learning environments for all science teachers. Creating such environments entails creating meaningful formal professional development programs and other opportunities for teachers to learn, as well as implementing policies and practices in schools that nurture cultures of learning for teachers and students alike.

As simple as this message may seem, the proverbial devil is in the details. As the new vision for the science education of K-12 students set forth in the *Next Generation Science Standards* (hereafter referred to as NGSS) and *A Framework for K-12 Science Education* (hereafter referred to as the Framework) has evolved, it is one that engages students in learning scientific and engineering practices, disciplinary core ideas, and crosscutting concepts. To achieve this new vision, teaching and learning in science classrooms will need to change, and so, too, will professional learning opportunities for teachers. This chapter summarizes the committee's major conclusions and recommendations for effecting the needed changes, which are based on the evidence reviewed in this report and on the committee members' collective expertise. We begin with the conclusions that flow directly from the analyses of existing literature in each chapter. We then lay out a set of conclusions the committee drew after looking across these analyses.

CONCLUSIONS

In reviewing the available research related to issues of contemporary science teacher learning, the committee drew a series of interrelated conclusions:

> **Conclusion 1:** *An evolving understanding of how best to teach science, including the NGSS, represents a significant transition in the way science is currently taught in most classrooms and will require most science teachers to alter the way they teach.*

This vision of science learning and teaching draws on a long tradition of reform in science education that has emphasized the need for all students to learn significant disciplinary core ideas, coupled with scientific and engineering practices that are part of inquiry. In addition, the vision emphasizes the need to integrate knowledge through crosscutting concepts. To teach science in these ways, teachers will need to move away from traditional models of instruction that emphasize memorizing facts and covering a large number of discrete topics, focusing instead on core ideas, studied in depth, through active student engagement in investigations and opportunities to reflect on and build scientific explanations for phenomena.

> **Conclusion 2:** *The available evidence suggests that many science teachers have not had sufficiently rich experiences with the content relevant to the science courses they currently teach, let alone a substantially redesigned science curriculum. Very few teachers have experience with the science and engineering practices described in the NGSS. These trends are especially pronounced both for elementary school teachers and in schools that serve high percentages of low-income students, where teachers are often newer and less qualified.*

Although professional development is available to all teachers, the committee found no evidence that elementary, middle, and high school science teachers have adequately rigorous opportunities to learn content related to the courses they teach, the new vision of science education, or how to teach to that new vision in challenging and effective ways. Instead, professional development appears to be more piecemeal, with few—if any—opportunities for the majority of teachers to engage in sustained study of science, scientific practices, and effective science instruction. High school teachers have some of these opportunities, while middle and elementary school teachers, who themselves may not have had much preparation in science and science teaching in their initial teacher preparation experiences, have fewer. Again, this situation is most pronounced in schools that serve high percentages of low-income students, and in which teacher turnover is especially high, leading to a less experienced and qualified workforce.

Conclusion 3: Typically, the selection of and participation in professional learning opportunities is up to individual teachers. There is often little attention to developing collective capacity for science teaching at the building and district levels or to offering teachers learning opportunities tailored to their specific needs and offered in ways that support cumulative learning over time.

While teachers in U.S. schools are required to participate regularly in professional development, mandated professional development tends to be generic, with little attention to systematically meeting the needs of science teachers. Many teachers pursue their own learning, taking summer professional development courses, volunteering to participate in curriculum development and/or review, working with preservice teachers, or taking on the role of professional developer or instructional coach. However, these individual pursuits are seldom linked to a well-articulated theory of teacher learning over time or a systemic vision of how to develop individual and collective teacher capacity.

Conclusion 4: Science teachers' learning needs are shaped by their preparation, the grades and content areas they teach, and the contexts in which they work. Three important areas in which science teachers need to develop expertise are

- *the knowledge, capacity, and skill required to support a diverse range of students;*
- *content knowledge, including understanding of disciplinary core ideas, crosscutting concepts, and scientific and engineering practices; and*
- *pedagogical content knowledge for teaching science, including a repertoire of teaching practices that support students in rigorous and consequential science learning.*

The set of professional knowledge and skills that informs good teaching is vast. Central to this knowledge base are the knowledge and skill needed to teach all students, mastery of science and science practices, and understanding and skill in teaching science. The committee acknowledges that there are other domains of knowledge equally essential to effective science teaching, and chose to focus on these three as there is considerable science-specific research on how these domains enable high-quality teaching. The capacity to teach all students science depends on teachers' respect for and understanding of the range of experiences and knowledge that students from diverse backgrounds bring to school, and how to capitalize on those experiences in crafting rigorous instruction. Knowledge of the sciences one is assigned to teach, of how those sciences are related to one another and to other fields like engineering, and knowledge and skill in how best to teach students science also are essential to high-quality instruction as envisioned in the NGSS and Framework.

This new vision of science teaching and learning will require new learning on the part of all teachers in all of these domains. The knowledge that students bring with them from their families and communities that is relevant to disciplinary core ideas, scientific and engineering practices, and crosscutting concepts is an area yet to be fully explored. In general, many teachers have had limited opportunities to engage in scientific and engineering practices themselves, much less to explore them in connection with the disciplinary core ideas and crosscutting concepts that animate the new vision. New curricula and instructional experiences will need to be crafted—with input from and the active engagement of teachers themselves—to bring that vision to life in U.S. classrooms. The knowledge demands of this new vision will require that the entire community—science teachers, teacher educators, professional developers, and science education researchers, as well as institutions of higher education, cultural institutions, and industry all of which invest in professional development— to create new, ongoing opportunities for teachers to rise to these new standards and to document what they learn from their efforts along the way.

> ***Conclusion 5:*** *The best available evidence based on science professional development programs suggests that the following features of such programs are most effective:*
>
> - *active participation of teachers who engage in the analysis of examples of effective instruction and the analysis of student work,*
> - *a content focus,*
> - *alignment with district policies and practices, and*
> - *sufficient duration to allow repeated practice and/or reflection on classroom experiences.*

The national interest in the power of professional development to enhance teacher quality has led to considerable investments in such programs and in research on what makes them effective. While the goal of linking professional development to student learning outcomes through research remains somewhat elusive, a great deal has been learned from the careful work of researchers and professional development leaders who have iteratively built professional learning programs for teachers. More research remains to be conducted in this area, but the research in science education, as well as mathematics, suggests that professional development of sufficient duration to allow teachers to deepen their pedagogical content knowledge and practice new instructional methods in their classrooms can lead to improved instruction and student achievement. Hallmarks of high-quality professional learning opportunities include focus on specific content that is aligned with district or school curriculum and assessment policies, as well as the proactive and professional engagement of teachers are hallmarks of high-quality professional learning opportunities.

> *Conclusion 6: Professional learning in online environments and through social networking holds promise, although evidence on these modes from both research and practice is limited.*

The potential to use new media to enhance teacher learning is undeniable. Social networking and online environments hold promise for meeting the "just-in-time" learning needs of teachers, and for providing access to science expertise and science education expertise for teachers in schools and communities that lack rich resources in these domains. While these areas have yet to be fully explored by teacher developers and science education researchers, the committee sees considerable potential for these resources as research accumulates concerning their effective use.

> *Conclusion 7: Science teachers' professional learning occurs in a range of settings both within and outside of schools through a variety of structures (professional development programs, professional learning communities, coaching, and the like). There is limited evidence about the relative effectiveness of this broad array of learning opportunities and how they are best designed to support teacher learning.*

Recently, there has been increasing commitment to creating schools where both students and teachers can learn. This heightened interest in "embedded professional learning" can take many forms, including professional learning communities; professional networks that reach across districts, the state, or the country; induction programs for early-career teachers; and coaching and mentoring for teachers wishing to improve their practice. Since teachers spend the majority of their professional time in classrooms and schools, it seems wise to capitalize on efforts to design settings that support their professional learning, both individually and collectively and to expand research in those settings.

> **Conclusion 8:** *Schools need to be structured to encourage and support ongoing learning for science teachers especially given the number of new teachers entering the profession.*

A growing body of research documents the generative conditions established for teacher learning when schools foster collective responsibility for student learning and well-being. However, the evidence base related to learning opportunities for teachers in schools and classrooms is weak, especially with regard to science. This, too, appears to be an area with too much potential to ignore. In particular, building school infrastructure that systematically develops the science and science teaching expertise necessary to engage all students meaningfully in the new vision embodied the Framework and NGSS can work proactively to ameliorate differences between schools that have ready access to such expertise and those that struggle to connect with it.

> **Conclusion 9:** *Science teachers' development is best understood as long term and contextualized. The schools and classrooms in which teachers work shape what and how they learn. These contexts include, but are not limited to school, district, and state policies and practices concerning professional capacity (e.g., professional networks, coaching, partnerships), coherent instructional guidance (e.g., state and district curriculum and assessment/ accountability policies), and leadership (e.g., principals and teacher leaders).*

Teachers' capacity to teach science well over time is intimately related to the environments in which they teach. The policies and practices that shape instruction vary from teacher evaluation to curriculum and accountability to teacher assignment. For example, teachers cannot teach science courses that do not align with their preparation. Nor is it productive for the feedback teachers receive concerning their annual evaluations to run counter to messages about effective science instruction embodied in curriculum policies.

> **Conclusion 10:** *School and district administrators are central to building the capacity of the science teacher workforce.*

Conditions in schools and districts can create contexts that allow teachers to take better advantage of professional learning opportunities both within the workday and outside of school. These conditions might include, for example, required professional development time and other learning opportunities designed to foster better understanding of how to teach the redesigned science curriculum. Administrators can direct resources (e.g., location of teachers, scheduling of classes, materials budget) toward science and teachers' learning in science. They also can send messages about the importance of science in schools. As instructional leaders, they need to understand the vision for science education in the Framework and NGSS and align policies and practices in the school to support this vision.

> **Conclusion 11:** *Teacher leaders may be an important resource for building a system that can support ambitious science instruction. There is increasing attention to creating opportunities for teachers to take on leadership roles to both improve science instruction and strengthen the science teacher workforce. These include roles as instructional coaches, mentors, and teacher leaders.*

Expertise in both science and pedagogy in science is an important component of building capacity in schools and districts. The development of science teacher leaders can be an important mechanism for supporting science learning for all teachers. The range of new roles for teacher leaders—lead teacher, curriculum specialist, mentor, collaborating teacher, instructional coach, professional development leader—holds considerable potential for enhancing the science teacher workforce. Not only do these teacher leaders engage in advanced study of science and science teaching themselves, but they also take on roles that involve helping fellow teachers learn. Such leaders can guide school- or district-based professional learning communities, identify useful resources, and provide feedback to teachers as they modify their instructional practices. While little research exists on the effects of these leaders on teacher learning more generally, the committee sees these new roles as a potentially powerful mechanism for improving science teacher quality collectively.

In addition to the above conclusions, all of which are drawn from chapter-specific analyses, the committee drew two additional conclusions based on the big picture emerging from these related, but separate analyses.

> **Conclusion 12:** *Closing the gap between the new way of teaching science and current instruction in many schools will require attending to individual teachers' learning needs, as well as to the larger system of practices and policies (such as allocation of resources, use of time, and provision of opportunities for collaboration) that shape how science is taught.*

The committee's view of science teacher learning is both individual and collective. That is, we see science teacher learning as an issue of building the capacity not only of individual teachers, but also of the science educator workforce more generally, particularly the capacity of science teachers in a school or district. The demands of schooling are such that distributed expertise is essential and building capacity across a group of teachers needs to be the goal. In addition, enhancing the collective teacher workforce is not simply a matter of ensuring that teachers, individually and collectively, have the necessary knowledge and skill. It is also necessary for schools, districts, school networks, and states to develop practices and policies including teacher hiring and retention, teacher evaluation, curriculum and accountability guidance, and school staffing and school/district leadership that enable good science teaching. Contexts shape the work of teaching, and enhancing science instruction in the United States will require new policies as well as well-prepared teachers.

> **Conclusion 13:** *The U.S. educational system lacks a coherent and well-articulated system of learning opportunities for teachers to continue developing expertise while in the classroom. Opportunities are unevenly distributed across schools, districts, and regions, with little attention to sequencing or how to support science teachers' learning systematically. Moreover, schools and districts often lack systems that can provide a comprehensive view of teacher learning; identify specific teacher needs; or track investments—in time, money and resources—in science teachers' professional learning*

This is not a new observation, but it is a continuing problem. Despite a wealth of opportunities for science teacher learning offered in schools and districts and through cultural institutions and industry—ranging from summer institutes to research apprenticeships to curriculum development to Lesson Study—the majority of the nation's science are impoverished in terms of targeted, coherent, aligned, and cumulative opportunities to enrich their understanding and practices in teaching all students challenging science. Piecemeal approaches have not redressed this well-established problem.

New incentives and investments to redesign/restructure science teachers' learning opportunities in schools, districts, school networks, and partnerships are needed. In particular, leadership by administrators at the school and district levels is critical to promoting and supporting the enabling conditions for science teachers to learn. Teacher leaders also play a critical role in these efforts. Approaches for elementary, middle, and high schools may need to vary, but in every case, school systems need ways to identify the myriad opportunities that exist for teacher learning, when and under what conditions these opportunities are aligned with one another, and how scarce resources can best be used to maximize opportunities for teacher learning and growth.

RECOMMENDATIONS FOR PRACTICE AND POLICY

Teachers matter, but they do not work in a vacuum. Their ability to elevate students' scientific understanding depends on the schools, districts, and communities in which they work and the professional communities to which they belong. The recommendations below are intended to address the issues identified in the conclusions with particular attention to the ways that the current education system needs to be changed in order to support teachers' ongoing learning as they respond to the demands placed by current reforms in science education.

Here, we focus on how schools and school systems (such as districts or charter networks) can improve the learning opportunities for science teachers. Focusing on this level of the system is essential, given the important roles played by principals and teacher leaders in connecting the rhetoric of visions such as that embodied in the Framework and NGSS to the realities of how teachers and students spend their time. Below we offer some specific recommendations for practices and policies we view as necessary to enhance ongoing teacher learning. Because the research base in this area is so uneven, often lacking science-specific studies related to the issues raised in this report, we think that these recommendations go hand-in-hand with research needs, and we offer recommendations for meeting these needs later in this chapter.

The following recommendations are not intended to be in chronological order—Recommendation 1, for example, does not have to be carried out first. Indeed, a plan for acting on recommendations toward the goal of enhancing science teacher learning to meet student learning goals is needed, and that plan might entail acting on a small number of recommendations, ordered in a way that capitalizes on current practice and policy and accelerates change.

In an ideal world, all these recommendations would be implemented. But in the real and complex world of schooling, it is important to start with one recommendation, building momentum, and with a long term goal of acting on the full set. Equally important is that acting on these recommendations will require additional resources (money, material, time, and personnel) or significant shifts in priorities. Such tradeoffs are inevitable, but investing in the individual and collective capacity of the workforce is essential to the improvement of science teaching in the United States. Finally, the committee presumes that acting on these recommendations will require the engagement of teachers, teacher leaders, and administrators as partners in creating strong systems of science teacher learning.

Recommendation 1:

Take stock of the current status of learning opportunities for science teachers: School and district administrators should identify current offerings and opportunities for teacher learning in science—using a broad conceptualization of teacher learning opportunities, and including how much money and time are spent (as well as other associated costs). Throughout this process, attention should be paid to the opportunities available for teachers to learn about

- approaches for teaching all students,
- science content and scientific practices, and
- science pedagogical knowledge and science teaching practices.

When identifying costs, administrators should consider both traditional professional development time and other supports for learning, such as curriculum, teacher evaluation, and student assessment/accountability. Given differences in the learning needs of elementary, middle, and high school teachers, expenditures and time allocations should be broken down by grade level and by school and district level. Plans to address any inequities across classrooms or schools should be developed with an eye toward policies and practices that will equitably distribute teacher expertise and teacher learning opportunities across the system.

Recommendation 2:

Design a portfolio of coherent learning experiences for science teachers that attend to teachers' individual and context-specific needs in partnership with professional networks, institutions of higher education, cultural institutions, and the broader scientific community as appropriate: Teachers and school and district administrators should articulate, implement, and support teacher learning opportunities in science as coherent, graduated sequences of experiences toward larger goals for improving science teaching and learning. Here, too, attention should be paid to building teachers' knowledge and skill in the sciences and scientific practices, in science pedagogical content knowledge, and in science teaching practices. It is critical to support teachers' opportunities to learn how to connect with students of diverse backgrounds and experiences and how to tap into relevant funds of knowledge of students and communities.

District personnel and school principals, in collaboration with teachers and parents, should identify the specific learning needs of science teachers in their schools and develop a multiyear growth plan for their science teachers' learning that is linked to their growth plan for students' science learning. Central to this work are four questions:

- In light of our school's/district's science goals for our students, what learning opportunities will teachers need?
- What kinds of expertise are needed to support these learning opportunities?
- Where is that expertise located (inside and outside of schools)?
- What social arrangements and resources will enable this work?

Using a variety of assessments/measures designed to provide the kind of concrete feedback necessary to support (teacher and program) improvement, school principals, in collaboration with teachers and school partners, should regularly consult data form such sources as (teacher observations, student work, and student surveys or interviews) to assess progress on the growth plan. It will also be important to consider the larger contexts in which the plan will unfold and how existing policies and practices regarding personnel (hiring, retention, placement) and instructional guidance (curriculum and assessment) can enable or limit the plan.

Recommendation 3:

Consider both specialized professional learning programs outside of school and opportunities for science teachers' learning embedded in the workday: A coherent, standards and evidence-based portfolio of professional learning opportunities for science teachers should include both specialized programs that occur outside of the school day and ongoing learning opportunities that are built into the workday and enhance capacity in schools and districts. Development of this portfolio will require some restructuring of teachers' work in schools to support new learning opportunities. School and district leaders will need to develop policies and practices that provide the necessary resources (fiscal, time, facilities, tools, incentives).

As school and district leaders identify professional learning opportunities for science teachers, they should work to develop a portfolio of opportunities that address teachers' varied needs, in ways that are sensitive to the school or district context. School and district leaders should not only make this portfolio of opportunities available to teachers; but also actively encourage, through their leadership and provision of resources, teachers' engagement in these opportunities, and provide time during the school day for teachers to engage meaningfully in them. Furthermore, school and district leaders should work with teams of teachers to build coherent programs of science teaching learning opportunities, tailored to individual teachers and the school as a whole. The portfolio of teacher learning opportunities should include structured, traditional professional development; cross-school teacher professional communities, and collaborations with local partners.

Recommendation 4:

Design and select learning opportunities for science teachers that are informed by the best available research: Teachers' learning opportunities should be aligned with a system's science standards, and should be grounded in an underlying theory of teacher learning and in research on the improvement of professional practice, and on how to meet the needs of the range of adult and student learners in a school or district. Learning opportunities for science teachers should have the following characteristics:

- Designed to achieve specific learning goals for teachers.
- Be content specific, that is, focused on particular scientific concepts and practices.
- Be student specific, that is, focused on the specific students served by the school district.
- Linked to teachers' classroom instruction and include analysis of instruction.
- Include opportunities for teachers to practice teaching science in new ways and to interact with peers in improving the implementation of new teaching strategies.
- Include opportunities for teachers to collect and analyze data on their students' learning.
- Offer opportunities for collaboration.

Designers of learning opportunities for teachers including commercial providers, community organizations, institutions of higher education and districts and states, should develop learning opportunities for teachers that reflect the above criteria.

When selecting learning opportunities for teachers, district and school leaders and teachers themselves should use the above criteria as a guide for identifying the most promising programs and learning experiences. District and state administrators should use these criteria to provide guidance for teachers on how to identify high-quality learning experiences.

District and state administrators should use (and make public) quality indicators to identify, endorse, and fund a portfolio of teacher learning opportunities, and should provide guidance for school leaders and teachers on how to select high-quality learning experiences in science appropriate to specific contexts.

Recommendation 5:

Develop internal capacity in science while seeking external partners with science expertise: School and district leaders should work to build school- and district-level capacity around science teaching. These efforts should include creating learning opportunities for teachers but might also include exploring different models for incorporating science expertise, such as employing science specialists at the elementary level or providing high school science department heads with time to observe and collaborate with their colleagues. When developing a strategy for building capacity, school and district leaders should consider the tradeoffs inherent in such choices.

School and district leaders should also explore developing partnerships with individuals and organizations —such as local businesses, institutions of higher education or science rich institutions—that can bring science expertise.

Crucial to developing relevant expertise is developing the capacity of professional development leaders. Investing in the development of professional developers who are knowledgeable about teaching all students the vision of science education represented in the NGSS (Next Generation Science Standards Lead States, 2013) and the Framework (National Research Council, 2012) is critical. It is not sufficient for these leaders to be good teachers themselves; they must also be prepared and supported to work with adult learners and to coordinate professional development with other policies and programs (including staffing, teacher evaluation, curriculum development, and student assessment).

Recommendation 6:

Create, evaluate, and revise policies and practices that encourage teachers to engage in professional learning related to science: District and school administrators and relevant leaders should work to establish dedicated professional development time during the salaried work week and work year for science teachers. They should encourage teachers to participate in science learning opportunities and structure time to allow for collaboration around science. Resources for professional learning should include time to meet with other teachers, to observe other classrooms, and to attend discrete events; space to meet with other teachers; requested materials; and incentives to participate. These policies and practices should take advantage of linkages with other policies For example, natural connections can be made between policies concerning professional development and teacher evaluation. Similarly, administrators could develop policies that more equitably distribute qualified and experienced science teachers across all students in school, districts, and school networks.

At the elementary level, district and school leaders should work to establish parity for science professional development in relationship to other subjects, especially mathematics and English language arts.

Recommendation 7:
The potential of new formats and media should be explored to support science teachers' learning when appropriate: Districts should consider the use of technology and online spaces/resources to support teacher learning in science. These tools may be particularly useful for supporting cross-school collaboration, providing teachers with flexible schedules for accessing resources, or enabling access to professional learning opportunities in rural areas where teachers may be isolated and it is difficult to convene in a central location.

As noted, the above recommendations focus on schools and districts/school networks, as the committee sees work at that level as a necessary condition for realizing the vision of the Framework and NGSS. Without the work of teachers, professional development leaders, and school leaders at the local level, the promise of these visionary documents cannot be realized.

Of course, working at that local level—while necessary—is not sufficient to change how science is taught across the United States and determining whether all children have access to high-quality science learning experiences. Within and across states, as well as nationally, science education needs to be elevated through policies, practices, and funding mechanisms. Without that kind of support, the local and essential work described in these recommendations will fall short. Other reports of the National Research Council (2014, 2015) include recommendations targeted to the state level that identify policies such as those related to assessment (National Research Council, 2014), high school graduation requirements (National Research Council, 2015), and teacher certification (National Research Council, 2015) that can help create supportive contexts for improving science education. The National Research Council (2013) also has issued recommendations for a national indicator system that would make it possible to track improvement in STEM education reforms, covering domains of state policy, curriculum, accountability, and teacher quality, and the National Science Teachers Association has issued a number of relevant position statements on accountability, teacher preparation and induction, leadership, and professional development.[1]

As states, districts, and schools move forward with initiatives aimed at improving supports for science teachers' learning, they should leverage these and other relevant resources that have been developed by such national organizations as the National Science Teachers Association, the

---

[1]See http://www.nsta.org/about/positions/#list [November 2015].

Council of State Science Supervisors, and Achieve, Inc. and are available online. These organizations also are creating networks of science educators who are exploring the Framework and NGSS and sharing ideas about implementation of the vision set forth in those documents. It is a massive undertaking to support all students, teachers, and schools in rising to the challenges of the new vision of science teaching and learning. And while the committee's recommendations focus on a set of strategic activities that schools and districts might undertake to make progress, the science teachers, scientists, science teacher educators, and professional development leaders who constitute the membership of these organizations can contribute much to an enriched understanding of how to support ongoing teacher learning.

RECOMMENDATIONS FOR RESEARCH

Considerable research exists, both in science education and in education more generally on which to draw, for insights into the wise development of policies, programs, and practices that will enhance teacher learning. At the same time, much remains to be learned. The committee identified several areas of research that would inform the work of school leaders interested in supporting ongoing teacher learning. Before offering our recommendations for future research, we reiterate the major gaps in the research literature.

- No system is in place to collect data on the science teacher workforce, their qualifications, experience, and preparation. This is due in part to differences across states in both teacher certification and data collection; the problem is exacerbated by a lack of measures that could be used to do comparative work. The authors of the National Research Council (2010) study of teacher preparation make a similar observation.
- No system is in place to collect data on general trends in science teaching and learning. This gap will challenge the collective capacity to assess any progress that may be made on meeting the challenges of the vision in the Framework and the NGSS. The observations in the National Research Council report *Monitoring Progress Toward Successful K-21 STEM Education* (2013) are similar. Studies vary in both their conceptions of good science teaching and how teaching is measured, compromising the capacity to ascertain general trends.
- No system in place to collect data about the myriad professional learning opportunities that teachers encounter in and out of

school. The committee found enormous variation in teacher learning opportunities, with no centralized way to determine general trends or the effectiveness of various programs or combinations of experiences. This observation is similar to a conclusion drawn by the authors of the National Research Council (2010) report on teacher preparation.

- While there is a body of research on formal science professional development, that research tends to focus on individual programs and to rely heavily on teacher self report. Few studies used research designs involving control or comparison groups and incorporating pre/post measures of teachers' knowledge and beliefs, instruction, and students' outcomes. Without such studies, it is difficult to draw strong conclusions about effectiveness. The field lacks consistently used, technically powerful measures of science teachers' knowledge and practice, as well as measures that capture the full range of student outcomes. There are a handful of noteworthy exceptions to this pattern (e.g., Heller et al., 2012; Roth et al., 2011).
- Substantially less research exists on other, potentially equally important opportunities for science teacher learning, including professional learning communities, mentoring and coaching, online learning, teacher networks, and teacher evaluation. In general, the evidence base related to learning opportunities for teachers that are embedded in schools and classrooms is weak, especially with regard to science.
- Almost no studies address school organization and context and how they might affect the impact of professional development programs. Little to no published research exists on the effects of recruitment, retention, and staffing policies on the quality of the science teaching workforce and of science instruction in schools and districts.
- Research on how and under what conditions principals and leaders affect the quality of science learning in their schools has yet to be conducted. Also lacking in the research literature are studies of how teachers learn to become leaders, as well as research that examines the role, expertise, or preparation of science professional development providers and facilitators.

Research Recommendation 1: Focus Research on Linking Professional Learning to Changes in Instructional Practice and Student Learning

In general, more research is needed to understand the path from professional learning opportunities to changes in teacher knowledge and practice to student learning and engagement in terms of both individual teachers and the teacher workforce more generally. To be maximally helpful, that research should attend to the contexts in which teachers learn and teach (see Figure 8-2). The contextual factors that shape and are shaped by teachers' learning opportunities, include teacher hiring, staffing, and assignment policies and practices; student and school demographics; resource distribution and use; instructional guidance; teacher evaluation; and school organization.

Research Recommendation 2: Invest in Improving Measures of Science Instruction and Science Learning

Fundamental to most research aimed at linking science teacher learning to student science learning and engagement is the development of publicly credible, technically sound, and professionally responsible measures of relevant teacher and student outcomes. Because teaching and learning also have subject-specific aspects, these outcome measures need to sample broadly from the practices, disciplinary core ideas, and crosscutting concepts outlined in the new vision of science teaching and learning. The committee cannot emphasize enough the centrality of good measures of teacher and student learning, particularly for addressing gaps in all of the domains cited above. This issue is noted in the National Research Council report *Monitoring Progress Toward Successful K-12 STEM Education* (National Research Council, 2013) as well. Lacking good outcome measures, considerable resources will continue to be devoted to professional learning opportunities with a limited ability to gauge their effects. Such measures would enable a great deal of needed research.

Research Recommendation 3: Design and Implement Research That Examines a Variety of Approaches to Supporting Science Teachers' Learning

The committee urges a broad conceptualization of professional learning and thus research that examines how teachers learn from portfolios of learning opportunities, including both off-site and embedded professional development (e.g., study groups, professional learning communities, lesson study). Of particular benefit would be research assessing the effects of the interactions among various learning opportunities, as well as the particular contributions of different kinds of learning experiences to teacher knowledge and practice. The conduct of such research would require having much better documentation of the range of learning opportunities in which teachers participate and that were designed intentionally to build upon, extend, and enhance one another. Moreover, any investment in teacher learning ought to be designed to document its effects; this would mean designing strong research in tandem with professional learning experiences, whether those experiences are based in cultural institutions, industry, universities, or schools. As is the case with all of the research recommended here, attention should be paid to contextual variation and how aspects of state, district, and school context mediate and/or moderate the effects of professional learning opportunities on teacher practice and student learning.

Typical research on professional learning is small scale, conducted by the program designers or providers, and uses locally developed measures. Although a growing number of studies entail carrying out large-scale, rigorous examinations of professional development interventions that link teachers' learning to student outcomes, the results of those studies are mixed. The collective body of small-scale research has produced some insights, but understanding of the nature and effects of the range of professional learning opportunities will remain limited without large-scale studies that include multiple programs and are not as dependent on teacher self-report. A wide range of research methodologies have important roles in shedding light on science teacher learning, as does the use of multiple measures of teacher knowledge and practice and student engagement and learning.

Research Recommendation 4: Commit to Focusing on Meeting the Needs of Diverse Science Learners Across All Research on Professional Development

The committee urges that research on science teacher learning focus on opportunities that help teachers meet the needs of diverse students while teaching to the standards. Accomplishing this goal will require developing and studying professional learning programs—in and outside of schools—that interweave attention to science content with attention to the needs and experiences of all students, including English language learners, special education students, gifted and talented students, and diverse learners. Compelling research exists in many of these areas. But teachers do not teach diverse learners on Tuesdays and science on Wednesdays; they teach the two together, and supportive professional learning experiences for teachers will integrate knowledge across a range of domains. For example, teachers would be aided in achieving the new vision by research documenting how they can tap into students' funds of knowledge when teaching a specific scientific practice or disciplinary idea. In other words, research that attends to the development of all three dimensions of teacher knowledge and skill discussed in this report—the capacity to respond to all learners, disciplinary scientific knowledge, and pedagogical content knowledge—is essential.

Research Recommendation 5: Focus Research on Exploring the Potential Role of Technology

When relevant, attending to the potential role of technology in enabling teacher learning would help schools and school districts take advantage of the capabilities of new technologies in enabling teacher learning. Such research could focus on online or hybrid professional development programs, face-to-face learning opportunities that take advantage of the use of technology in pursuit of ambitious instruction, the use of technology to teach to the new vision of science learning, or the support of online professional networks of teachers.

Research Recommendation 6: Design and Implement Research Focused on the Learning Needs of Teacher Leaders and Professional Development Providers

The field also needs research on the development of teacher educators, professional development leaders, and teacher leaders more generally. Learning to teach teachers is related to but distinct from learning to teach. Research documenting and explaining how skilled teacher developers acquire relevant knowledge and practice would help improve the quality of professional learning across the myriad settings in which it takes place.

FINAL REFLECTIONS

First, given current efforts toward developing new curriculum and assessment materials aligned with the Framework and NGSS, it would be strategic to design research that documents what teachers learn in developing and implementing those materials, especially in their classrooms and with the range of supports provided to help them. As teachers and schools embrace the new vision for science teaching and learning, teachers, teacher leaders, principals, and professional development staff will be learning a great deal. Research should document that learning so that efforts to reform science instruction can learn productively from that experimentation.

Second, many fields of research relevant to science teaching and learning currently do not address what science teachers and their students learn. Science education would benefit greatly from being integrated into programs of research concerning instructional reform, English language learners, how to reach and teach diverse student populations, teacher preparation, and teacher evaluation.

Finally, given that many schools and school networks are currently engaged in efforts to improve teacher learning opportunities, some of the research envisioned here might draw on design-based implementation research, networked improvement communities, strategic education partnerships, or other research designs. These research traditions—which are designed as collaborations among various stakeholders (schools, teachers, policy makers, and researchers) and committed to responding quickly to data and shifting course when necessary—holds great promise for helping teachers and schools respond in a timely fashion to the mandate to raise standards and teach all children scientifically rich curricula.

REFERENCES

Heller, J.I., Daehler, K.R., Wong, N., Shinohara, M., and Miratrix, L.W. (2012). Differential effects of three professional development models on teacher knowledge and student achievement in elementary science. *Journal of Research in Science Teaching, 49*(3), 333-362.

National Research Council. (2010). *Preparing Teachers: Building Evidence for Sound Policy.* Committee on the Study of Teacher Preparation Programs in the United States, Center for Education, Division of Behavioral and Social Sciences and Education. Washington, DC: The National Academies Press.

National Research Council. (2012). *A Framework for K-12 Science Education: Practices, Crosscutting Concepts, and Core ideas.* Committee on a Conceptual Framework for New K-12 Science Education Standards, Board on Science Education. Division of Behavioral and Social Sciences and Education. Washington, DC: The National Academies Press.

National Research Council. (2013). *Monitoring Progress Toward Successful K-12 STEM Education: A Nation Advancing?* Committee on the Evaluation Framework for Successful K-12 STEM Education. Board on Science Education and Board on Testing and Assessment, Division of Behavioral and Social Sciences and Education. Washington, DC: The National Academies Press.

National Research Council. (2014). *Developing Assessments for the Next Generation Science Standards.* Committee on Developing Assessments of Science Proficiency in K-12. Board on Testing and Assessment, Board on Science Education, Division of Behavioral and Social Sciences and Education. Washington, DC: The National Academies Press.

National Research Council. (2015). *Guide to Implementing the Next Generation Science Standards.* Committee on Guidance on Implementing the Next Generation Science Standards. Board on Science Education, Division of Behavioral and Social Sciences and Education. Washington, DC: The National Academies Press.

Next Generation Science Standards Lead States. (2013). *Next Generation Science Standards: For States, By States.* Washington, DC: The National Academies Press.

Roth, K., Garnier, H., Chen, C., Lemmens, M., Schwille, K., and Wickler, N.I.Z. (2011). Videobased lesson analysis: Effective science PD for teacher and student learning. *Journal of Research in Science Teaching, 48*(2), 117-148.

Appendix

Biographical Sketches of Committee Members and Staff

Suzanne M. Wilson (*Chair*) is a professor and Neag endowed professor of teacher education Department of Curriculum and Instruction at the University of Connecticut. Previously, Dr. Wilson was a university distinguished professor at Michigan State University (MSU), where she served as chair and professor in the Department of Teacher Education. While at MSU, she has collaborated on several large-scale research projects, including the National Center for Research on Teacher Education, the Educational Policy and Practice Study, and the National Partnership for Excellence and Accountability in Teaching. She has written on teacher knowledge, curriculum reform, educational policy, and teacher learning. Her interests include exploring various measures of teaching and teachers' understanding that might be used for teacher education and education research documenting the effects of professional development on science teachers' professional knowledge and practice, and a study of the contemporary and jurisdictional battles over who should control teacher education and licensure. Dr. Wilson served on the National Research Council's Committee on the Study of Teacher Preparation Programs in the United States and the Center for Education's advisory board and is currently a member of the National Academies of Sciences, Engineering, and Medicine's Board on Science Education. Dr. Wilson has a B.A. in history and American studies from Brown University and an M.S. in statistics and a Ph.D. in educational psychology from Stanford University.

Elizabeth A. (Betsy) Davis is a professor at the University of Michigan, School of Education. Her research integrates aspects of science education, teacher education, and the learning sciences. One major focus of Dr. Davis' work is the use of educative curriculum materials in supporting elementary teachers in ambitious science teaching, building on earlier work on how preservice and new elementary teachers learn to teach inquiry-oriented science and how curriculum materials and technology can support those teachers' learning. Dr. Davis is also interested in how coherent practice-based teacher education experiences support beginning elementary teachers in this learning, through the development of content knowledge for science teaching and high-leverage science teaching practices. Most recently, she chaired the Elementary Teacher Education Program at the University of Michigan for 4 years and helped lead the reshaping and redesign of this program. Dr. Davis received the Presidential Early Career Award for Scientists and Engineers at the White House in 2002 and the Jan Hawkins Early Career Award in 2004. Dr. Davis earned a B.S.E. in engineering and management systems at Princeton University, and an M.A. and Ph.D. in education in mathematics, science, and technology from the University of California, Berkeley.

Zoe Evans is an assistant principal at Villa Rica High School in Villa Rica, Georgia. Before becoming an assistant principal in 2012, she served as a middle-grades science teacher for 19 years in Florida and Georgia. Ms. Evans is a National Board Certified teacher in early adolescent science and a Georgia master teacher. She is the 2005 Georgia recipient of the Presidential Award of Excellence in Mathematics and Science Teaching. Ms. Evans has served as a member of the Georgia Department of Education Science Frameworks writing team, which created instructional models designed to help guide Georgia teachers in the implementation of the Georgia Performance Standards. Additionally, she is a member of the Georgia Science Education advisory committee. Most recently, Ms. Evans served as a member of the writing team for the *Next Generation Science Education Standards*. In addition to her work at the local, state, and national level, she serves as an active member of the Georgia Science Teachers Association having served as president from 2012-2015. She has held several executive board positions and is currently president-elect of the organization. Ms. Evans earned a bachelor's degree in middle grades education, master's degree in middle grades science, and specialist's degree in middle grade science from the University of West Georgia. Additionally, she has received certification in Educational Leadership from the University of West Georgia.

Adam Gamoran is president of the William T. Grant Foundation, which supports research on the education and development of young people. He was formerly the John D. MacArthur professor of sociology and educational policy studies and the director of the Wisconsin Center for Education Research at the University of Wisconsin–Madison. His research interests include school organization, stratification, and inequality in education. He recently concluded a large-scale randomized trial, supported by the National Science Foundation, on the impact of professional development to improve teaching and learning in elementary science in the Los Angeles Unified School District. Dr. Gamoran is a member of the National Academy of Education, and he has served on several National Research Council panels, including the Board on Science Education. In that capacity, he chaired the Committee on Highly Successful Schools or Programs in K-12 STEM Education and the Committee on the Evaluation Framework for Successful K-12 STEM Education. For the U.S. Department of Education, he chaired the congressionally mandated independent advisory panel of the National Assessment of Career and Technical Education, and he was twice appointed by President Obama to serve on the National Board for Education Sciences. Dr. Gamoran earned his Ph.D. in education from the University of Chicago.

Kris D. Gutiérrez is professor of language, literacy, and culture at the University of California, Berkeley. She was most recently, distinguished professor and professor of learning sciences literacy and the inaugural provost's chair at the University of Colorado, Boulder. She is also professor of social research methodology at the Graduate School of Education and Information Studies at the University of California, Los Angeles. Her research examines learning in designed learning environments, with attention to student from nondominant communities and English learners. Specifically, her work focuses on the processes by which people negotiate meaning in culturally organized contexts, using language and literacies that are embedded within socio-historical traditions. Issues of equity and excellence are recurrent themes in her work. Dr. Gutiérrez is a past president and a fellow of the American Educational Research Association (AERA) and an elected member of the National Academy of Education. She has been an Osher fellow at the Exploratorium and is a fellow at the National Conference on Research on Language and Literacy and at the National Education Policy Center. She has served on numerous policy-making and advisory boards, including the U.S. Department of Education Reading First Advisory Committee and as a member of President Obama's education policy transition team. She has received numerous awards, including the AERA Hispanic Research in Elementary,

Secondary, or Postsecondary Education Award and the inaugural AERA Award for Innovations in Research on Diversity in Teacher Education. Dr. Gutiérrez holds an M.A. in English education, reading and English from Arizona State University, and a Ph.D. in English and education from the University of Colorado.

Paula Hooper is senior science educator and learning research scientist in the Institute for Inquiry at the Exploratorium. Dr. Hooper has been an elementary classroom teacher; worked on the design and teaching of inquiry-oriented science professional development experiences for K-8 teachers, administrators, and museum educators; and worked with youth in informal settings on robotics and using digital design fabrication for their creative activism. Her research and teaching addresses the uses of digital media to support science, technology, engineering, and mathematics (STEM) learning in formal and informal learning settings from a sociocultural perspective. She is also interested in the design and facilitation of online communication and cyberlearning projects that complement STEM professional development. Dr. Hooper has worked for TERC, the Massachusetts Institute of Technology, and Shaker Heights Public Schools. She has served on advisory boards for the Science Museum of Minnesota and the Technology Committee of the American Educational Research Association and was a Warren Weaver fellow at the Rockefeller Foundation. Dr. Hooper holds a Ph.D. from the Massachussettes Institute of Technology Media Lab in media arts and sciences with a focus on epistemology and learning with digital media.

Judith Warren Little is dean of the Graduate School of Education and professor of policy, organization, measurement, and evaluation at the Univeristy of California, Berkeley. Before becoming dean in 2010, Dr. Little had been on the University of California, Berkeley, faculty since 1987. Her research interests center on the organizational and occupational contexts of teaching, with special attention to teachers' collegial relationships and to the contexts, policies, and practices of teachers' professional development. In pursuing these interests, she attempts to balance attention to the daily life of schools and the search for locally situated meanings, identities, and relationships with a broader view of the larger social, institutional, and policy environments in which the work of teaching resides. An elected member of the National Academy of Education, she has received numerous awards, including being named a fellow of the American Educational Research Association, the Frank H. Klassen Award for scholarly contributions in teacher education, and the Spencer Foundation Faculty Mentor Award. Dr. Little has a B.A. from the University of Colorado, and a Ph.D. in sociology from the University of Colorado.

Julie Luft is the inaugural athletic association professor of mathematics and science education at the University of Georgia. Her previous professional experience includes teaching science in middle and high school. Dr. Luft's areas of research expertise are science teacher education (preservice and inservice), mixed-methods research, and science teacher beliefs and practices. She has served as a board member and president of the Association of Science Teacher Educators (ASTE), and she has been the research director, board member, and council member of the National Science Teachers Association. She has received the ASTE Outstanding Science Teacher Educator Award, the ASTE Mentor Award, the Journal of Research on Science Teaching Award, and she is an American Association for the Advancement of Science fellow. Dr. Luft has a B.S.Ed. in life sciences from the University of New Mexico, an M.S.T. in science education and ecology from the New Mexico Institute of Mining and Technology, and a Ph.D. in science education from the University of Iowa.

Barbara Miller is a vice president at Education Development Center (EDC) and associate director of EDC's Learning and Teaching Division. A national expert in professional development for districts and schools, Dr. Miller conducts research on professional development and teacher leadership; provides technical assistance to programs and districts; and creates materials for teachers, teacher leaders, and administrators. Dr. Miller directed the award-winning *Success at the Core* project, a video-based professional development toolkit designed to improve instructional quality in classrooms and among school leadership teams. She has conducted research on knowledge management for the National Science Foundation's Math and Science Partnership Program, by synthesizing and sharing knowledge from the field around teacher leadership and professional learning communities; consulted with numerous districts on leadership development efforts; evaluated systemic reform initiatives; and provided assistance to underperforming schools and districts. A former middle school teacher and teacher educator, Dr. Miller has co-authored numerous articles, chapters and books on teacher leadership and school reform. Dr. Miller has a B.A. from Carleton College and an Ed.D. from Harvard University.

Kathleen Roth is a principal investigator at California State Polytechnic University, Pomona, where she is engaged in building on a line of research about videocase-based, analysis-of-practice professional development for elementary science teachers. In earlier work, she was principal investigator of a series of National Science Foundation-funded studies that developed and tested the effectiveness of this professional development approach on upper-elementary teachers' science content learning, their pedagogical content knowledge, their science teaching practice, and their students' science learning. An example of this is the Science Teachers Learning from Lesson Analysis Program, which demonstrated significant effects on teacher knowledge, teaching practice, and student learning. Later, as a teacher educator and researcher at Michigan State University, she taught elementary school science and studied her own practice and her students' learning. She also served as director of the LessonLab Research Institute, where her research examined science teaching in classrooms. Dr. Roth received a B.S. in biology from Duke University, an M.S. in secondary science teaching from Johns Hopkins University, and a Ph.D. in science education from Michigan State University.

Irwin Shapiro is the Timken University professor at Harvard University and a senior scientist at the Smithsonian Institution. Dr. Shapiro is the former director of the Harvard-Smithsonian Center for Astrophysics (CfA), where he was instrumental in the Center's research initiatives including the development of powerful telescopes and the establishment of a science education department. Prior to joining the CfA, Dr. Shapiro spent 28 years at the Massachusetts Institute of Technology on the research staff, as a professor of geophysics and physics, and the Schlumberger professor. He is a member of the National Academy of Sciences and other honorific societies. He has been active on a number of academic and government advisory boards, including the NASA. Dr. Shapiro has served as a member of the Radio Science teams for the Mariner, Viking, and Pioneer Venus spacecraft missions. More recently, Shapiro has devoted some of his interest to precollege and college science education, and has for years worked on curriculum development and teacher training. Dr. Shapiro has been the recipient of a number of awards, among them the Dannie Heineman (1984) and the Fred Whipple (1989) prizes of the American Astronomical Society, the Charles A. Whitten (1991) and William Bowie medals (1993) of the American Geophysical Union, and the Einstein Prize of the American Physical Society (2013). Dr. Shapiro received a B.S. in mathematics from Cornell University, and an M.A. and Ph.D. in physics from Harvard University.

Patrick M. Shields is executive director of the Learning Policy Institute. Previously, he served as the executive director of SRI Education. Dr. Shields' research focuses on effective educational policies and teaching practices for economically poor and ethnically diverse populations. Currently, he is the co-principal investigator of the Science Learning Activation Lab, a national research and design effort to strengthen science teaching and learning in the United States. Since 1999, he has served as the director of research for state-wide policy and research initiative to improve the teacher workforce in California. Dr. Shields is also principal investigator of a national randomized trial assessing the efficacy of the National Writing Project, a professional development program to improve the teaching of writing. Dr. Shields has served on the National Research Council committees on the Influence of Standards in Mathematics, Science, and Technology and Lessons Learned from Large-Scale Reforms in K-12 STEM Education. He was a senior policy advisor to the Center for Research on Educational Diversity and Excellence at the University of California and a member of the National Council for Teacher of Mathematics Standards Impact research group. He is currently a member of the committee of visitors for the Center for Informal Learning and Schools and is a member of the editorial board of *Education Evaluation and Policy Analysis*. Dr. Shields holds a Ph.D. in educational policy from Stanford University.

Warren Simmons is executive director of the Annenberg Institute and co-directs its work in community-centered education reform at Brown University. He also co-chairs the Aspen Urban Superintendents Network and the Working Group on School Transformation in New York City. Before joining the Annenberg Institute, he was founding director of the Philadelphia Education Fund, a local reform support organization that helped the School District of Philadelphia to fund, develop, and implement new academic standards, content-based professional development, standards-based curriculum resources, and comprehensive school reform. Previously, at the Annie E. Casey Foundation, he developed and funded initiatives on community development and urban school reform. He also served as director of equity initiatives for the New Standards Project and as special assistant to the superintendent of schools in Prince George's County, Maryland, where he planned and/or implemented district-wide initiatives on improving the achievement of traditionally underserved students. He is a recent recipient of the Distinguished Citizens Award from the National Governors Association and has served on the advisory groups or boards of several national organizations for science education. He was chair of the Rhode Island Urban Education task force and a member of the National Commission on Civic Investment in Public Education. Dr. Simmons received a B.A. in psychology from Macalester College, and a Ph.D. in psychology from Cornell University.

Mark Windschitl is a professor of science teaching and learning at the University of Washington. His research interests deal with the early-career development of science teachers—in particular, shaping their trajectories toward ambitious and equitable pedagogy. He has recently been principal investigator on two projects that tracked science teachers from preparation through their first year of teaching. His research group has prototyped a set of high-leverage practices for K-12 science instruction that represent a "'beginner's repertoire" and has tested the conditions under which these core practices, with the help of specially designed tools to support the intellectual work of teaching, can be appropriated as novices begin their professional careers in high-needs schools. His most recent funded work by the National Science Foundation is the *Mapping Clinical Experience* project in which he is collaborating with multiple institutions to do analyses of the advice and information networks that teacher candidates rely on when in their school placements. He is the recipient of the 2002 AERA Presidential Award for Best Review of Research and an author of the chapter on Science Teaching in the new American Educational Research Association *Handbook of Research on Teaching*. Dr. Windschitl received a B.S. in zoology, an M.S. in education research and evaluation, and a Ph.D. in education in curriculum and instruction from Iowa State University.

James Wyckoff is a Curry Memorial professor of education, professor of policy and director of EdPolicyWorks at the University of Virginia. Currently, his research examines a variety of issues in the preparation, recruitment, development and retention of effective teachers. Dr. Wyckoff has written widely on issues of education finance, including teacher compensation, teacher recruitment and retention of teachers in New York State, New York City, and the District of Columbia. He has served on several National Research Council committees, including the committee on the Study of Teacher Preparation Programs in the United States. He serves on the editorial board of *Education Finance and Policy* and several other advisory panels. Dr. Wyckoff received a B.A. in economics from Denison University, and a Ph.D. in economics from the University of North Carolina.

Carla Zembal-Saul is a professor of science education in the College of Education at the Pennsylvania State University. She holds the Gilbert and Donna Kahn endowed professorship in science, technology, engineering, and mathematics education, and she was recently named a NSTA fellow by the National Science Teachers Association. Her research takes place in the context of specially designed content courses for nonscience majors who are preparing to be teachers and in school-university partnerships where she investigates the long-term development of elementary teachers' knowledge and practices for supporting children's meaningful science learning and scientific discourse. She has developed online video-based cases of reform-oriented science teaching, used video analysis tools with preservice and practicing teachers, examined the use of software scaffolds to support meaningful science learning, and implemented electronic teaching portfolios in teacher education. She is an elected member of the executive board for the National Association for Research in Science Teaching, and she chairs the organization's publications advisory board. Her previous experience includes teaching science in middle school. Dr. Zembal-Saul received a B.S. in science education from the University of Michigan, an M.S. in science education from the University of Houston, and a Ph.D. in science education from the University of Michigan.

Staff

Heidi Schweingruber (*Study Director*) is the director of the Board on Science Education (BOSE) at the National Academies of Sciences, Engineering, and Medicine. In this role, she oversees the BOSE portfolio and collaborates with the board to develop new projects. She has worked on multiple Academies' projects on science, technology, engineering, and mathematics education including co-directing the study that resulted in the report *A Framework for K-12 Science Education*. She co-authored two award-winning books for practitioners that translate findings of Academies reports for a broader audience: *Ready, Set, Science! Putting Research to Work in K-8 Science Classrooms* (2008) and *Surrounded by Science* (2010). Prior to joining the Academies, she was a senior research associate at the Institute of Education Sciences in the U.S. Department of Education and the director of research for the Rice University School Mathematics Project, an outreach program in K-12 mathematics education. She holds a Ph.D. in psychology (developmental) and anthropology, and a certificate in culture and cognition from the University of Michigan.

Natalie Nielsen (Study Director until January 2014) was a senior program officer with the Board on Science Education (BOSE) at the National Academies of Sciences, Engineering, and Medicine, and acting director of the Board on Testing and Assessment (BOTA) from December 2013 until June 2015. While at BOSE, she directed studies on K-12 and undergraduate science, technology, engineering and mathematics education, including the studies that produced the reports *Successful K-12 STEM Education* and *Monitoring Progress Toward Successful K-12 STEM Education*. As BOTA director, she oversaw the completion of projects related to assessing Next Generation Science Standards and evaluating governance reforms in the District of Columbia's public schools, and the launch of projects related to NAEP achievement levels, character education, and inter- and intrapersonal competencies in postsecondary education. Before joining the Academies, she was director of research at the Business-Higher Education and a senior researcher at SRI International. Dr. Nielsen holds a B.S. in geology from the University of California, Davis; an M.S. in geological sciences from San Diego State University; and a Ph.D. in education from George Mason University.